THE BOOK OF THE YEAR 2018

Praise for *The Book of the Year 2017*

'Laced with their dry wit, and likely to end up in
many a pub-quizzer's Christmas stocking.'
Daily Telegraph

'*QI* is such an institution that even the programme's
researchers are taking over the world. Fully justified
that is, too, as anyone who's heard their podcast,
No Such Thing As A Fish, will confirm. It's packed
with killer facts – and so is this book.'
Daily Mail

'If you love funny facts as much as we love funny
facts then you should get your funny fact-loving
faces in front of *The Book of the Year*.'
Comedy Central UK

'Hugely enjoyable . . . Its tone is just right:
deadpan, sharp and disarmingly offbeat.'
Mail on Sunday

'Bitesize chunks of truth in a year of fake news. If you
love fact-based trivia, you'll get a kick out of this.'
Irish Times

THE BOOK OF THE YEAR 2018

YOUR DEFINITIVE GUIDE TO THE WORLD'S WEIRDEST NEWS

James Harkin, Andrew Hunter Murray, Anna Ptaszynski
and Dan Schreiber

Illustrations by Adam Doughty

BOOKS

5 7 9 10 8 6 4

Random House Books
20 Vauxhall Bridge Road
London SW1V 2SA

Random House Books is part of the Penguin Random House
group of companies whose addresses can be found at
global.penguinrandomhouse.com.

Penguin
Random House
UK

First published by Random House Books in 2018

www.penguin.co.uk

A CIP catalogue record for this book is available
from the British Library.

ISBN 9781847948397

Typeset in 9.5/13 pt ITC Cheltenham Std by Jouve (UK), Milton Keynes
Printed and bound in Great Britain by Clays Ltd, Elcograf S.p.A.

Penguin Random House is committed to a sustainable future
for our business, our readers and our planet. This book is
made from Forest Stewardship Council® certified paper.

MIX
Paper from
responsible sources
FSC® C018179

INTRODUCTION

Welcome back to your annual anthology of the world's weirdest news.

In 2017, when we wrote the first *Book of the Year*, we thought nothing could match the unrelenting absurdity of that year's news. How wrong we were. Since then, not only have the main issues like Brexit and Trump got bigger and madder by the day, thousands of new brilliant, bizarre stories have come to light.

We've spent the last twelve months gathering up the lesser-known facts behind the year's headlines. For instance, we discovered which dictator travels with a personal potty (see **Singapore Summit**), who predicted that leaving the EU might lead to an outbreak of super-gonorrhoea (see **Brexit**), and how half-naked women and tinned peas helped Vladimir Putin stay in power (see **Russian Election**). And obviously we couldn't have written this without mentioning the biggest name of the year (see **Berdymukhamedov, Gurbanguly Mälikgulyýewiç**).

As well as finding the best bits from the main events, we mined the news for the curious and quirky stories that never made it to the front pages. Like the fact that a woman called Crystal Methvin was arrested for possessing crystal meth (see **Names, From the Sublime . . .**); that an ice hotel in Canada caught fire (see **Irony**); and that a snail racing competition was postponed because the snails were too 'sluggish' to take part (see **Animal Races**).

Of course, we wouldn't have learned any of this if it weren't for the world's journalists and fact-finders who dug out the news in the first place. We dedicate this book to all of them, from the investigators who broke the vital news of a government which censored its own policies (*see* **China**) to the reporters who covered the nearly-as-vital campaign to preserve a historic British street name (*see* **Bell End**).

Reading the news every day, it's easy to think the world is a gloomy and frightening place. This book intends to show that it's full of bright, eccentric, uplifting spots too. We hope the stories that follow inspire you to do something great – or if not great, at least something so unbelievably daft that you're guaranteed a place in next year's book (*see* **Urine Trouble**).

So, here we go again – in a year dominated by Kim Jong Un, #MeToo, and Three Lions, we four fact-hunters present to you *The Book of the Year 2018*, your guide to what on earth just happened.

Dan, James, Anna & Andy
Covent Garden, London, 2018

In which we learn . . .
Why flies can't fly with American Airlines, whose
reputation might be tarnished by working with the
White House, who bought Russell Crowe's jockstrap,
how to tell your astronauts from your astron-nots, and
why the Belgian army are such mummy's boys.

AA

American Airlines banned passengers from travelling with emotional support insects.

American Airlines changed its rules on emotional support animals (companion animals prescribed to people with disabilities). Emotional support insects are now prohibited, along with emotional support animals with hooves (apart from emotional support miniature horses, which are allowed). Other banned animals include emotional support amphibians, emotional support ferrets and emotional support hedgehogs. The move was a response to an 84 per cent rise in urine-, faeces- and aggression-related incidents involving animals since 2016.

AA

A man who bought the original Alcoholics Anonymous document waived his anonymity to help alcoholics.

The founding book of Alcoholics Anonymous, dating to 1935, was sold this year for $2.4 million at an auction in Los Angeles. The text, which is known to its members as the 'big book' due to the thickness of its paper, was bought by the owner of the Indianapolis Colts NFL team, who has been battling his own addictions over the last few years. Jim Irsay decided to go public over the sale, saying that he plans to make a cabinet for the book, and display it for part of the year at Alcoholics Anonymous's headquarters in New York in order to help inspire alcoholics to give up drink.

AA ▶

Scientists invented a battery that never runs out.

The AA-sized battery was created by Ossia,
a wireless technology company based in
Washington state. Forever Battery comes
with a transmitter that constantly keeps
it fully charged via Wi-Fi-like waves,
provided that battery and transmitter are
within 10 metres of each other. The hope
is that one day such set-ups will be available
for use in every home.

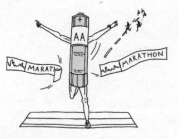

AA ▶

*The Automobile Association found there was one
breakdown they couldn't fix.*

A former executive chairman at the Automobile
Association sued the company for wrongful dismissal
after he was fired for gross misconduct. He said he
was stressed and overworked when he got into a fight
with a colleague, and that the company had no regard
for his mental well-being. Essentially, his argument
appears to be that the AA couldn't deal with his
breakdown.

AA ▶

For American Airlines, *see* **AA**; for Alcoholics
Anonymous, *see* **AA**; for AA batteries, *see* **AA**; for the
Automobile Association, *see* **AA**; and for a pointless list
of all the other AAs, *see* **AA**.

ADVERTISING

Roger Federer lost the rights to his own initials.

The 'RF' logo, famously embroidered into Federer's tennis gear, is owned by Nike, who have been his sponsor for the past 24 years. This means that when he switched allegiance to Japanese company Uniqlo this year, the initials remained the property of his former sponsor. He's currently trying to reach an agreement with Nike to get them back because, as he (rather petulantly) put it, 'They are my initials. They are mine.' The one bit of comfort that he can draw in the meantime is that Uniqlo is paying him $300 million just to wear their clothes on court over the next 10 years.

While Uniqlo and most other advertisers hope to maximise their public exposure, the company that makes Skittles produced an advert that will only ever be seen by one person: teenager and Skittles fan Marcos Menendez. As a publicity stunt, Menendez was shut in a room and shown the advert made specially for him, while his reaction was streamed live on Facebook to thousands of viewers. He revealed afterwards that the ad featured *Friends* star David Schwimmer shooting lasers from his mouth at Marcos's mother and turning her into Skittles.

There's one company, however, that was less than happy with the way its goods were being advertised. Tea manufacturer Twinings complained to the Advertising Standards Authority after Poundland decided to publish a tweet last Christmas showing a 'naughty elf' squatting over a female doll, holding a Twinings tea bag above her face. The accompanying caption read, 'How do you take your tea? One lump or two?' The Advertising Standards Authority ruled in February that the ad was irresponsible.

An advert for women's razors, made by the Billie razor company, became the first one actually to show women's body hair – in the past, women have always been shown shaving already-smooth body parts. And in other underarm advert news, an agency started selling ad space on women's armpits. The Japanese company Wakino paid women to wear stickers as they held onto the overhead handles on the Metro.

Meanwhile, the truth of the old advertising mantra that 'sex sells' was demonstrated in the monkey world this year. A group of male macaques was shown pictures of either dominant male macaque faces, subordinate male faces or female macaque hindquarters, alongside the logos of brands such as Pizza Hut and Adidas. They displayed a very clear preference – for logos they associated with the females' bottoms.

ADVICE, BAD

For turning off your smoke alarms as you cook, *see* **Obituaries**; for submitting your intimate pictures to Facebook, *see* **Send Nudes**; for changing your passwords to 'Nutella', *see* **Twitter**; and for al-Qaeda's tips on how to be a perfect wife, *see* **Women's Rights**.

ADVICE, WORSE

The government advised people being deported to Jamaica to put on a Jamaican accent.

Labour MP David Lammy drew attention this year to a leaflet given to British residents being deported to Jamaica, published when Theresa May was home secretary. As he pointed out, it included such tips as 'Try to be "Jamaican" – use local accents and dialect.' The pamphlet's existence came to light during the Windrush scandal, when it was revealed that hundreds of British subjects who had arrived in the UK between 1948 and 1970 had been wrongly detained, denied legal rights, lost homes, jobs and benefits, and in at least 63 cases had been deported, even though they had originally been given an automatic right to remain permanently in the UK. To make matters worse, the government had destroyed all their landing cards back in 2010 to cut

Goa's agricultural minister advised farmers not to use fertiliser on their fields but to try out 'cosmic farming', which involves chanting ancient Hindu mantras at crops.

back on stored paperwork, so the Windrush generation had no way of proving their status.

Meanwhile, in preparation for the World Cup, Argentina's football association issued a manual to its players and officials that contained a chapter on how to pick up women while they were in Russia. Tips included 'Make sure you're clean, smell good and dress well' and 'Russian girls hate boring men. Never ask trite questions. Be original . . . they don't like to be seen as objects.' The Argentine Football Association insisted the section had been mistakenly included, and when it was noticed they had the booklets returned – and hurriedly ripped out the offending pages.

ALEXA ▶

Alexa got in trouble for laughing at her owners.

The Church of England launched an app that allows you to ask Alexa questions like 'Where is my nearest church?', 'Please read me the Lord's Prayer', 'What is the Bible?' and 'Who is God?' The app proved surprisingly popular. One in ten people who downloaded it now ask Alexa to say grace before meals for them.

Numerous customers reported that Amazon's voice-activated assistant was breaking out into spontaneous laughter when she wasn't even supposed to be switched on. Amazon fixed the glitch, explaining it was caused by Echo devices mistakenly misinterpreting words it overheard as the phrase 'Alexa, laugh'. However, Amazon was not able to explain why one device started telling 'random jokes' without being asked, and why another woke its owner up around midnight and announced 'He's home, he's home' for no apparent reason.

In some cases Alexa even went so far as to place orders for unwanted products. One woman tried to have an Alexa TV advert banned, claiming that her Echo Dot had ordered pet food because it overheard someone on the advert asking for it. And White House press secretary Sarah Huckabee Sanders tweeted that her two-year-old son had inadvertently ordered a Batman toy by shouting 'Batman' repeatedly into their device. Perhaps even more unnervingly, one couple discovered Alexa had recorded their private conversation and sent it to one of their contacts. They only realised when he phoned to inform them he'd just received a recording of them discussing hardwood floors.

Given all this, customers may not be reassured by the news that Amazon have filed a patent for 'voice-sniffing' technology, which would theoretically let its Echo speakers listen to people all the time to ascertain their likes and dislikes. It's no wonder, perhaps, that the name Alexa has declined in popularity by 33 per cent in the US since 2015.

ALL-YOU-CAN-EAT

An all-you-can-eat restaurant had to shut after two weeks because customers ate all they could.

Jiamener, a restaurant in Chengdu, China, shut its doors for good after launching an all-you-can-eat membership card which, for 120 yuan (£13), guaranteed unlimited food for a month. The owners said they were aware they might lose some money initially, but hoped that their loyalty scheme would not only attract clients, but would also allow them to negotiate discounts from food and drink suppliers.

What they didn't count on was how many customers would take advantage of the deal. In the first 14 days, the restaurant attracted more than 7,000 diners, many of whom were repeat customers or people who had borrowed cards from family and friends. After just two weeks the restaurant had fallen into debt to the tune of £50,000 and was forced to shut. The owners cited their 'poor management' as the problem.

Brighton's Big Cheese festival ran out of cheese, due to bad weather that delayed traders. One person wrote on social media, 'Hmmm, was expecting more cheese', while another said, 'I'd rather have gone to the super-market: less queues more cheese.' A couple of months later, an all-you-can-eat pizza festival in Notting Hill ran out of pizza.

AMAZON

For giggling robots, *see* **Alexa**; for the worst way to spend your Amazon vouchers, *see* **Bombs**; for deliveries that will avoid you if you're screaming, *see* **Droning, Dangerous**; for a bracelet that will tell you where to go, *see* **Inventions**; for Sly attempts to tell Amazon where to go, *see* **Offices**; and for a queueless shop that's well worth queuing for, *see* **Queuing**.

ANIMAL RACES

A snail racing competition was postponed because the snails were too 'sluggish'.

Protest group Lambentations persuaded 15,000 people to sign their petition against an event that they believed would involve pigs being raced and lambs being ridden by children at the Swan Inn in Dorset. As the pigs and lambs were actually humans in fancy dress, the occasion went ahead as planned. Lambentations said that the advertising material should have been clearer.

The race was due to take place in February at the Dartmoor Union pub in Plymouth, but when organisers went to the pet shop to collect the snails they were told that the cold weather had made them 'extra sleepy'. The pub should probably have taken advice from the organisers of the World Snail Racing Championships, which always takes place in July, in Norfolk: they use a special damp cloth to keep their snails happy. The human competitors involved, though, don't always show the same compassion – the owner of the winner, Jo Waterfield, said, 'I pulled him out this morning and told him if he didn't win I would squash him.'

The animal race with the youngest participants was undoubtedly 'The Great Hihi Sperm Race' set up by a New Zealand charity to raise money for the hihi bird, an endangered yet relatively unknown species. Sperm samples were taken from four different hihi colonies, and people were encouraged to place a NZ 10-dollar bet on which of the samples would swim the fastest. According to the website: 'The male with the fastest sperm was CP11870 from Tiritiri Matangi Island . . . also known as the male who was "famous for his natty pink leg bands, but secure in his masculinity".'

ANTARCTIC

Every minute, the Antarctic loses enough ice to keep the UK in slushies for an entire year.

In fact, in the time it took you to read that sentence, Antarctica lost 12 Olympic swimming pools' worth of ice, with more than a gigaton (a billion tons) of ice disappearing every two days. Things are definitely getting worse. According to a study published this year, the Antarctic is losing three times more ice than it was as recently as 2012. And as if that weren't bad enough, we've also recently discovered that there's a volcano going off under the South Pole, which is only adding to the effects of climate change.

In better news for the Antarctic this year, researchers discovered a 'supercolony' of 1.5 million previously unknown penguins on the Danger Islands, after noticing streaks of penguin poo in NASA satellite imagery of the islands. Until now, it was thought that this particular species of Adélie penguins was on the decline, but population levels are, in fact, relatively healthy.

Another good piece of Antarctic news came in the form of the first-ever harvest at the South Pole. It was

In July, a 4-billion-year-old particle landed in Antarctica. The neutrino had been ejected from a black hole and had flown through space, unmolested, until it smashed into a science experiment – creating a detectable particle called a muon in the process. Physicists were able to work out exactly which galaxy it had come from, and could effectively map out its entire life.

grown in a giant 'greenhouse' that uses a special liquid nutrient instead of soil, and LEDs rather than sunlight, and whose technology may one day allow us to farm on other planets that are less fertile than our own. The first Antarctic crop was modest, consisting of 18 cucumbers, 70 radishes and 8 pounds of salad leaves.

ARCTIC

China called itself a 'near-Arctic state', despite the fact that its nearest border ends a thousand miles south of the Arctic.

China would love to increase its influence in the Arctic, both because it could then take advantage of shorter trade routes, and because the Arctic contains a third of the world's natural gas reserves and various other tempting resources. So this year China attempted to charm two key regional powers by opening a joint observatory with Iceland, and by lending Finland a couple of pandas. China's first polar cruise ship will launch next year.

It's not just China that is invading the Arctic: this year it was discovered that the Atlantic Ocean is doing the same. Since 2000 the northern Barents region of the Arctic Ocean has been heating very rapidly. As its ice cover has diminished, so has the salinity of the water, turning it into an ocean with qualities very similar to those of the Atlantic. The result has been that Atlantic fish have started to invade traditionally Arctic areas of sea.

But it's not all bad news for the Arctic. A group of students from Bangor University created prototype ice-rebuilding machines that spray water on to existing ice, causing it to freeze, thicken existing ice layers, and hopefully reverse the effects of climate change. A similar technique has been tried in Canada, but the Canadian machines are

Apps

This year, apps were made for the following people:

Stoners: Scientists at the University of Chicago developed a prototype app designed for cannabis users so they can determine whether or not they are actually high. Am I Stoned assesses the effects of the drug on cognitive ability by providing users with a series of tasks to test memory, reaction time and attention span.

Future fathers: A new app called YO has been developed that allows men to check their sperm count without having to see a doctor. It comes with a slide on which men can place a drop of their semen, and the app then takes a picture of the deposit, analyses it and assesses whether the sperm count is normal.

Future farters: Australian scientists invented an indigestible electronic pill which, when paired with a pocket-sized receiver and a mobile app, allows users to monitor their fart development in real time as it passes from the stomach to the colon. The aim is to collect gut data and give us a better understanding of which foods cause digestive problems.

Terrorist organisations: Islamist militant group Hamas built two dating apps, GlanceLove and WinkChat, in which they pretended to be attractive young Israelis in order to lure soldiers into installing malware, compromising their data. Another spying program they built for the same purpose was a World Cup app called 'Gold Cup', which one senior Israeli Defence Force officer described as 'actually very good'.

powered by petrol engines, whereas the new Bangor method is wind-powered and therefore much more environmentally friendly. Sadly, on the day it was first trialled, there wasn't any ice in the Welsh water, meaning it couldn't be fully tested. But it certainly works in *theory*.

ARDERN, JACINDA ▶

New Zealand's prime minister gave birth to a prime miniature.

This year Jacinda Ardern became only the second world leader ever to have a baby while in office (the other was Benazir Bhutto back in 1990). Ardern gave birth to her daughter on 21 June* and then took six weeks of maternity leave.

Which, coincidentally, was also Benazir Bhutto's birthday.

Ardern first discovered she was pregnant with the 'prime miniature' (as the baby was dubbed on Twitter) only six days before she became prime minister-elect and barely two months after she had been handed the Labour Party leadership. Labour at the time was in real difficulties: its popularity in the polls was at a 20-year low of 23 per cent, and the party had just run through four leaders in four years. Ardern told reporters, 'Everyone knows that I have just accepted, with short notice, the worst job in politics.'

However, only a few weeks into the campaign 'Jacinda-mania' (as the press called it) kicked in, and she ended up increasing her party's vote by 50 per cent. In October 2017, aged 37, she became the world's youngest female leader.

Ardern named her daughter Neve Te Aroha Ardern Gayford. Te Aroha is a tiny farming community with a population of 3,900, near to where Ardern grew up. The townspeople were so excited by the news that they announced plans to paint all of their buildings pink and invited Ardern to visit so she could take part in the traditional Maori practice of burying the afterbirth in the earth. Jacinda did not respond to the offer, perhaps because she was considering her options: earlier in the year another Maori tribe had suggested she bury her placenta at the spot where Britain signed the treaty that led to the founding of modern New Zealand.

As well as putting a small town on the map, this year Jacinda fronted a nationwide campaign to help put New Zealand *back* on the map. As she pointed out in a video she made with comedian Rhys Darby, world maps produced in other countries have a worrying tendency to leave out New Zealand – the board game *Risk*, a map in Central Park Zoo, a John Lewis tablecloth and an episode of *The Simpsons* are just four of the places you won't find it, according to online communities that have been monitoring the problem for some years.

In other pregnant Kiwi politician news, Julie Genter, New Zealand's Minister for Women and Associate Minister for Health and Transport, cycled to hospital to give birth.

ARMENIA

Armenians held a snowball fight in temperatures of 25 degrees Celsius.

The snow was transported from the Armenian mountains in an enormous dump truck specifically to celebrate the fact that Prime Minister Serzh Sargsyan

Armenia's new government launched an anti-corruption drive. As part of this, Vachagan Ghazarian, a former bodyguard of Sargsyan's, was arrested after being stopped leaving a bank with more than $1 million in cash, and Republican MP Manvel Grigoryan was arrested after being accused of stealing food sent by children for the Armenian army and feeding it instead to the tigers and bears in his private zoo.

had stepped down in the face of huge public protests. Some said the white snow showed the demonstrators' purity and their desire for democracy in the country – but most saw it as actually just a way to have a bit of fun.

In 2015, the Armenian people voted to swap their presidential system for a parliamentary one, with the country run by a prime minister. This year, Sargsyan, who had been president for the previous 10 years, said he would not try to become prime minister, and indeed the opposition planted a 'farewell tree' to say good riddance to him. Two days later, though, the Republican Party of Armenia (RPA) confirmed it would nominate Sargsyan to be the country's next prime minister – a role that, thanks to new laws, meant he would be even more powerful than he had ever been as president.

During the protests that ensued, opposition leader Nikol Pashinyan led a 200-kilometre march from Armenia's second city of Gyumri to the capital Yerevan, where he was promptly arrested. Further marches followed, in which some 20 per cent of the country took part. Sargsyan eventually bowed to pressure, saying, 'I was wrong, while Nikol Pashinyan was right.' Pashinyan became Armenia's new prime minister.

ARMIES

American soldiers gave away the location of secret military bases by going jogging.

There's a GPS tracking company called Strava which employs satellite information to map the location of people using Fitbits and other wearable fitness devices all over the world. In Europe and America, the devices are ubiquitous – but in countries such as Iraq or Syria, US soldiers are almost the only people using them. This, of course, means that wherever the Strava map lights up red in those areas, there's almost certainly a military base there. The publicly available information on the map has therefore given away daily patterns, supply routes and even patrol routes. The worst part of it is that in 2013 the Pentagon gave out 2,500 Fitbits to its soldiers to help fight obesity, hence unwittingly compromising its own bases.

At least US army personnel are trying to keep fit. The Chinese army has had to ban fat soldiers from promotion after a fifth of would-be recruits failed the weight test: in some brigades, 40 per cent of soldiers failed to complete a 5-kilometre cross-country run. (Last year the official state newspaper blamed failure to get into the army on young men's poor diets and excess masturbation.) As for the Spanish army, it was announced in January that 180 legionnaires from the elite rapid reaction force were too overweight to fight. They have been put on a diet.

But this year's prize for the most mocked armed force goes to the Belgian army, which announced plans to let recruits sleep at home during training – so they don't get homesick. One horrified former paratrooper said, 'You don't go to a war zone with men who miss their mummies.'

───── ▼ ─────

It was revealed this year that the US has built a digital North Korea, where American troops can practise fighting in virtual reality on enemy terrain before doing it for real.

ARRESTS

For the MP who was charged with stealing from army privates and giving to his private zoo, *see* **Armenia**; for illegally impersonating a spaceman, *see* **Astronauts**; for why crime doesn't pay if you have pants on your head, *see* **Bank Robbers**; for how the 'mop' got 'in the bucket', *see* **Catalonia**; for illegally criticising the Thai prime minister's music, *see* **Chan-o-cha, Prayuth**; for things you shouldn't do outside your car, *see* **Drake**; for things you shouldn't do *inside* your car, *see* **Driving, Dangerous**; for a salad-based dressing-down, *see* **Excuses**; for a DIRTBAG, *see* **Licence Plates**; for a man caught red-faced, *see* **Meatballs**; for a man caught with his fingers in the Play-Doh, *see* **Shoplifters**; for forbidden love, *see* **Valentine's Day**; and for viral tattoos, *see* **Yakuza**.

ARTIFICIAL INTELLIGENCE

Scientists exposed their AI machine to an online forum, and it became a psychopath.

The team from MIT fed the comments from a particularly angry message board into the machine, which they called Norman. After doing so, they showed Norman ink blots from the Rorschach test, which are often used to give clues about a subject's personality, and compared Norman's responses to those of another computer that had not seen the Internet comments. Where a normal AI saw 'a black and white photo of a baseball glove', Norman saw 'a man is murdered by machine gun in broad daylight'; and where the normal AI saw 'a person is holding an umbrella in the air', Norman thought of 'a man is shot dead in front of his screaming wife'.

In more constructive technology innovations this year, it turns out that AI programs can be better than doctors at spotting cancer. In one test, machines were pitted against doctors in a competition to spot and diagnose skin cancer. The machines got it right 95 per cent of the time; the doctors only managed 87 per cent. And Nissan invented an AI that trundles around and scans the ground, looking for a flattish clear space large enough for a football pitch. It then paints the markings on that area, ready for a game. It's the robot equivalent of putting your jumpers down as goalposts.

Art

The Book of the Year *Art Awards are as follows:*

Hyperrealism: In Hong Kong, cleaners accidentally threw away a piece of art. In their defence, it looked like rubbish: Swiss artist Carol May had made an 'Unhappy Meal' by recreating a discarded McDonald's box with a frown instead of the trademark smile. 'Initially I didn't find it funny at all,' May said, 'but later I realised it meant my imitation had been a success.'

Street Art: The Royal Academy rejected a work by Banksy, which he had submitted to their summer exhibition under the pseudonym 'Bryan S. Gaakman' (an anagram of 'Banksy anagram'). A month later, the Academy contacted Banksy asking if he might submit a piece to the exhibition – so he sent them a slightly revised version of the same piece, which they accepted.

Kinetic: A fire broke out in London's Hayward Art Gallery when the exhibit *Majestic Splendor* – consisting of a collection of rotten fish covered in sequins – spontaneously combusted.

Performance: Australian artist Mike Parr had himself buried alive in a steel box under an open road for 72 hours to symbolise the 'burial' of Aboriginal history. The unimpressed chief of the Tasmanian Aboriginal Centre said, 'The idea of our Aboriginal history being hidden . . . is a valid point. The most effective way of bringing it out is not climbing under the road.'

A group from IBM, meanwhile, unveiled Project Debater – a new artificial intelligence program that they said could successfully debate against humans. It uses a library of millions of documents from around the world to create its arguments. The one problem with it is that it does tend to hammer its points home. It was reported that 'During the space debate, for example, it repeated the point that space exploration is beneficial to the economy several times using slightly different words.' So it's not a perfect technique, but at least that should not preclude Project Debater from becoming president of the United States.

ASTEROIDS

Scientists concluded that birds escaped death by asteroid thanks to their inability to fly.

According to a team of evolutionary scientists, the fossil record shows that the asteroid that wiped out the dinosaurs 66 million years ago destroyed so much tree life that all flying birds, who lived in trees, died out. Only flightless, ground-dwelling, emu-like ones survived, and those survivors must therefore be the common ancestors of all birds today. Birds didn't relearn to fly until thousands of years later, when the forests returned.

To avoid being hit by giant asteroids in the future, Russian scientists blasted tiny, centimetre-wide rocks with lasers, simulating the effect of a nuclear bomb. They hope to be able to scale this up to work on asteroids that are even wider than an inch in future. Not to be outdone, NASA announced plans for an eight-tonne spaceship called HAMMER which will be able to push an asteroid out of Earth's path.

Japan also deployed asteroid-striking technology, but for different reasons. Its *Hayabusa2* spacecraft, which has spent the last four years travelling through space, arrived at its target, the Ryugu asteroid, currently located about 200 million miles away, between Earth and Mars. The plan is that next year, *Hayabusa2* will release a projectile that will smash into the asteroid at a mile a second, making a crater that will be filmed and beamed back to Earth so that astronomers can better understand how craters are formed. According to one scientist, the *Hayabusa2* projectile is 'a kinetic impactor, which is what we say in polite company when we don't want to say the word "bomb"'.

The largest asteroid to come close to hitting Earth in recent memory came within a mere 192,317 kilometres of us as it flew by in April. It was the size of a football pitch, six times bigger than the one that injured 1,200 people in Russia in 2013 – and astronomers didn't even notice it was coming until the day before it arrived.

ASTRONAUTS

NASA sent a man with a fear of heights to the International Space Station.

Astronaut Andrew Feustel, who flew up to the ISS in March, confessed to this mild phobia not long before leaving on his six-month space mission. Fortunately his fear of heights doesn't affect him too badly when he is 250 miles above the planet, 'but it is there,' he said.

Three months into his mission Feustal became the commander of the ISS, and while on board conducted over 250 science investigations and technology demonstrations. He also started a band called AstroHawaii, which featured five of the ISS's astronauts and cosmonauts. Their instruments included two guitars, two flutes – and an improvised drum, which is actually a metallic unit that stores all of the Russian cosmonauts' faeces.

In other astronaut news, the world said goodbye to two Apollo moonwalkers. In January, John Young died. He was a member of the Apollo 16 lunar mission, and was not only the ninth person to stand on the Moon, but also sparked a review into the safety of crumbs in space after he sneaked a corned beef sandwich up there. Five months later, we lost Alan Bean, who as well as being the fourth man to stand on the Moon was also a painter. 'Buzz Aldrin will call me up sometimes,' Bean once said, 'wanting to talk about space stuff, cos he's really into space stuff. And I say, "Quit talkin' to me, Buzz . . . I'm not an astronaut any more. I don't phone you to ask you what colours to paint these things."'

Meanwhile, in India, a father and his son were arrested after conning a businessman out of £160,000 by pretending to work for NASA. The pair successfully convinced the man they had invented a device that could generate electricity from thunderbolts. They even performed a demonstration for him in silver spacesuits. After the businessman realised he had been duped by the pair, the police were called and the astro-nots were arrested.

ATTORNEYS ▶

Numerous lawyers refused to represent the US president for fear he'd damage their reputation.

When Donald Trump's lead attorney, John Dowd, resigned over a disagreement with his client, the president hunted for a replacement to represent his interests in the Robert Mueller-led investigation into alleged Russian meddling in the US 2016 election. However, a number of lawyers who were approached later said they turned the offer down because they were concerned that defending him might damage their professional reputation. According to Ted Boutrous, one of LA's top lawyers, Trump is a 'notoriously difficult client who disregards the advice of his lawyers and asks them to engage in questionable activities'. Trump was eventually left with only two lawyers on his legal team – Ty Cobb* and Jay Sekulow – neither of whom come from traditional law firms.

Eventually the former mayor of New York Rudy Giuliani joined the team. He's had dealings with Donald before: a video from 2000 resurfaced this year, showing him at a charity event dressed as a woman and calling Trump a 'dirty boy' for nuzzling into his fake breasts.

The breast-touching video was not the only problem with Trump's new lawyer. The DC Bar website lists Giuliani as an 'Inactive Attorney', meaning he's not licensed to practise in the District of Columbia. Consequently, should Trump ever have to appear in court during the Mueller investigation, his own lawyer won't be able to attend.

Lawyers and breasts met again this year when, owing to a computer malfunction, every single lawyer in Utah received a photo of a woman's naked breasts. The Utah State Bar sent an event invitation and somehow managed to attach the image by mistake. But despite

*In May, Cobb left the legal team set up to advise Trump during the Russia investigation. He was replaced by Emmet Flood – who represented Bill Clinton during his impeachment.

technological hiccups, courts increasingly rely on machines to replace humans. For instance, the Serious Fraud Office in the UK announced they'd be using evidence-sifting robots on all their casework in future, since one robot can scan more than half a million documents a day.

AUCTIONS ▶

Russell Crowe held an auction called 'The Art of Divorce' on his wedding anniversary.

The auction, held at Sotheby's Australia, included a car used on the day of Crowe's wedding and some jewellery that once belonged to his ex-wife, Danielle. Crowe said the reason he had decided to go ahead with it was that he was keen to try to turn something bleak into something joyful. The auction was streamed live on Facebook and lasted five hours, during which time members of the public were able to bid on 227 lots that also included a leather jockstrap and a life-sized rubber horse.

$79,788 of the $3.7 million Crowe made in the auction came from comedian John Oliver's TV show *Last Week Tonight*, which bought numerous bits of Crowe memorabilia, including the jockstrap which the actor wore in the movie *Cinderella Man*. Oliver then lent the underwear to an Alaskan Blockbuster video store in the hope that by displaying it, the jockstrap might attract more customers for them. The store has since closed. A joke feud then broke out, with Crowe returning the gesture by using the $79,788 to fund a ward at Australia Zoo's wildlife hospital to treat chlamydia in koalas. A plaque on the wall of the ward now reads: 'The John Oliver Koala Chlamydia Ward'.

Other auctions around the world featured a broken teapot originally bought for £15 which was sold for

£575,000; the original map of Winnie the Pooh's Hundred Acre Wood which sold for £430,000, setting a new world record for a book illustration; a 1973 job application by Steve Jobs which fetched $174,000 despite not identifying what job Jobs was applying for; and a lunch with billionaire Warren Buffett* which was auctioned for $3.3 million. A postcard from a passenger aboard the *Titanic* failed to sell when it didn't meet its reserve of £10,000. Addressed to a Miss Green in Birmingham, it included the words 'wish you were here, it is a lovely boat & it would do you good'.

Sadly, it wasn't a buffet.

AUSTRALIA

For the Aussie who went down under a road, *see* **Art**; for koala chlamydia, *see* **Auctions**; for sportsmen on the run, *see* **Commonwealth Games**; for sportsmen who did disgusting things with their balls, *see* **Cricket, Just Not**; for a part-man, part-travelcard, *see* **Cyborgs**; for swimmers saved by a flying lifeguard, *see* **Droning, Dangerous**; for animals who are dying for sex, *see* **Endangered**; for a global convention that fell a bit flat, *see* **Flat-Earthers**; for teaching bees nothing, *see* **Honeybees**; for a 132-year-old letter, *see* **Messaging, Very Much Not Instant**; for the place where prostitutes can't advertise via skywriting, *see* **Queensland**; for the world's fastest flying, *see* **Quokkas**; for the world's fastest centenarian, *see* **Records, Broken**; for an oyster that wasn't quite big enough, *see* **Records, Unbroken**; for a lost piece of North America, *see* **Rocks**; for ARSE, *see* **Space Exploration**; for secret docs in furniture shops, *see* **Spies**; and for free pornography in the town of Blowhard, *see* **XXX**.

In which we learn . . .
Why terrorists don't carry plastics with their
explosives, why 50 Cent doesn't have a penny to his
name, why there was a ding-dong over Bell End, who
fell foul of the Botox Bandits, and the worst way to
spend a 'Student of the Year' voucher.

BABIES

A baby in Abu Dhabi was given a government job as 'Happiness Executive'.

The Public Prosecution Office in the United Arab Emirates summoned government officials to explain themselves after a video was posted online of eight-month-old Mohammad Al Hashimi sat at a desk with aeroplanes and rubber ducks, shaking hands with the director general of the General Civil Aviation Authority. The video announced that he was the 'Youngest Employee in the World'. The GCAA later backtracked and said that, of course, the baby had not been given an *actual* job, as that would break children's rights laws. It was, they said, simply an activity run by the department's nursery.

A child was born on the Brazilian island of Fernando de Noronha for the first time in 12 years. They have no maternity ward there, and so it is official government policy to get expectant mothers off the island before they give birth. In this case, though, the woman had no choice but to flout the ban, as she hadn't previously realised she was pregnant.

Another baby to enter public life was Prince Louis, the third child of the Duke and Duchess of Cambridge who was born in April. Louis became the first male royal ever to be ranked behind a sister in the line of succession. He was baptised in July with water flown in from the River Jordan. Louis was a surprise choice for his name: James, Albert, Philip, Alexander and Henry were the ones most commonly predicted, along with Arthur, which was considered so likely by some that one bookmaker actually paid out on bets made on that name a few days before Louis was announced.

If it was a slightly leftfield decision, it wasn't quite as leftfield as Lucas Skywalker Scott, the name selected for their new baby by an American couple. They'd chosen it not only because they are huge *Star Wars* fans but because he was born on 4 May (known as 'Star Wars Day' due to the pun 'May the Fourth be with you'). The name was originally intended for their first son who was born two years before, but unfortunately he ended up being born on 3 May.

BANK ROBBERS

Sweden is running out of bank robbers because most banks no longer have anything to rob.

Bank robberies used to be very common in Sweden. In fact, cash heists in general were worryingly frequent. Partly in response, the country has become one of the world's most cashless – Stockholm's buses, for example, abandoned cash payments after a particularly robbery-heavy year in 2006. The move towards electronic payment acquired such momentum that cash accounts for just 2 per cent of the value of all payments. Today fewer than half of the country's banks have any cash in them. The result has been an extraordinary decline in the number of bank robberies: from 110 in 2009 to only 11 in 2017.

Unfortunately, the move away from bank jobs has led to increases in other crimes, including smash-and-grab raids, muggings, and heists on moving trucks full of high-value products. Not only that, the black market in endangered species is booming – there's been a surge in both orchid smuggling and owl thefts. A contraband great grey owl is worth about a million Swedish kronor, or £85,000.

Countries such as America, on the other hand, still have plenty of old-fashioned bank robbers. One such example is the Connecticut man who fancied Taylor Swift so much that he allegedly robbed a bank and then drove 60 miles to her house to throw the money over her fence in an attempt to impress her. Given that Swift earned $54 million in just the first five cities of her latest tour, and that he managed to steal only $1,600, his gesture probably wouldn't have done the trick, even if he hadn't then been immediately arrested.

In Britain, an armed robber who took on a G4S van came a cropper when the underpants he'd placed over his head to disguise his face proved such an effective mask that he proceeded to walk straight into a parked van. He was later arrested and jailed.

BANNED

Terrorist group al-Shabaab announced a complete ban on all single-use plastic bags.

According to the group's official radio station, plastic bags have been banned in all Somali territories run by al-Shabaab because they 'pose a serious threat to the well-being of humans and animals alike'. The logging of indigenous trees has also been prohibited. Plastic bags join a growing list of items outlawed by al-Shabaab that so far includes (among other things) Western music, cinemas, smartphones, fibre optic services and humanitarian agencies.

Other authorities who have issued surprising bans this year include:

▶ The Chinese government, who banned all online videos of people whispering, brushing their hair, and eating ice cubes to stop the rise of ASMR. Standing for 'autonomous sensory meridian response', ASMR describes the tingling, relaxing or sleep-inducing feeling that some people get when watching these videos. Suspicious of the phenomenon, the government has decided to order the removal of them from China's biggest streaming sites.

▶ A Maryland prison, which banned all *Game of Thrones* books. According to Kimberly Hricko, an inmate at the Maryland Correctional Institution for Women, the books have been permanently banned because they contain maps. They may be invented maps pinpointing the location of imaginary places, but they are still considered contraband.

▶ A Mexican court, which banned the sale of Frida Kahlo Barbie dolls. The court ruled the dolls couldn't be sold, as the Kahlo family are the sole owners of her image. The family objected to the doll, saying that it should have looked more Mexican. The Mattel doll was too light-skinned, they said, and was missing Kahlo's trademark monobrow.

BAYEUX TAPESTRY ▶

An Oxford professor became the first person to count all of the horses' penises in the Bayeux Tapestry.

— ◆ —

France announced it will lend the Bayeux Tapestry to the UK in 2022, having refused British requests in 1953 and 1966. It will be first time the tapestry has left France in 950 years.

At least, he's the first we know of. Professor George Garnett, of St Hugh's College, wrote in *BBC History Magazine* that of the 93 penises that feature in the tapestry, 88 are equine, suggesting that horses' genitals must have had a symbolic significance.

As evidence of this, Professor Garnett pointed out that while King Harold is 'mounted on an exceptionally well-endowed steed . . . the largest equine penis by far is that protruding from the horse presented by a groom to a figure who must be Duke William, just prior to the battle of Hastings'. William the Conqueror, of course, went on to win the battle. According to the professor, the fact

28

that he did so on this enormously hung horse 'cannot be simply a coincidence'.

BEANO ▶

The Beano ordered Jacob Rees-Mogg to stop looking and acting like a cartoon character.

The character Walter the Softy is distinguished by his side parting, round glasses and all-round 'snootiness', as well as his 'bullish behaviour with peers and stopping others from having fun'. The similarity with the hard-line Brexiteer is striking, and so the creators of the comic said, in a letter addressed to the Houses of Parliament, that Rees-Mogg had 'adopted trademarked imagery and brand essences of the character to the benefit of enhancing [his] career and popularity'. Rees-Mogg declared he thought the letter was 'very jolly stuff', though he rebutted some of the allegations, insisting he's actually in favour of people having fun.

BEARDS ▶

False beards were banned in Copenhagen.

Gal Vallerius, a well-known competitive beard grower, was arrested on his way to a beard-growing contest and charged with running one of the biggest drug-trafficking sites on the dark web, under the pseudonym 'OxyMonster'. A fellow beard-grower expressed his sorrow, saying, 'He always seemed like a fun, carefree person. I don't know anything about what other stuff he did but as far as his beard goes, it's really awesome, long, and bright red.'

When Denmark banned the wearing of full-face veils this year, many saw the move as an illiberal measure that unfairly targeted Muslim women. But because the new rules had to be consistent so as not to breach anti-discrimination legislation, it wasn't just this form of face covering that was made illegal: balaclavas and fake beards were prohibited too. Exceptions are being made, however, for those who can demonstrate a 'worthy purpose' – i.e. if it's very cold. Incidentally, the total number of women estimated to have been wearing full-face burqas and niqabs in Denmark when the legislation was passed was about 200.

In Iran, it was women who were wearing the fake beards – to get around a ban on attending football matches. An enterprising group of women bearded up in Tehran and saw their team win 3–0. And in Kyrgyzstan's capital, Bishkek, the mayor has been wearing a false beard and old clothes as he tours the city in disguise to witness his people's problems first hand and 'see how things actually are'.

In *real* beard news, meanwhile, the SAS joined the US army in banning soldiers from growing them – though the US army did allow one sergeant to keep his beard because of his Norse pagan faith. An Islamic preacher, meanwhile, warned that men had a *duty* to grow beards, as the sight of clean-shaven men might provoke 'indecent thoughts' in other men's minds.

BECKER, BORIS

Boris Becker announced he was an ambassador to a country he'd never visited.

The former tennis star was declared bankrupt in 2017 and court proceedings against him were due to start this summer. Just before they did, Becker suddenly claimed he'd been made sports, culture and humanitarian attaché to the Central African Republic, which, according to his lawyers, gave him diplomatic immunity against any attempts to enforce his bankruptcy. Confusion ensued as the CAR's government denied such a role existed, while its envoy in Brussels seemed to confirm that it did.

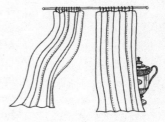

Becker then produced a diplomatic passport, saying that the CAR's ambassador to Germany had given it to him, and that he'd had an official inauguration and multiple conversations with the president. The CAR's foreign ministry claimed the passport was a forgery, pointing out that the document's serial number corresponded to one of a batch stolen in 2014. Becker did acknowledge he'd never actually been to the country, but said he'd very much like to visit when his schedule allowed it.

As the bankruptcy case continued, bailiffs visited Becker's home to seize his assets, but were unable to find the most valuable ones – his three Wimbledon trophies. One was eventually tracked down at his mother's house, but the other two remained missing. An official handling the bankruptcy said, 'There are a lot of trophies so it's possible one might forget where a couple of them are, but these are perhaps the highest value ones and it's particularly unfortunate that he can't remember where they are.'

BELL END

Residents of a West Midlands town launched a petition to save their Bell End.

Bell End is an unfortunately named street in Rowley Regis which, in 2014, was named the fourth-rudest street name in the UK, beaten only by Minge Lane, Slag Lane and Fanny Hands Lane. In January, some local residents started a petition to have the name changed, concerned at the effect it was having on house prices, and the fact that children who lived on Bell End were a target for bullies.

They suggested changing it to something similar but less offensive, such as Bell Road. However, they managed to attract just 23 signatures in four weeks, while a rival petition, 'Leave the Historic Name of Bell End Alone!', eventually received almost 5,000.

In the end, the local council told journalists there was no plan to change the name of Bell End because, apart from anything else, they had not received copies of either petition.

BERDYMUKHAMEDOV, GURBANGULY MÄLIKGULYÝEWIÇ

Citizens of Turkmenistan were told not to use pictures of the president's face as toilet paper.

The secretive state reportedly employed janitors to search people's rubbish for newspapers with Gurbanguly Berdymukhamedov's face on them, and report what they found to the police. Berdymukhamedov runs the country as a near-celebrity cult and people are forced to subscribe to the state newspaper. But toilet roll is in short supply and so they tend to wipe with the only paper that is in plentiful supply. As the BBC reported, 'It is difficult not to soil the Turkmen leader's photos because his pictures dominate all newspapers.'

One reason Berdymukhamedov was in the news this year is that he won an international motor race qualifier. He had actually turned up at the venue in the Karakum Desert to meet one of his ministers, but upon hearing that his BMW car met the entry requirements for the race, he decided to take part – and won. Whether the win was down to his skills or the fact that nobody dared beat him is not clear, but it was noted that the car was navigated by his son Serdar, who is also Turkmenistan's foreign minister.

On Berdymukhamedov's birthday, state media announced that his favourite presidential horse had broken a world record by running for 10 metres on its hind legs.

BITCOIN

A Miami bitcoin conference stopped accepting bitcoin.

The organisers of the North American Bitcoin Conference in Miami informed attendees that they wouldn't be able to buy their tickets with bitcoin because of processing problems and the high transaction fees involved. Conversely, a mosque in London became the

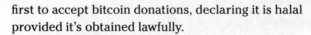

first to accept bitcoin donations, declaring it is halal provided it's obtained lawfully.

The mosque is right to be cautious, as bitcoin and crime seem increasingly to go hand in hand. In Britain's first bitcoin heist, robbers broke into the house of currency trader Danny Aston and demanded he transfer huge amounts of it over to them. Thankfully, the transfer failed, and the robbers left the house without realising it hadn't gone through.

But this incident pales into insignificance in comparison to the theft of $534 million-worth of various crypto-currencies in Japan, when hackers broke into a digital storage area known as a 'hot wallet' and siphoned off the assets. The crime represents the biggest single theft in the entire history of the world.

Cryptocurrency prices fluctuated throughout the year, but nobody went through quite as much of a financial roller coaster as rapper 50 Cent. Tabloid news website *TMZ* claimed he'd acquired a few hundred dollars of bitcoin in 2014, then forgotten about it, and that it was now worth $7.5 million. When he filed for bankruptcy a month or so later, he was forced to admit the original story wasn't true. He explained he hadn't denied it at the time because he doesn't tend to deny reports that are favourable to his image.

Bitcoin may be the most successful cryptocurrency, but there are many others, and new ones are being created all the time. One such newcomer is Banana-coin, a unit of which is equivalent in value to the export price of a kilo of premium bananas in Laos. The tokens can be traded either for that sum of money or for a kilo of actual bananas. And a new crypto-coin called Prodeum was recently offered to investors, only for its website to disappear, leaving just the word 'penis' in its place.

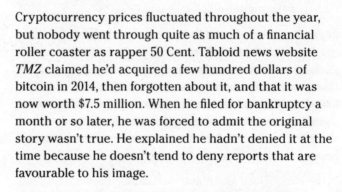

Strippers in Las Vegas started accepting bitcoin payments via a QR code temporarily tattooed on to their bodies. Patrons pay by scanning it with their phones.

BLUE ICE ▶

The Canadian aviation coordinator denied that Canadian planes were dropping poo on Canadian people.

This year Transport Canada received 18 complaints from people in Western Canada about mysterious down-pours of what appeared to be human excrement that had fallen on them. One victim said, 'It's definitely not something anybody should experience. Ever.'

Transport Canada denied any planes had been overhead at the times of the various incidents, and went on to say that the reports they had received did not tally with descriptions of 'blue ice' – frozen excrement that occasionally falls from planes. Despite multiple incidents of foul-smelling matter falling from the sky, officials declared the matter officially closed.

Environmental scientist Robert Young, on the other hand, said that, judging from the smell and the fact that someone had caught conjunctivitis from the falling matter, faeces were probably involved. 'It's just a matter of identifying the perpetrator . . .' he said, adding, 'I don't think this will be one of the great mysteries of the universe.' So far, however, the reason for the deluge remains unknown.

Plane poo proved much more welcome in India – initially, at least – when a 12-kilogram lump of 'blue ice' fell from the sky and was mistaken by the residents of the village of Fazilpur Badli for a UFO or a piece of space rock. They took it home, but soon regretted their decision. As one resident told the *Times of India*, 'Villagers who kept it inside their refrigerators are disappointed and are now busy cleaning their houses.'

— ▼ —

A plane carrying over 80 plumbers had to turn around because of a problem with the toilet. The passengers would have happily tried to fix it, but unfortunately it was a fault that needed to be repaired from the outside.

BOMBS ▶

The Parsons Green bomber paid for the explosives using a voucher he'd won for being 'student of the year'.

Police were called to Gothenburg airport when a man tried to pass through security with two jars and a bottle that he claimed were filled with yoghurt and honey. Security officials scanned the containers twice, and identified the contents as TATP, an explosive commonly referred to as 'Mother of Satan'. Parts of the airport were closed for five hours, flights were diverted and the objects were taken to a secure outdoor location for testing. Expert analysis revealed that the contents were, indeed, yoghurt and honey.

Ahmed Hassan, who was responsible for the 2017 explosion that injured 29 people, was convicted in March this year. During his trial it was revealed he'd bought some of the chemicals for his home-made bomb with a £20 Amazon voucher that his college in Surrey had presented to him as a prize for being a model student.

A number of bomb scares this year were allegedly triggered by misunderstandings. One man waiting for a flight from Mumbai to Delhi was arrested for saying 'bomb hai', meaning 'there is a bomb', during a call to airport authorities. He insisted he'd been saying 'Bom–Del' – referring to Bombay, the former name of Mumbai. Coincidentally, a couple of months later, a woman travelling from Mumbai to Australia also caused an alert when it was noticed that she'd written 'Bomb to Brisbane' on her bag. Again, she claimed to have used the old word for the city, this time with an unfortunate abbreviation. And in another case of careless abbreviating, a bakery in London called Bombetta was raided by police after a bread delivery was left outside with the first four letters of the establishment's name written on the bag.

BOOKS OF THE YEAR ▶

For why *Game of Thrones* isn't allowed in jail, *see* **Banned**; for why Sean Penn shouldn't pen novels, *see* **Celebs**; for the sports book in the 'true crime' section, *see* **Cricket, Just Not**; for a 10-year-old book that accidentally became a bestseller, *see* **Fire and Fury**; for a tale with one sentence, *see* **Literary Prizes**; for *A Tale of Two Sisters*, *see* **Markles, The**; for controversial recipe books, *see* **Obituaries**; for what 'real men' don't eat, *see* **Quiche**; for a group who don't know how to use books, *see* **Schoolchildren**; and for how the cockiest author in the world got too cocky, *see* **Trademarks**.

BOTOX ▶

A man who hadn't burped for 34 years was finally cured by Botox.

Doctors had long been baffled by a mysterious condition that left the patient in agony after meals, with his stomach bloating to twice its normal size and his throat emitting a strange gurgling sound. He said he'd become extremely good at farting as a way of releasing gas after eating. But after enduring excruciating pain for more than three decades, he was finally offered relief in the form of Botox injections in his larynx, which relaxed it and so allowed gas to escape. Now he says he has been 'burping like a frog' – an appropriate simile for a man whose name is Neil Ribbens.

More conventional Botox use became a police matter when three 'Botox bandits' in south-east England ran away without paying for the extensive treatments they'd had. But because they agreed to pose for the first stage of 'before and after' pictures, police at least had something to go on and were able to release reasonably

In Saudi Arabia, 12 camels were disqualified from the annual camel beauty contest when it was discovered they'd been injected with Botox to make them better-looking.

up-to-date photos, as well as a description of two women, and a man with a 'neat beard, puffy cheeks and trimmed eyebrows'. A restaurateur in the area recognised the man immediately, saying he'd once demanded a free meal from her, and that in any case she knew it was him because 'there's no way you would ever forget that face'.

BOXERS ►

An American boxer tried to intimidate his Mexican opponent by wearing shorts with 'America 1st' printed on them. He came 2nd.

Unfortunately for Rod Salka, his plan to unnerve Mexican boxer Francisco Vargas backfired when Vargas used the pro-Trump shorts (which were also decorated with images of bricks to symbolise the proposed border wall) as extra motivation to beat the American senseless. The match ended with Salka's team throwing in the towel after six rounds.

It wasn't the first time Salka has been vocal about his political views. In 2016, he attempted to swap the boxing ring for the political ring by running as a Republican for the Pennsylvania House of Representatives. He came second then, too.

Donald Trump himself racked up an honourable mention in boxing news when he announced he was thinking of posthumously pardoning Muhammad Ali. In response, Ali's lawyer, Ron Tweel, released a statement saying that while the family appreciated the sentiment, a pardon wouldn't be necessary, as there was no offence on the record for which Ali needed to be pardoned.

BREXIT

The government denied that a project called 'Brexit Operations Across Kent' had anything to do with Brexit.

The plan is to turn a 13-mile section of the M20 into a car park, where backed-up lorries can park if they're delayed in reaching Dover to cross the English Channel. The government said it was part of 'standard procedure designed to improve cross-channel transport', unrelated to any predicted disruption caused by Brexit. It then emerged that the name of the project was Operation Brock, short for Brexit Operations Across Kent.

Theresa May's own Brexit operations faced tough opposition in Parliament. A series of extremely close votes put MPs under huge pressure to attend. In June, MP Naz Shah discharged herself from hospital in Bradford, missing an operation she was due to have, and came to Westminster while high on morphine and carrying a sick bucket. Two other Labour MPs arrived in wheelchairs due to illness, and the pregnant Lib Dem Jo Swinson voted while two days past her due date. Swinson, a Remainer, was on maternity leave for an even closer vote in July, and so Brexiteer MP Brandon Lewis was 'paired' with her. According to parliamentary protocol, this means he shouldn't have voted, to balance out the fact that she couldn't. He controversially went against this long-established rule and did so anyway.

The Cabinet was no more united than Parliament. The *Sun* reported that at a meeting in June, Michael Gove tore up Theresa May's plan for a European customs partnership in a fit of rage. And during a crucial summit at Chequers on 6 July, May's spin doctors warned ministers that if they resigned over May's proposals they would lose car privileges and have to pay for a taxi home. Taxi business cards were left at the foyer at Chequers to emphasise the threat.

In July, a toilet at Westminster that had been out of order for six weeks was given a sign that read, 'If we cannot fix a toilet in six weeks, what are our chances of negotiating Brexit in eight months?'

The long-term effects of Brexit remain uncertain. According to Niall Dickson, chief executive of the NHS Confederation, a no-deal Brexit could cause medical shortages, leading to a rise in super-gonorrhoea. And the people in the Devon town of Totnes showed their displeasure at the UK's exit from the EU by declaring their independence from Britain and blu-tacking their treatise to the church door. Meanwhile, EU nationals in the country were understandably upset when it turned out the government's Brexit app, designed to help them apply for settled status in post-Brexit Britain, didn't work on iPhones. The official advice if you're an Apple user is to 'use someone else's phone'.

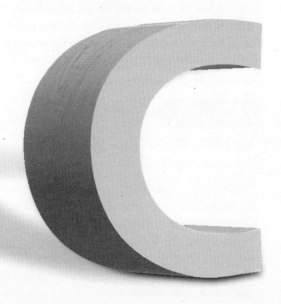

In which we learn . . .
How a Thai football team emerged from the tunnel,
why Barbra Streisand can't tell the difference between
her puppies, what prompted a crumpet crisis, why
you shouldn't insert chips into your body, and how a
grumpy cat got 500,000 reasons to be cheerful.

CANADA

For planes dropping poo on Western Canada, *see* **Blue Ice**; for farmers dropping poo in *Eastern* Canada, *see* **G7**; for the ice hotel that caught fire, *see* **Irony**; for a bakery that refused to put 'cum' on a cake, *see* **Vulgar**; for a French waiter who was fired for being too French, *see* **Waiter, Waiter**; for an American building which moved to Canada, *see* **Weather, Severe**; and for taking a bear to get ice cream, *see* **Zoos**.

CATALONIA

Catalonia's president got in a fight over a cartoon pig that looked like him.

This year, as well as facing 30 years in prison for holding an independence referendum the Spanish government ruled illegal, Catalonia's ousted president Carles Puigdemont also had to endure the indignity of seeing Puigdemont-themed ham going on sale. 'Pig Demont' ham features a pig mascot in glasses, with mop-like hair just like Puigdemont's. The man who runs the company said it is all a coincidence – that 'Pig Demont' just means 'Pig from the Mountain' and that 'If he [Puigdemont] sees himself reflected in the caricature of a pig that is more his problem than mine.' It's worth noting that the company also sells a wine called 'Rufian', which has the same name as another pro-independence MP. The Spanish patent office suspended sale of the ham while it considered the case.

Ever since Catalonia's controversial vote, the struggle for (and against) independence has been ongoing. Supporters of Puigdemont, who fled abroad in the immediate aftermath to avoid being arrested for sedition, initially suggested he could rule the region from his self-imposed exile in various European cities. This earned him the nickname 'the hologram president' in the press. But Spanish secret service agents managed to put a tracking device on his car and the hologram was eventually apprehended while driving across Germany. The coded message sent back to the Spanish authorities on his arrest referred to his hair, reading: 'The mop is in the bucket.'

Puigdemont has been succeeded by a politician named Quim Torra, who is pressing on with demands for independence, and who has called the Spanish rule of Catalonia 'infinitely pathetic and repulsive'. But Catalonia also has a faction who want the region to remain part of Spain. This year they invented a new country called Tabania that they joke will break away from Catalonia if Catalonia ever breaks away from Spain. It has its own flag, currency, anthem and an appointed 'president'. Thousands have gone on marches for the fake country.

CATS ▶

The world's most famous cat won over £500,000 in a California lawsuit.

Grumpy Cat is the name the Internet gave to Tardar Sauce, a cat with a genetic condition that makes her look very moody all the time. She became an online phenomenon, and has earned millions of dollars for endorsing various products. But with success has come controversy: for the past two years Grumpy Cat has been caught up in a legal battle with one of her business associates, US coffee company Grenade Beverage. Her people claimed that the company had been selling T-shirts featuring the cat's face without permission. The coffee firm then counter-sued, alleging that the cat's

A Cambridgeshire woman climbed a tree to save a cat, got stuck halfway up the tree and had to be rescued by the fire brigade.

people hadn't mentioned the coffee brand nearly often enough. Grenade also said they'd been promised the cat would be appearing in a film with Will Ferrell and Jack Black, but that this hadn't come to pass.

Grumpy Cat's representatives finally proved victorious this January, and the cat's firm was awarded $710,000. The reaction of Tardar Sauce herself was not known – she was in court for the trial but was not present for the verdict.*

*While the Grumpy Cat trial was going on, a member of the Wu-Tang Clan was busy legally challenging a dog-walking company over a potential breach of copyright. The dog-walking firm, who said they walked 'the illest group of dogs in New York City', had named themselves the Woof-Tang Clan.

In cheerful cat news, a hundred cats were shipped from Yorkshire to London this year. London has a shortage of cats and lots of people who want to adopt them, while Yorkshire has a large surplus of unwanted cats, so they were brought down and immediately adopted. And in cat survey news, Washington DC doesn't know how many homeless cats it has – so the city has launched a three-year, $1.5-million project to count all the cats in the DC area. The census will involve high-tech solutions, such as 50 cameras in key locations, and low-tech solutions, which involve people walking around and making a note when they see a cat.

CAVE RESCUE

Divers first located the trapped Thai football team by smelling them.

The mission to get the 12 junior football players and their coach out of the flooded Tham Luang cave involved 10,000 people. John Volanthen, one of the divers who first found them, told how he and his colleagues swam through tunnels, surfacing at air pockets to shout, listen and sniff for signs of life. He said they smelled the children before they spotted them.

The boys had explored the cave before, sometimes getting as far as 8 kilometres in and writing the names of new team members on the walls. This time, they were celebrating a birthday party in there, but were pushed back by floodwaters and ended up stranded on a ledge behind a spot called Pattaya Beach. Their coach was a Buddhist monk, who taught them to meditate to keep calm during the two weeks they were trapped. They drank moisture off the cave walls and even dug a 5-metre-deep cavern in the shelf in an attempt to tunnel their way out.

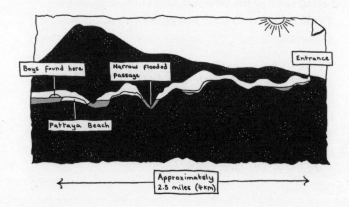

Numerous ideas were put forward as to how to save them. One involved setting up a series of corrugated pipes the children could crawl through. Another was to tunnel in from above. Elon Musk commissioned a child-sized mini-submarine, but by the time it arrived eight of the thirteen had been rescued, and it was, in any case, deemed unsuitable for the task at hand. While all this was going on thousands of people congregated outside the caves, their numbers eventually swelling to create a makeshift town at the cave entrance, with toilets, a laundry to wash the mud off divers' clothes, and numerous food stalls, some staffed by Thailand's royal chefs.

Meanwhile, work was going ahead on the rescue attempt. Four hundred water pumps were sourced from all over the country, many donated by fish farms, and 200 million litres of water were pumped out to stabilise water levels within the cave system. (An unfortunate side effect was that the pumped water flooded surrounding farms and destroyed their crops.) Then the divers gave the boys breathing equipment, placed them on stretchers and carried them via a system of winches, pulleys, rafts and zip lines. Some parts of the 4-kilometre escape route were so narrow, the divers had to remove the boys' air tanks and send them through first, then push the boys themselves through afterwards.

When the team finally emerged, they were in relatively good health, although they had to wear sunglasses until their eyes became accustomed to the light. Tragically, there was one fatality during the mission: one of the rescuers died when the oxygen in his air tank ran out underwater. He was cremated in a ceremony paid for by the King of Thailand himself.

This year in celebrity gossip . . .

It was revealed that *Sherlock* star Benedict Cumberbatch stopped a motorcyclist from being mugged just down the road from Baker Street; Hugh Grant got married so that he and his partner could get through airport immigration more easily; Sandra Bullock revealed she keeps herself looking young with 'penis facials' (where a person's skin is injected with a serum derived from discarded foreskins of newborn Korean babies); Danny Dyer revealed that in between takes on *EastEnders*, he knits; Victoria Beckham celebrated her birthday with a watermelon instead of a cake; Shia LaBeouf filmed a movie about Shia LaBeouf, but didn't play Shia LaBeouf; Pierce Brosnan was threatened with jail in India after a legal dispute over a mouth freshener advert; Margot Robbie revealed she had a Harry Potter-themed stripper at her hen do; French film director Agnès Varda couldn't go to Los Angeles for an award ceremony, so she sent cardboard cut-outs of herself instead; Gordon Ramsay revealed he goes speeding around Los Angeles at night, but avoids speed cameras by wrapping his plates in cling film; Woody Allen claimed his track record with female stars is so clean he should be made the poster boy for the #MeToo movement; both Patrick Stewart and Snoop Dogg invested in the same Oxford-based cannabis company; Sean Penn released his debut novel, about a man who goes around the world killing old people with a mallet to stop them farting out noxious gases; the actor who played Barney the Dinosaur revealed he is now a tantric sex guru; and a former *EastEnders* star criticised a restaurant for being so pretentious that her husband tried to eat his napkin.

CHAN-O-CHA, PRAYUTH

Thailand's military dictator released his fifth pop single.

'Diamond Heart', the fifth song Prime Minister Prayuth Chan-o-cha has uploaded to YouTube since he led a military coup in 2014, met with unfavourable reviews. Penned by Prayuth, and sung by an army officer who said, 'I may not be the best singer available but I was the best choice at the time', the song is about overcoming obstacles as a nation. Prayuth has made many creative attempts to overcome whatever those obstacles might be since the military coup, offering the masses not just his five heartfelt songs, but free haircuts and puddings.

Despite his efforts, the Thai public expressed their dislike for the song by giving it 40,000 more 'thumbs down' than 'thumbs up'. As soon as the backlash was spotted, the video's comment bar was disabled. This is probably for the best, as Prayuth doesn't have a great history of dealing with criticism. In the past he has had an activist arrested for criticising his single 'Returning Happiness to Thailand' on Facebook, has had six other people arrested for spreading false news about him, and has told journalists that he has the power to execute them if they write reports critical of him.

The main thing the journalists want to know from him, as do most of the Thai population, is when he plans to hold an election. He promised one for November this year, but it now looks as though nothing will happen until 2019 at the earliest. To avoid questions on the subject, Prayuth has once again harnessed his creative powers. At a press conference this year, instead of answering questions himself, he produced a life-sized cardboard cut-out and told those assembled, 'If you want to ask any questions on politics or conflict . . . ask this guy.'

CHARITY ▶

For fast-swimming semen, *see* **Animal Races**; for motor-boating a lawyer, *see* **Attorneys**; for breaking into piggy banks, *see* **Debt, National**; for flying home to vote, *see* **Eighth Amendment**; for walking on LEGO, *see* **Records, Broken**; and for making great whites great again, *see* **Sharks**.

CHEDDAR MAN ▶

Cheddar Man was allergic to cheese.

Cheddar Man, the oldest known Briton for whom we have a complete skeleton, hit the headlines when it was discovered that in life he probably had 'dark to black' skin. The first full DNA analysis of the 10,000-year-old human revealed he had specific skin pigmentation genes usually found in sub-Saharan Africans. This suggests the fair skin of Europeans today is a much more recent phenomenon than previously thought. The researchers also learned that Cheddar Man had dark, curly hair and blue eyes, and that his nearest ancestors came to Britain from the Middle East.

Images of his skull were captured using a high-tech scanner originally designed for use on the International Space Station. Identical twins Adrie and Alfons Kennis, who are both prehistoric model makers, then used these scans to help them build a replica of his head to give an idea of how he would have looked in life.

Geneticists did point out that our understanding of DNA isn't yet advanced enough to use it to predict skin colour for certain, so these conclusions aren't definitive. But as one archaeologist who worked on the project pointed out, something we *do* know is that Cheddar Man wouldn't have been able to enjoy Cheddar cheese. He died just before humans evolved the genes for lactose tolerance.

CHINA ▶

The Chinese government censored its own anti-censorship plan.

───── ▼ ─────

A woman in China was barred from graduating as a teacher because she is too short. Height restrictions for would-be teachers apply in many Chinese provinces; in the Shaanxi region, where she hoped to teach, female applicants have to be over 150cm tall.

───── ▼ ─────

A couple in China who were desperately trying to conceive learned from their obstetrician that they had been having sex the wrong way for four years.

Authorities in the Chinese tourist island of Hainan announced this year that, to boost tourism, it would allow visiting foreigners to access websites blocked in mainland China, including Facebook, Twitter and YouTube. There was such outrage from Chinese citizens at the unfairness of the idea that the official announcement was deleted, search terms relating to it were blocked, and the policy was binned.

The country also censored its own economic policies. News media in China were instructed not to mention the 'Made in China 2025' campaign – an industrial masterplan to make the country a high-tech superpower – because President Trump has cited it as evidence that China is poaching intellectual property and breaking international trade rules. Since he is now raising tariffs and ramping up the threat of a trade war, it's not a campaign the authorities are keen for news outlets to discuss.

China also prohibited its citizens from watching John Oliver, after the comedian's show *Last Week Tonight* described President Xi Jinping as a 'creepy uncle who imprisons 800,000 people in his basement'. Within days, not only was Oliver's show blocked, but the whole HBO network had become mysteriously unavailable in China. One of Oliver's main criticisms was that Xi can't cope with dissent.

One thing that definitely *wasn't* banned was the film *Amazing China*, which was all about the fantastic achievements of President Xi. After its release it became the country's highest-grossing documentary of all time. However, this could be because many state employees were required to watch it, and employers were instructed to block-book cinemas so they could send their staff to see it. On the Chinese ticket-booking platform Maoyan, the film had an average rating of 9.6 out of 10. On the Western website IMDb, it scored only 1 out of 10.

CLOCKS ▶

Microwave clocks across Europe ran six minutes slow due to an argument in the Balkans.

This year, the energy grid across Europe slowed down, thanks to a political dispute between Kosovo and Serbia. After Kosovo declared independence from Serbia in 2008, Serbia agreed to meet Kosovo's energy needs. But the two don't get along, and when a power plant in Kosovo failed in January, Serbia refused to make up the difference. As a result, the energy grid supplying 25 countries across the Continent, which should run at a speed of 50 hertz, ran at 49.996 hertz instead.

One knock-on effect of this was that lots of clocks across Europe – mostly digital clocks like radio alarms, or microwave and oven clocks, which base their timings on oscillations in the electricity they receive and are calibrated to 50 hertz – started to run very slightly slow. Eventually, they lost up to six minutes. Four months later, exactly the same thing happened again and the clocks ran slow a second time.

A six-minute delay would have completely ruined the most monotonous experiment published this year. A group of scientists at the National Institute of Standards and Technology in Colorado set 12 extremely accurate atomic clocks going, in a temperature- and humidity-controlled room, in November 1999. They then kept them going for 450 million seconds, until

▬▬▬▬ ▼ ▬▬▬▬

Amazon billionaire Jeff Bezos announced plans to build a giant clock inside a Texas mountainside, which will keep going for 10,000 years without any human intervention. Members of the public will be able to visit it, but to save energy it won't show the right time – visitors will have to turn a wheel to get the dial to update.

2014, in an attempt to test whether the laws of physics were changing over time, and have now published their results. The good news is their report confirms that the laws of physics remained stable. Even so, they are now planning to repeat the experiment, with even better clocks.

CLONING ▶

Barbra Streisand cloned her dog. Twice.

────── ▼ ──────
It was revealed that the world's smallest living dog, a chihuahua named 'Miracle Milly' who is 3.8 inches tall and could fit into a teaspoon when she was first born, has been cloned 49 times in a South Korean lab.

This year singer Barbra Streisand revealed that two of her dogs, Miss Violet and Miss Scarlett, are clones of her previous dog Samantha, who died in 2017. Streisand added that because the doppel-dogs look so similar, she has to dress them in different-coloured clothes to tell them apart. The experiment attracted criticism from animal rights groups, as the whole field of cloning pets is widely seen as ethically dodgy: owners are often disappointed to learn that cloned dogs can have very different personalities to the original; and the cloning process often generates less similar-looking dogs which are surplus to requirements (Streisand herself received a third puppy which she gave to the 13-year-old daughter of her PR officer). The *Washington Post* summed up the objections by saying, 'What a dog-cloning expert would have told Barbra Streisand: "Nooooooo!"'

In other cloning news, a green activist and writer called Mark Lynas revealed that in 1998 he was part of a failed plot to kidnap Dolly, the first ever cloned sheep. According to Lynas, campaigners broke into her pen only to discover she was being kept with a lot of other sheep, and they had no idea which one was Dolly.

CO2 ▶

Despite there being more carbon dioxide in the atmosphere than ever before, Britain still managed to run out of it.

There hasn't been this much carbon dioxide in the atmosphere for at least a million years. Despite that, a carbon dioxide shortage hit the UK this summer, resulting in pubs finding it hard to get hold of carbonated beer, supermarkets running out of fizzy drinks, and supplies of all kinds of food running low, including salad, chicken and pork (carbon dioxide is pumped into sealed packaging to boost food's shelf life, and it's used in animal slaughter too). Worst of all, Warburtons had to temporarily stop making crumpets, because the gas is used to fill crumpet packets to keep the contents fresh. And because frozen carbon dioxide – or dry ice – is used to preserve frozen food, ice cream was under threat too (there was no word on whether *Strictly Come Dancing* would be hit by the dry ice crisis).

The problem was caused by a break in the manufacture of ammonia, which is a key element in carbon dioxide production. Ammonia plants usually shut down for maintenance between April and June, but because ammonia prices were so low this year – and the product therefore so unprofitable – producers in Europe decided to stay closed for longer. Given all the concern about carbon dioxide in the environment, some might think the logical alternative would have been to extract the gas from the air around us, but in fact although the level of CO_2 is indeed rising it still only constitutes 0.04 per cent of the air and so is prohibitively expensive to extract.

The crisis eventually eased, but it was 'the worst supply situation to hit the European carbon dioxide business in decades', according to the industry's trade journal, *gasworld*.

▼

NASA have offered a prize of $1 million to the person who can work out how to turn CO_2 into glucose, the idea being that such a process would help future astronauts live on Mars. (Terms and conditions apply.)

COMEY, JAMES

While investigating Hillary Clinton for inappropriately using a private email account, former FBI Director James Comey inappropriately used a private email account.

This was one of the headlines of a Justice Department report that dealt with Comey's handling of the last presidential election and found a number of problems with his professionalism, but did not find any evidence of political bias on the part of the former FBI boss. Hillary Clinton was obviously not convinced: back in 2016, Comey reopened an investigation into her emails just 11 days before the election, which was widely seen as a factor in her losing to Donald Trump. When the Justice Department report was published she tweeted a link to it accompanied by the three words 'But my emails'.

Comey's number-one bestseller, *A Higher Loyalty*, contained a number of personal attacks on Donald Trump, and he rarely missed an opportunity to criticise the president in the press. In response, the Republican Party allegedly bought up at least 17 web domains insulting James Comey, including lyingcomey.com, comeyisaliar.net, comeylies.org and creepycomey.com.

COMMONWEALTH GAMES

A third of the Cameroonian athletes at the Commonwealth Games ended up doing a runner.

Eight of the 24 athletes – five boxers and three weightlifters – representing Cameroon at the Games in Australia disappeared while there, one of the boxers not even bothering to compete before he vanished. This left just two other weightlifters and the country's basketball team to catch the flight home. There was something of an African exodus from the games: six Ugandan athletes also vanished, and one Rwandan coach never returned from a bathroom break. In total, about 250 African athletes and officials, constituting 3 per cent of those who attended from abroad, overstayed their visas after the competition.

Most who outstayed their visas went on to formally seek asylum, and this can sometimes work. Cameroonian weightlifter François Etoundi, for example, was given refugee status after the Melbourne Commonwealth Games in 2006 and now competes for Australia. This year he won a bronze medal. Unfortunately, he injured his shoulder in the process, leaving him in pain for the rest of the tournament. During the medal ceremony he had to have his arm in a sling, but this didn't stop officials patting him on his injured shoulder 23 times to congratulate him.

One surprising winner at the games was Norfolk Island. Despite having a population of only 1,700, less than 35 square kilometres of land and just one bowls club, it took bronze in the men's lawn bowls. The team, which included a 62-year-old taxi driver and a 55-year-old

Welsh table tennis player Anna Hursey won three of the matches she played at the Commonwealth Games. At just 11 years of age, she's the youngest person ever to participate.

farmer, managed to beat Canada, which has a population of 36 million.

CORBYN, JEREMY

See **Vegetables**.

CRICKET, JUST NOT

After he was caught cheating, a bookshop put Australian cricketer Steve Smith's autobiography in its 'true crime' section.

The Brisbane store's reaction was typical of the country as a whole: people were horrified to discover that *The Australian* newspaper's Australian of the Year 2017 could possibly be guilty of ball-tampering during Australia's Test match against South Africa. Smith didn't actually alter the ball himself: it was rookie batsman Cameron Bancroft who, on the orders of veteran player David Warner, hid sandpaper in his trousers and used it to scuff up the ball.* But as the captain, who was aware that the deception was taking place, Smith had to accept responsibility.

*A scuffed ball swings more when bowled, which makes it more likely that the batsman will be fooled into making a mistake.

Crazes

The biggest fads of 2018 included:

The Tide Pod Challenge: In the first two weeks of 2018 alone, at least 39 people required medical treatment after consuming Tide laundry detergent pods – a product about which Democratic Party statesman Chuck Schumer once said, 'I don't know why they make them look so delicious.' The blue, white and green capsules ended up inspiring a number of edible imitations including shots, pizzas and doughnuts.

The Neymar Challenge: After Brazilian footballer Neymar Jr was widely ridiculed for diving and exaggerating his injuries in the World Cup, people filmed themselves rolling around as dramatically as possible.

The 24-hour Challenge: Kids in America and Europe were dared to stay in a shopping centre for a full day. Police issued a warning against the craze after a massive hunt was sparked by an 11-year-old who hid in IKEA.

Plogging: A craze that began in Scandinavia which involved picking up litter while jogging. The word is a combination of 'jogging' and the Swedish term '*plocka upp*', meaning 'pick up'.

Brieing: An Ecstasy-based craze among middle-class women in London for wrapping their Es in cheese before swallowing them.

Umpires did not catch them out to begin with. It was South African cameraman Zotani Oscar who drew their attention to what was going on when he caught Bancroft in the act and then played the sandpaper footage on the big screens in the stadium. Oscar was already something of a cult figure in South Africa – he always operates his camera in a full suit and brogues, regardless of the weather – but now he became a national hero. Incidentally, it's not the first time television cameras have caught people cheating, and with cameras everywhere these days it's becoming increasingly difficult to get away with it. Some cricket commentators noted, though, that no *home team* has ever been caught out by its own television cameras.

CRISPS ▸

Doritos announced a new, slightly less crunchy crisp just for women.

Indra Nooyi, the CEO of PepsiCo, which owns Doritos, appeared on the *Freakonomics* podcast this year, to discuss company market research that had found that women dislike crunching loudly when eating crisps in public, and that they don't like licking their fingers in front of other people either. The firm, she said, was therefore exploring the option of manufacturing 'snacks for women that can be designed and packaged differently' – in other words, less crunchy crisps, which aren't quite so finger-licking good, and which would also come in smaller packets to fit into women's handbags. Nooyi added that 'we're getting ready to launch a bunch of them soon'. There was instant, frenzied outrage online, and within a day, PepsiCo had publicly cancelled the plans. The so-called 'Lady Doritos' were scrapped.

Soon after the crisis, in a totally unrelated move definitely not designed to earn PR points, Doritos said they wanted to find a superfan to award £18,000, a year's supply of Doritos, and an invitation to taste future flavours. The competition was won by a woman.

Meanwhile, the Crisp Hero of the Year award goes to the Oregon lorry driver who got stranded in the woods with a lorry full of crisps, but refused to eat them. The 22-year-old trucker, Jacob Cartwright, had to abandon his stuck vehicle and walk for three days without any food or water, after going off course due to a GPS mistake. Even so, he didn't eat any of the crisps. He later told his boss, 'That stuff's worth something, that's the load – I'm not gonna touch it.'

CROYDON CAT KILLER ▶

A violent cat murderer continued to fox detectives.

This summer it was reported that a notorious psychopath, known in the press as the 'Croydon Cat Killer', had murdered and decapitated their 400th cat. The killer's modus operandi is always the same: the cat is found without its head and the body is left in plain sight to 'horrify' people. One psychologist said that the killer may one day get bored with cats and kill people instead, and so, with attacks reported as far afield as Southampton and Cornwall, the Met Police took the threat seriously enough to launch Operation Takahe to investigate the incidents.

Environmental scientist Stephen Harris has other ideas though. According to an article he wrote in *New Scientist*, the 'murders' are actually the work of foxes whose jaws are not strong enough to rip up cats' bodies or heads, but are capable of decapitating the pets by chewing around the softer neck area first. Professor Harris should know: he was part of the team who worked out that foxes were responsible for a spate of cat decapitations in the 1980s, so disproving the contemporary theory that they were the work of satanic cults.

HUNT, JEREMY

*For the third time, a BBC presenter mispronounced
Jeremy Hunt's surname with a rogue 'c'.*

Justin Webb, presenter of Radio 4's *Today Programme*,
made the mistake while reading an article about how
the then health secretary favoured a cap on social care.
He was the second host of the *Today Programme* to
make that error, after the appropriately named James
Naughtie in 2010, and the second person to make the
mistake on Radio 4 that very day, after Andrew Marr
blundered on the weekly discussion programme *Start
the Week*.

It was a good year for Hunt. He became the longest-
serving health secretary in the history of the NHS in
June, clocking up almost six years in the job, and a
few months earlier he won a humanitarian award at
the World Patient Safety Summit – an event that Hunt
himself helped to organise.

And so, when Theresa May had to replace Boris Johnson
as foreign secretary she went with Hunt – who almost
immediately made a blunder worthy of a Radio 4
presenter. At a meeting with his Chinese counterparts, he
mistakenly said that his Chinese wife was Japanese. He
explained that he got his words mixed up when trying to
explain his wife's nationality while his brain was preoccu-
pied with the fact that he and the Chinese foreign minister
had earlier conversed in Japanese. Hunt is fluent in Japanese. Even if he's not always quite so fluent in English.

CUT-OUTS, CARDBOARD

For the director who sent one to an awards ceremony,
see **Celebs**; for the prime minister who let one take a
press conference, *see* **Chan-o-cha, Prayuth**; for one that

made it to the World Cup, *see* **Football Fans**; and for 100 of them on the White House lawn, *see* **Zuckerberg, Mark**.

CYBORGS ▶

A cyborg won the right to implant his travelcard in his body.

Meow-Ludo Disco Gamma Meow-Meow is an Australian geneticist and biohacker (someone who uses technology to upgrade their own body). Last year, Mr Meow-Meow had the chip from his electronic travelcard implanted in his hand, so he would never lose it. But when a ticket inspector asked to see a valid travelcard, Meow-Meow was unable to comply, and so was duly fined for travelling without a ticket. Even more annoyingly for him, the travel authorities then cancelled his chip while he was away at a convention about cyborg rights.

Meow-Meow went to court, lost, and was fined £680, including costs, for tampering with the travelcard's terms of use. He appealed and managed to have his conviction (but not the fine) overturned. Meow-Meow was delighted, saying 'cyborg justice has been served'. He also clarified that he wouldn't implant a chip in himself again without permission from the New South Wales transport authorities, and advised people not to try it at home, 'unless you know what you're doing'. (He actually has two other implants already, one of which he uses to store important documents.)

In which we learn . . .
Why Stormy Daniels stomps on crusty orange
snacks, whether old dogs can learn new tricks,
why you shouldn't serve shoe pastry in Japan, who
should have ducked Drake, and who uses a quiz
to split their family's fortune.

DANIELS, STORMY

The porn star who claimed to have slept with Donald Trump went on a national tour called Make America Horny Again.

One month before winning the 2016 presidential election, Donald Trump allegedly had his personal lawyer, Michael Cohen, pay $130,000 in hush money to an adult film actor named Stormy Daniels, whose film credits include *Good Will Humping* and *Porking with Pride 2*. In return, Daniels (real name Stephanie Clifford) signed a non-disclosure agreement promising not to mention that she had had sex with the president-to-be at a golf tournament in 2006 – a year after he married Melania.

However, in March Daniels filed a lawsuit against Trump claiming the agreement was invalid because Trump had never personally signed it. Since then we have learned a lot about the two times they allegedly got together. According to Daniels, the first encounter involved her having sex with Trump, spanking his bottom with a magazine that had a picture of his face on it (journalists have since worked out it would have been the very first issue of *Trump Magazine**) and, before leaving his hotel room, signing his copy of her X-rated film *3 Wishes*. The second time they met up they didn't sleep with each other, but instead watched TV documentaries all night long (*see* **Sharks**).

Thanks to the revelations, Daniels has become a household name in America. She has appeared as a guest on numerous talks shows; she has had 'fans' turn up at strip clubs requesting that she stamp on some Cheetos (the orange snack supposedly representing Trump); she was approached by a sex robot company who wanted to license her image for a fleet of Stormy dolls; and she was given the keys to the city of West Hollywood by the mayor in a ceremony that took place in a sex shop.

*Coincidentally, it is partly thanks to Trump Magazine *that we know what the president's porn name would be if he decided to have one. In response to a journalist who asked him, at a party thrown by the magazine's publisher, Trump said 'Big' or 'The Trump Tower'.*

Daniels decided to capitalise on her fame by embarking on a grand tour of US strip clubs with a show called *Make America Horny Again*. One poster for the tour included a picture of Stormy with Trump with the line: 'He saw her live – you can too!'

DEAD, BACK FROM THE ▶

A Russian journalist faked his own murder to avoid actually being murdered.

A Romanian man who went to court to try to prove that he was alive had his case thrown out because he didn't submit his appeal in time. The late, not-late Mr Constantin Reliu, who blamed a bureaucratic mix-up for his predicament, said, 'I am officially dead, although I'm alive. I have no income and because I am listed dead, I can't do anything.'

The killing of Arkady Babchenko, a Russian anti-Putin journalist, was reported by the Ukrainian government, and much of the world's press. However, the next day, he turned up at a news conference in Kiev. The Ukrainian secret service claimed to have faked his death to expose his would-be assassins, explaining that they hoped the news of their target's 'death' would prompt the Russians on his tail (whom they had under surveillance) to get in touch with their bosses to find out what was going on. The media was less than impressed. Reporters Without Borders spoke of 'its deepest indignation after discovering the manipulation of the Ukrainian secret services', adding, 'it is always very dangerous for a government to play with the facts.' Former chess champion and anti-Putin activist Garry Kasparov disagreed, joking that 'people who are resurrected have a track record of doing great things'.

The fake assassination was meticulously planned. Babchenko practised falling over in order to make the 'shooting' more convincing. He wore a shirt with pre-existing bullet holes, and utilised pig's blood and a make-up artist to make it look as though he had a mortal wound. He was then bundled into an ambulance and taken to a morgue, where he watched news coverage of his death. When he finally re-emerged and was asked what he was going to do next, he said he wanted to become a Ukrainian citizen, and to carry on with his life by 'getting drunk' and writing a book. He also said that despite needing to spend his life under round-the-clock surveillance, he intends to live until 96 after having 'danced on Putin's grave'.

DEBT, NATIONAL

The British government tried to claim a donation from someone who died in 1928.

In 1928 an anonymous donor gave the British government a gift of £500,000, with the instruction that it was to be left in a bank account, earning interest, until it could pay off the country's whole national debt. At the time, the UK's total government debt was £7.6 billion. Since then, the initial £500,000 has grown to £400 million – but unfortunately, the UK's national debt now stands at £1.6 trillion, almost 4,000 times as much as the pot.* (The fund is gaining on the debt, though: back in 1928 the debt was greater by a factor of 15,000.)

* At no time in the last 90 years has the fund grown above 0.066 per cent of Britain's total borrowing.

The National Fund, as it is known, is technically a charity – in fact, it's now become one of the UK's largest charities – but the nature of the bequest has meant that those responsible for administering it haven't been able to do anything with the money it holds. The fund's sole corporate trustee has said that it's been trying to shut the charity down and give the money away for nearly a decade, and in May the UK government even went to court to try to get hold of the cash.

While the UK looked to a dead citizen to reduce its debt, Malaysia's very-much-alive citizens tried to do their bit. The new Malaysian government inherited a national debt of $250 billion, and so a crowdfunding page was set up so that people could contribute. It made

$2 million in the first day, which sounds impressive. Unfortunately, at that rate, the debt will take 342 years to pay off, even without interest – $2 million is approximately the amount of interest accrued on the debt every three hours. Within two months, $37 million had been contributed – enough to pay two days' worth of interest.

DESSERTS, DIPLOMATIC

By serving the prime minister of Japan his pudding in a shoe, the Israelis really put their foot in it.

Shinzō Abe was the guest of honour at a dinner hosted by Israeli Prime Minister Benjamin Netanyahu when he was presented with a somewhat pretentious pudding served in a large leather shoe. It was a spectacular faux pas, as shoes are considered extremely unhygienic in Japan. Or, as one diplomat put it, 'There is nothing more despised in Japanese culture than shoes.'

Amazingly, this wasn't the only dessert-based diplomatic faux pas involving Japan this year. At a banquet during the historic talks between North and South Korea in April, a dome-like mango dessert – known as 'Spring of the People' – was served. When split open, it revealed a chocolate map of the Korean peninsula. Unfortunately it also contained marzipan versions of the Takeshima/Dokdo Islands, the ownership of which is currently highly disputed between Japan and South Korea. Japanese officials were convinced that the dessert was making some kind of political point and demanded it be taken off the menu. Leaders Kim Jong Un and Moon Jae-in enjoyed it anyway.

DIVING FOOTBALLERS

For the underground Thai football team, *see* **Cave Rescue**; for the underhanded Neymar Jr, *see* **Crazes**.

DIVORCE

Chinese couples can now get faster divorces by failing a quiz about their spouse.

Divorce rates are rising in China, and the government is concerned that society might become more unstable as a result. Unhappy couples in at least two provinces have therefore been asked to participate in a quiz before they split up, answering questions about the date of their wedding anniversary, their partner's favourite food and so on. If they score more than 60 out of 100 they are informed by the authorities that the marriage has 'room for recovery' and that they should go away and work on their relationship. In at least one case a husband and wife have actually been refused a divorce because they scored so highly.

'Sham' divorce is also a problem in China. Many married couples live and work in different cities from each other, but because children's school places tend to be allocated first to husbands and wives living in the same educational district as one another, people are applying for divorces so that the parent living closer to the better school will receive priority treatment.

But while marital bureaucracy is becoming harder for many Chinese couples, it's getting considerably easier for those living in Guangdong province. People living there can now book their divorce registration via the instant messaging service WeChat.

DODD, KEN ▶

The world said goodbye to a comedian who told jokes at a speed of 7.14 titters per minute.

*'Some people say my tickle sticks are a sex symbol. I say that's a fallacy.'

Sir Ken Dodd (1927–2018) was a comedian and singer known for his one-liners, his famous tickle stick prop,* and his marathon-length live shows. In 1974, he set a Guinness World Record when he told more than 1,500 jokes in three and a half hours, averaging roughly 7.14 laughs a minute (TPM, or titters per minute, as he called it). That was considered one of his shorter gigs. An average Ken Dodd show could run for well over five hours, much to the annoyance of theatre staff. 'The sooner you laugh at the jokes,' he would tell his audience, 'the sooner you can go home.' Once, when he was told that a group of pensioners had to leave the theatre at 11 p.m., he responded, 'What . . . before the interval?'

Dodd kept a comprehensive record of every show he played. He graded audience reactions to every joke and built a 'giggle map of Britain', which showed that Nottingham audiences liked picture gags, Scots liked one-liners, and in the West Midlands jokes had to be delivered slowly or audiences wouldn't understand.

His lifelong obsession with the history and psychology of comedy resulted in a library of over 10,000 books on the subject. One of his favourites was Sigmund Freud's *Wit and Its Relation to the Unconscious*, which he often quoted in interviews, though he didn't always agree with what he read: 'Freud said, "Laughter is the outward expression of the psyche",' Ken recounted. 'But he never played the Glasgow Empire on a Saturday after both Celtic and Rangers lost.'

Even in his final years, Dodd was still clocking up to 80,000 kilometres per annum as he travelled from venue to venue. After each performance, no matter the time he finished, he was driven back to Knotty Ash, Liverpool, to the home in which he was born, lived his entire life, and eventually died, aged 90.

For another sadly missed entertainer, *see* **To Me**.

▼

In 1989, Dodd was charged with tax evasion by the Inland Revenue. He joked that he didn't owe them a penny as he lived by the sea. He was acquitted after a three-week court hearing.

DOGS ▶

Scientists discovered that old dogs can learn new tricks.

Not only that, they benefit from learning the 'new tricks' in question – specifically, playing touchscreen video games with their noses. Elderly dogs that were taught to play the games were not only rewarded with treats, but, according to researchers from the University of Veterinary Medicine, Vienna, became more engaged, happy and alert.

Sniffer dogs, meanwhile, were being taught lots of new tricks. The Boston Museum for Fine Arts announced that its newest member of staff, a puppy

After yet another dog died on a United Airlines flight (see *Book of the Year 2017*), this time after being put in an overhead compartment, two US senators introduced a bill to stop this ever happening again. The bill was called the Welfare Of Our Furry Friends Act, or WOOFF.

named Riley, would be set to work smelling out insects and other pests hiding in the museum's collection. Elsewhere, the US set up a 'K-9 Artifact Finders' programme that involves training dogs to sniff out ancient treasures that criminals are attempting to smuggle out of Syria. And Britain got its first-ever water-sniffing dog, trained to smell the chlorine in leaks from faulty underground pipes, while Northern Irish police announced they are trying out a special fire-fighting dog which will detect the chemicals used by arsonists.

Perhaps the bravest sniffer dog of the year was Sombra (or 'Shadow'), a Colombian sniffer dog who has sniffed out almost 10 tonnes of a gang's cocaine and led to 245 arrests over her career so far. Sombra hit the headlines after she had to be moved off her regular beat on Colombia's coast and reassigned. The reason was that the gang in question – the Urabeños – had been so annoyed by her skills they had put a 200-million-peso (£53,000) bounty on her head.

DOORBELLS

Indian and Pakistani diplomats started ringing each other's doorbells and running away.

Relations between India and Pakistan are very poor at the moment. Officials in each other's countries have complained of harassment, and of diplomatic residences having their utilities cut off. And this March, India's high commission in Islamabad complained to Pakistani officials that the doorbell of the deputy high commissioner had been rung at 3 a.m. The Indian diplomats who answered the door found nobody there, but strongly suspected the Pakistani security forces were responsible.

A few days later, the doorbell of the *Pakistani* deputy high commissioner in New Delhi, 400 miles away, was rung at 3 a.m. in what seems to have been a case of tit for tat (or tit for rat-a-tat-tat). Other pranks and annoyances have included the two sides following each other to work, harassing and filming each other in the street, and making obscene phone calls. A fortnight after the doorbell debacle, the two countries agreed to resolve the diplomatic tensions, so there is a chance the region may avoid a sudden outbreak of whoopee cushions or cling-filmed toilet seats.

The alternative might be to deploy more technology. 'Smart doorbells' which film the doorway are one possibility, though even these don't always deter miscreants: a thief in California who opportunistically tried to steal packages from someone's doorway and then realised the home's smart doorbell was filming him, promptly tried (and failed) to steal the doorbell itself. Alternatively, doorbells in future might be missing entirely: some British property developers have said they're no longer bothering with them on new-build homes, partly because millennial visitors tend just to text when they've pitched up outside. Something that Indian and Pakistani diplomats might like to bear in mind.

Five years ago, Jamie Siminoff pitched the idea of a doorbell that people can monitor via their smartphones on the US reality TV show *Shark Tank* (known in the UK as *Dragon's Den*). He failed to get the backing he was hoping for, but this year sold his company to Amazon for a reported $1 billion.

DRAKE ▶

Israel's finance minister got in trouble for dancing to a song by Canada's most famous musician.

The 'Kiki Challenge' is an Internet meme in which someone jumps out of a moving car while Drake's song 'In My Feelings' plays, before dancing alongside the vehicle for a little while, and then jumping back inside. The whole video is then posted on the Internet. In order to show he was down with the kids, Finance

Minister Moshe Kahlon had a go, but it has to be said his performance lacked a certain something: it was more of a walk than a dance, and when he got back in the car, he spoiled it even more by saying to the camera, 'Never mind all this nonsense. We have a lot of work to do' – referring to his efforts to reform Israel's economy. Israel's National Road Safety Authority was not amused, and demanded that Kahlon 'immediately take the clip down from all his social media platforms'. Which he did.

The craze caused problems across the world. Officials in the US, India, Spain and the UAE all warned against the dance, which obviously places people in severe danger, while Cairo police actually arrested a university student who tried it. Egypt premier Abdel Fattah al-Sisi found the whole business quite amusing, though: he said the government shouldn't worry so much, and should instead make the most of the trend by raising fuel taxes.

*Drake wasn't the only avian artist to have a big 2018. The Eagles' Their Greatest Hits album overtook Michael Jackson's Thriller as the best-selling album of all time. The band achieved this just one week before what would have been Jackson's 60th birthday.

Drake himself had a huge year.* The Canadian rapper's album Scorpion smashed records as it became the first to be streamed more than a billion times in its first week. All 25 tracks from the album debuted in the US Top 100 Billboard Chart, including 7 in the top 10, beating a record set by the Beatles in 1964. And according to one marketing expert, the artist was responsible for about 5 per cent of his hometown of Toronto's total income from tourism.

DRONING, DANGEROUS

New Jersey made it illegal to 'drink-drone'.

It's now illegal to fly a drone in the state of New Jersey if your blood alcohol level is 0.08 per cent or higher (the same level that applies to drink-driving). Offenders face up to six months in jail, a $1,000 fine or both.

Driving, Dangerous

Dangerous drivers of the year included:

Someone who wasn't actually driving: A driver travelling on the M1 put his electric car on autopilot and got into the passenger seat. He was subsequently banned from driving.

A woman with an extremely concealed weapon: Anika Witt was arrested for speeding in Missouri. Suspicious police strip-searched her and discovered she had heroin in her bra and a loaded gun in her vagina.

A man who tried to get off on a technicality: Earle Stevens Jr sought to avoid a charge of drink-driving by claiming that he wasn't drinking *while* driving. He told the officer that stopped him that he had only downed the bourbon found in his possession when his car was at stop signs.

Fans of The Fast and the Furious films: According to researchers, fans are responsible for a marked increase in cases of speeding – especially near cinemas – the weekend after the latest instalment is released.

A fan of 'Netflix & Grill': A Frenchman was arrested after being caught driving while watching a film on his laptop and eating foie gras on toast.

Someone who used their phone while driving: A man from Massachusetts was pulled over because he was driving a scooter in the dark with no lights. He argued that he had made improvised headlights by strapping his mobile phone to the front of his vehicle.

The move was felt necessary not simply because remote-controlled aircraft have now become hugely popular, but because they're also potentially dangerous – one commentator said that the fast-spinning blades effectively make a drone a flying blender.

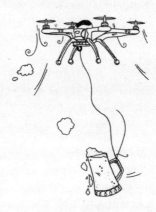

To make matters worse they're also notoriously difficult to control, as evidenced by a demonstration in Russia this year, when a postal drone crashed into a wall and broke into pieces. Reuters reported that it happened 'in front of a small crowd of spectators who were heard uttering expletives'.

Such very public crashes have not, however, deterred Amazon from continuing its research into delivery drones. This year the company patented a machine that can interpret human gestures such as a thumbs-up, a scream of panic, or the flailing of arms in an unwelcoming manner. According to which gesture it receives on arrival, the drone will either deliver the package it's carrying, avoid the person screaming at it, or abort the mission altogether.

Other drone innovations this year included an anti-drone gun invented by the US military that fires small drones at bigger drones to knock them out of the sky, and the drone lifeguard that rescued two swimmers in Australia by dropping a flotation pod on to them. And then there's the drone that delivered the body and blood of Christ at a service held by the São Geraldo Magela church in Brazil. Not everybody was impressed by this: some Catholics called the stunt 'scandalous' and a 'profanation'.

DRUGS ▶

A suspected drug dealer spent seven weeks in custody while police waited for him to poo.

Twenty-four-year-old Lamarr Chambers was accused of swallowing drugs in his possession in order to dispose of the evidence. The police held him in custody while they waited for the evidence to emerge at the other end – but it didn't. Eventually, after 47 days of bowel non-activity, the authorities, citing 'medical and legal advice', gave up and dropped the charges.*

Not all drug suspects were so lucky. In Manchester, the ringleader of the gang behind the city's largest-ever drugs haul, involving £63 million-worth of heroin hidden in tables, received a 25-year sentence despite his claim that he'd only got involved so that he could collect intelligence on other criminals to give to the police. He was known as Mario, due to his resemblance to Super Mario, and so the undercover sting was called Operation Cartoon. And in Cambridgeshire, two men arrested for growing cannabis failed to persuade a sceptical court that they thought they had been growing bonsai trees. In fact, they had so many cannabis plants under cultivation that when the police raided their house the suspects were able to hide among them.

Some of the year's drug users were comically incompetent. A man who had taken an illegal high ended up

A Girl Scout managed to sell 300 boxes of cookies by setting up her stall outside a San Diego marijuana dispensary.

He was, though, rearrested on the separate charge of being concerned in the supply of a Class A drug.

illegally high when he climbed 32 feet up a lamp post in Birmingham, got stuck and had to be rescued by authorities. A dealer in Virginia accidentally texted a police officer offering to sell him drugs. And a rapper in Rhode Island whose songs include 'Sell Drugsz' was sentenced to three years in prison for selling drugs.

DURIAN ▶

An Australian college was evacuated by a single smelly fruit.

When Chinese consumers on the shopping website Tmall were allowed to buy durian fruit this year, 80,000 were purchased in the first minute.

Melbourne's fire brigade received a report of a gas leak at the Royal Melbourne Institute of Technology, after a terrible smell was noticed wafting through the building. Five hundred students and staff were immediately evacuated and 40 specialists and firefighters were summoned to the scene. After they had cautiously made their way in, they discovered that the smell had been caused by a single durian fruit, which someone had left to rot in a cupboard. Durians are delicious and creamy, but they are so foul-smelling they're banned from public transport in Singapore.

The durian's legendary bad smell didn't deter Thailand's space agency from sending four specimens into space on a US rocket in July. They stayed there (thankfully shrink-wrapped) for a grand total of five minutes, before being brought back to Earth, where they were analysed to establish if they had undergone any changes in texture. Thailand hasn't actually been to space yet, but the country's space agency is keen to ensure that there'll be some decent Thai food on offer when they do eventually get there – although it's not clear why the supremely smelly durian makes such a good candidate.

In which we learn . . .
Who thought no newts was good news,
how babies love to listen to 'We Will Rock You',
what caused India's sandal scandal, how salad
can get you tossed out of a nightclub, and why
Ethiopian planes are like London buses.

ED SHEERAN VS NATURE

Ed Sheeran had his planning permission refused due to fake newts.

─────── ▼ ───────

In July, Sheeran, who was famously home-less for part of his life, got permission to put anti-homeless railings outside his London home.

The singer's problems began in March, when he requested permission to build a chapel on his estate in the hope that he could get married there. His plans were foiled, however, when it was suggested that the site might already be home to a colony of great crested newts, which are a protected species. Sheeran brought in experts to prove that there were no newts present, only to be refused permission a second time – because the council decided it didn't want it to look like there were two churches in the village.

A few months later, the natural world thwarted Sheeran again when he had to cancel a concert in Germany because it was believed his music would disturb a population of rare skylarks that were nesting nearby. And his first choice of alternative venue had to be changed when organisers discovered they would need to fell 104 trees to accommodate the crowd.

Sheeran then had a fourth struggle with nature at a show in Cardiff, when he had to respond to its urgent call and run off stage in front of 60,000 people – twice – to use the toilet. Finally, Sheeran was sued by a bush – well, a 'Busch'. Lawyer Richard Busch represented Sydney songwriters Sean Carey and Beau Golden, who claimed that one of Sheeran's hits was too similar to one of his clients' songs.

EGYPT

The only candidates in Egypt's presidential election were the president . . . and a vocal supporter of the president.

Egypt's incumbent president, Abdel Fattah el-Sisi, sought re-election this year, but because all other potential candidates had been bullied, intimidated, jailed or physically attacked until they withdrew their nominations, he faced the slightly embarrassing prospect of competing in a one-horse race. Clearly, a rival candidate had to be found quickly so that the whole vote didn't become a (complete) farce. Unfortunately – or fortunately – the only competitor the government could come up with was Mousa Mostafa Mousa, a member of the pro-government Ghad Party who had previously said he was a proud supporter of President Sisi, and that he hoped Sisi would win 90 per cent of the votes at the next election. Last year, Mousa even founded a campaign called 'Supporters of President el-Sisi's nomination for a second term'.

Incredibly, even though Mousa did not announce his candidacy until the day before the deadline, he still managed to gather the 47,000 signatures required by law for him to stand, completing his registration just 15 minutes before the deadline. Sisi expressed regret that there were not more rivals, and that he wished there were 'one, or two, or three, or ten candidates' standing against him. 'We are not ready,' he said, 'isn't it a shame?'

In the end, Mousa got his wish: Sisi won with 97 per cent of the votes, on a turnout of just 41 per cent. One of the unofficial runners-up was Liverpool and Egypt footballer Mo Salah: on a fair chunk of the million spoiled ballots, voters crossed out the names of the two official candidates and wrote Salah's name instead.

EIGHTH AMENDMENT

Budget flights to Ireland on the day of their abortion referendum were £100 more expensive than on the days before and after.

Ireland voted in two further referendums later in the year. One asked whether blasphemy should remain an explicit offence; the other, whether the statement that a woman's life is 'within the home' should be removed from the constitution.

The eighth amendment of the Irish constitution recognised the equal right to life of the pregnant woman and the unborn child, so cementing the country's position as one of the few in Europe to make abortion completely illegal except to save a mother's life. That is, until this year, when the amendment was repealed after a landslide referendum result in favour of a change to the law.

Any Irish citizen who had lived in the country in the previous 18 months was eligible to take part in the referendum, and thousands of Irish emigrants duly flew home to cast their vote. Unfortunately, because many budget airlines work on a strict supply-and-demand basis, increased demand led to skyrocketing ticket prices. Flights between London and Cork, which had been just £40 return the week before, were now on sale for over £100 each way. Financial help was on hand for some, though. Students at various British universities, including Oxford and Cambridge, were able to apply for bursaries, and many Irish expats in Australia were helped out by local campaigning charities. In the end, more than two thirds of the votes cast were in favour of the law change.

Of course, some found it hard to accept the result. One priest, for example, said that anyone who voted 'yes' in the abortion referendum shouldn't be allowed to marry in a church. And there was dissatisfaction in the victors' camp, too, among those who felt they'd won a battle but not yet the war: they next set their campaigning attentions on Northern Ireland, where abortion is still illegal. In fact, some activists planned to use robots to deliver abortion pills to women in the North – claiming that what they were planning was not illegal, because the robots would be operated from the Netherlands.

EL CHAPO

A Mexican drug lord who famously escaped jail through an underground tunnel requested to return to court through another one.

In July 2015, Joaquín 'El Chapo' Guzmán managed to escape from the most secure wing of Mexico's most secure prison via an intricately built mile-long tunnel that ran from the outside world to a shaft emerging from the floor of his shower. He would have got out sooner had his henchmen not initially missed their target and surfaced in the wrong cell.

Six months after his escape, El Chapo was caught again, and was extradited to the US to stand trial on drug trafficking and other charges. Pre-trial hearings involved driving him from 'Little Gitmo', the jail where he was being held, to court in a motorcade so large it forced the closure of the Brooklyn Bridge, drawing huge attention from locals which, his lawyers argued, could potentially prejudice the trial. Guzmán's team therefore attempted to simplify things by requesting the court move their client's case to Manhattan's Southern District, where El Chapo could avoid public attention by using the 200-metre underground tunnel that connects the courthouse to the jail. The judge declined to make the change.

If El Chapo's pre-trial hearings have proved complex, that's nothing compared with what the full trial promises. The judge has announced plans to call between 800 and 1,000 potential jurors, each of whom is required to fill out a lengthy questionnaire. Because there are fears for the jury's safety, he has ordered that their identities should be kept secret. According to El Chapo's lawyers, though, their client has solemnly promised not to have any of them murdered.

EMOJIS

For 📱 *see* **Messaging, Instant**; for 💩 *see* **Poo, Dog**; and for 🥑 *see* **Vegans**.

ENDANGERED

Two Australian species are now officially endangered thanks to their marathon sex sessions.

The black-tailed dusky antechinus and the silver-headed antechinus are mouse-like marsupials, discovered in 2013, that have become famous for their suicidal sex lives. They indulge in such frantic sex during the mating season (which lasts for several weeks) that males and females alike go from peak health to virtual collapse as their systems are poisoned by lethal levels of testosterone. This year, both species were put on the official list of endangered animals. According to Dr Andrew Baker, the man who discovered them, 'They're honestly like the walking dead towards the end.'

ESCAPES, SUCCESSFUL

For flying Frenchmen, *see* **Jails**; for fleeing fridges with frozen food, *see* **Sausages**; and for flinging faeces in faces, *see* **Shoplifters**.

ESCAPES, UNSUCCESSFUL

A man was arrested after burgling an escape room – and finding himself unable to escape.

An escape room is an interactive game in which participants are locked in a room and have to solve a number of challenges in order to free themselves. So when Rye Wardlaw of Washington state broke into one and attempted to steal a mobile phone, he was temporarily defeated by the room's puzzles. He did eventually manage to get out, but not before ringing the police four times in panic. Consequently, when he finally did emerge, officers were waiting for him.

In Texas, meanwhile, an escaped prisoner was caught trying to break *back into* jail, smuggling with him 'a large amount of home cooked food'; and in Oxford, a tortoise who escaped from its home was recaptured six months after her escape, 322 metres away. Tallulah's average speed, calculated by *The Times*, was 0.00005 miles per hour.

ETHIOPIA ▶

No planes flew from Ethiopia to Eritrea for 20 years, then two came along at once.

The two countries have been at war since 1998 over the precise position of their shared border, so it came as a welcome surprise this summer when Eritrean President Isaias Afwerki and Ethiopian Prime Minister Abiy Ahmed finally signed a peace agreement. The first commercial flight between the two countries' capitals took place soon afterwards, on 18 July. Many of those aboard were journalists, who were served champagne and given celebratory red roses, but there was such high demand for seats that a second flight had to be put on just 15 minutes after the first. Among the passengers were a large number hoping to be reunited with family members they hadn't seen in years. Phone lines between the countries were also reopened, with some people in Ethiopia ringing random strangers in Eritrea, just so they could exchange congratulations.

The impetus for change has much to do with Ethiopia's new leader, Abiy Ahmed.* However, his time as prime minister didn't begin quite so successfully, as just three months into the job he was stood up by a robot. The plan had been for him to have dinner with Sophia, arguably the world's most famous android (she's been awarded Saudi citizenship, has been on a date with Will Smith and played Rock, Paper, Scissors with Jimmy Fallon). But the get-together had to be postponed when baggage handlers at Frankfurt airport lost half of her body. Fortunately, replacement parts were found and a few days later the two were able to meet. Sophia greeted the prime minister in Amharic, Ethiopia's official language and only the second language (after English) she's ever learned.

*At 42, Abiy is the youngest leader in Africa. His popularity in his home country is such that it has been dubbed 'Abiymania', and up to 4 million people attend his rallies. However, he is not universally liked: in June, a grenade was thrown at him as he spoke in Addis Ababa, killing at least one bystander. He responded by saying, 'Love always wins . . . To those who tried to divide us, I want to tell you that you have not succeeded.'

EXAMS

Indian schools banned shoes and socks from their exam halls.

Cheating is such a widespread problem in the Indian state of Bihar that in the past schoolchildren have even been arrested for it. This year, students were therefore monitored by video as they sat their exams. In addition, they were searched before they entered the exam hall and told the only footwear they would be allowed was sandals or slippers. Shoes and socks were banned on the grounds that they could be used to conceal crib sheets and notes.

Elsewhere in India, a gunman armed with a pistol forced invigilators to remain outside one exam hall while students inside quickly copied from answer sheets. And students at another university who had got hold of a leaked exam paper took to a rooftop next to their exam hall and yelled the answers to their friends through a megaphone.

India is hardly alone in facing a cheating epidemic. In Algeria the problem proved so severe that this year the authorities completely shut off access to the Internet for several hours a day during exam season. The one problem with this approach was that it left hundreds of businesses and millions of citizens equally unable to get online.* And in one of the biggest cheating takedowns ever, the Swedish authorities busted a father and his two sons for allegedly charging students sitting university entrance exams up to £14,300 to have the answers relayed to them via concealed earpieces. Apparently, those who took part in the scheme were offered a choice of perfect answers, or slightly wrong ones if they wanted to seem more convincing.

The no-Internet strategy has been tried before in countries such as Syria, Iraq, Ethiopia, Mauritania and Uzbekistan.

EXCUSES ▶

Roseanne claimed that sleeping pills made her racist.

After her TV show was cancelled because she had written a racist tweet, the American comedian Roseanne Barr immediately announced she was leaving Twitter. She then proceeded to tweet more than a hundred times over the next 24 hours. She admitted that her original tweet had been 'indefensible' and that she had 'made a mistake', but she also blamed 'Ambien tweeting' – her suggestion being that the sleeping medication she was taking might have provoked her remark. Sanofi, the company that makes Ambien, denied this could be the case. 'While all pharmaceutical treatments have side effects,' a spokesperson said, 'racism is not a known side effect of any Sanofi medication.'*

The leaflet provided with Ambien does, however, warn of various other bizarre side effects, including sleep-eating, sleep-driving and sleep-sex.

In other excuse news:

▶ A salad company boss who was arrested for behaving violently blamed his conduct on the salad. The chief executive of Tossed, Vincent McKevitt, claimed his low-calorie diet had lowered his alcohol tolerance, which, he argued, explained why he had punched two bouncers outside a nightclub.

▶ An Irish man charged with dangerous driving failed to turn up to court because he was too sunburned. His lawyer said, 'I never thought I'd have to say that in Ireland.'

▶ Eight Argentinian police officers who were being investigated after 540 kilos of marijuana went missing from a police warehouse blamed mice for the disappearance. Forensics experts pointed out that if rodents had been responsible, their corpses would have been lying around everywhere. The officers were sacked.

▶ And after provoking accusations of treason with his remark that he didn't see 'any reason why it would be' Russia who'd hacked the US election, Donald Trump explained that he hadn't meant to say 'would'. He had, of course, intended to say there was no reason it *wouldn't* be Russia.

EXPERIMENTS

Scientists tested whether or not fruit flies enjoy orgasms.

First their neurons were altered in such a way that the flies ejaculated when exposed to red light. It was noted that once the insects realised red light brought them to fly-max, they flocked to it in preference over other coloured lights, suggesting their orgasms must be giving them pleasure. Then the team from Bar-Ilan University in Israel offered them alcohol and discovered those that had already been to the red-light district were less keen to drink than those that hadn't. They therefore concluded that flies that have already had an orgasm have satisfied their reward systems to the point where they don't need a drink as well. The experiment was only conducted on male fruit flies, so we still don't know whether female flies enjoy sex, or want to get drunk after it.

Scientists who played music to foetuses to see what they liked discovered that unborn babies are partial to Queen, but don't like Shakira or the Bee Gees.

In another insect experiment, biologists in Sweden tied stalks to the backs of bogong moths, tethered them inside a flight simulator, applied magnetic fields, and pointed them towards a felt cut-out of a mountain. They then monitored which direction the moths flew in as they moved the fake mountain around, and altered the magnetic field. The moths adjusted their flight based on both the visual and the magnetic cue, providing the first evidence that insects use the earth's magnetic field to navigate.

Meanwhile in an experiment conducted in Belgium, human volunteers were given the choice of letting five mice receive severe electrical shocks, or, if they opted to push a button, just one mouse being electrified. It was a real-life version of the well-known 'trolley problem' that asks the theoretical question: if you saw a runaway train carriage about to run over five people, would you be prepared to pull a lever that would divert the train and kill one other, unsuspecting bystander? In the event, 84 per cent of people chose to press the button and hurt the single mouse, though many admitted afterwards they didn't believe the scientists would really let a rodent be harmed (which they didn't).

EXTERMINATE ▶

Three terriers walked 2,500 kilometres searching for a single rat.

The hope was that they wouldn't find one. It was all part of a mission to ensure the Atlantic island of South Georgia is clear of rats (and mice). The British-owned territory is one of the world's last great wildernesses, and home to thousands of endangered seabirds, but since humans first arrived 250 years ago, invasive rodents have been destroying the birds' eggs and threatening their populations, hence the decade-long fight against them.

The programme was mostly funded by private philanthropy and by schemes such as 'sponsoring a hectare', whereby you could help pay for the dropping of hundreds of tonnes of rat poison by helicopter across 108,000 hectares (an area eight times larger than any other previous eradication zone). For a long time rats evicted from one area tended just to pop up elsewhere. But after 4,600 rodent-detecting devices, including camera traps and chewsticks coated in peanut butter, had failed to find anything, and the sniffer dogs and their handlers – aka 'Team Rat' – had walked for 2,500 kilometres (and climbed the equivalent of Mount Everest more than 12 times over) without encountering a single rat, the project was declared a success.

EYEWEAR

Scientists invented contact lenses that can fire lasers from your eyes.

The lenses, which shoot out a 'well-defined green laser beam', have been developed by a team at the School of Physics and Astronomy at the University of St Andrews. They haven't been given to humans to wear yet, but they have been tested on cows' eyeballs. The scientists aren't yet sure what the practical uses for ultralight eye-lasers might be, but because it's possible to make each laser unique, they might one day serve as wearable security tags.

Scientists wanted to test whether puffin beaks glow under UV light (they do). But to safeguard the puffins' eyes, they had to put tiny sunglasses on the birds first.

Eyewear is already playing a security role in China, where police have been issued with glasses that can scan the faces of passers-by and compare them with a central database, to help the authorities recognise – and so apprehend – known criminals. Seven people were arrested this way by officers at the Zhengzhou East railway station during this year's New Year celebrations.

It's not just humans and cows who are being offered augmented eyeballs. In a recent experiment, praying mantises were fitted with glasses to see if they were able to enjoy 3D movies. In fact, it emerged that insects' vision is not quite the same as humans' – while we can enjoy the 3D effect with still images, the praying mantises can only perceive depth when the image is moving. But they did enjoy the films, which starred insects that they like to feed upon. Some praying mantises even tried to catch the digital bugs.

In which we learn . . .
Which computer game was making $150 million every
fortnite, why people flocked to see a giant lump of
fat, who nailed the record for the longest fingernails,
and which of the world's hemispheres has the best
flat-earth conventions.

FACEBOOK

For a perfectly safe place where you can send naked pictures that absolutely won't spread on the Internet, *see* **Send Nudes**; and for the founder of a company that accessed and shared the private data of over 90 million of its users, *see* **Zuckerberg, Mark**.

FACIAL RECOGNITION

Police in South Wales revealed that their facial recognition technology wrongly flagged 2,000 people as potential crooks.

A robot has been invented that can solve a *Where's Wally?* puzzle in less than five seconds, using facial recognition. The machine takes a photo of the page, captures every face, and then checks each one against the robot's idea of what Wally looks like. Its success rate is higher than 95 per cent.

The new software was trialled at 2017's Champions League final in Cardiff, but this year it was revealed that it had wrongly identified more than 2,000 people at the event as criminals. Of 2,470 flagged, 2,297 were false positives. Thankfully, nobody was incorrectly arrested.

The American Civil Liberties Union also suffered from the false positive problem when they tried Amazon's version of the software: 28 members of Congress were wrongly identified as people who had previously been arrested, and much more problematically, it disproportionately misidentified people of colour. (Amazon, it should be said, disputed the ACLU's conclusions.)

Despite these teething problems, the march of FR seems unstoppable. A fertility clinic in Spain is using the technology to match people with egg donors who look like them, ensuring mothers will get a child who resembles the rest of the family. And in China FR is making its way into every aspect of life: schools are using it to check whether pupils are paying attention; hotels use it to allow guests to check in; and, unsurprisingly, the police are using it a lot. At one concert, in the Eastern city of Zhejiang, the technology was used to spot and arrest a man who was wanted for the alleged theft of £12,000-worth of potatoes.

FAMILIES ▶

A Swedish mother changed her son's name to match her misspelled tattoo.

Johanna Sandström thought she had asked for the name of her infant son, Kevin, to be tattooed on her arm, but when she got home, she realised she'd ended up with 'Kelvin'. Rather than undergo the multiple treatments it would take to remove the tattoo, she decided to change the two-year-old's name instead. She says she now prefers Kelvin to Kevin.

As Sandström competed for 'Mum of the Year', the media gave the 'Dad of the Year' award to the motorist who, en route from western Germany to Lake Garda in Italy, drove off from a service station without noticing he'd left his 10- and 14-year-old daughters behind to use the bathroom. He realised his mistake an hour and a half later, when he checked his phone to find he had 48 missed calls from the police. By then he was 170 kilometres away in Austria.

Meanwhile, the 'Son of the Year' award goes to 30-year-old Michael Rotondo, who so steadfastly refused to get a job or move out of his parents' house that they finally felt they had no option but to take him to court to get rid of him. They won their case and Rotondo was evicted. He then immediately called the police on his father, claiming he hadn't been allowed to re-enter the house to retrieve his eight-year-old son's LEGO from the basement.

——— ▼ ———

In the space of one week, Trump claimed twice that his father was born in Germany, despite the fact that he was actually born in New York. The president's uncertainty on the subject might explain why, on his visit to Britain, Theresa May gave him a gift of a chart showing his family tree.

FAST FOOD ▶

A crowd gathered in Wisconsin to watch a man eat his 30,000th Big Mac.

———— ▼ ————

Burger King Russia apologised for offering free burgers to women who were impregnated by World Cup players. They explained that their hope had been that the promotion would lead to Russian babies with foreign football-playing genes.

Don Gorske began eating Big Macs on a daily basis back in 1972 and in all that time has only gone without on a couple of occasions. One of these was in 1988, when he refrained out of respect for his mother's request that he avoid burgers on the day she died. He keeps all the evidence of his meals – receipts, sandwich wrappers and containers – although he did lose 7,000 styrofoam cartons in a tornado in 1990. Now something of a local celebrity, he delivered a half-hour presentation about his Big Mac journey to onlookers before he consumed his 30,000th in May. He says he's eaten only one Burger King Whopper in his life, after his friend bet him $5 he wouldn't, and afterwards he immediately went across the road to McDonald's to buy some Big Macs with the money he'd won.

Another American burger chain, Jack in the Box, teamed up with Snoop Dogg this year to create the Merry Munchie Meal for stoners. Described as 'infused with the most craveable and snackable products', it became available at select locations in California, just as the state legalised recreational marijuana.

And while meals for stoners were available in the US, meals for loners thrived in the UK, as Tesco increased its range of meals-for-one by 40 per cent because so many of us now live or eat alone. Among its new 'single serve' meals are solitary burgers and steaks, and shrunk-down bottles of wine.

FATBERGS

A 250-metre-long lump of sewage got its own range of merchandise.

Fatbergs, which are made up of congealed fats, cooking oils, wet wipes, nappies, condoms and other waste, are a big problem for London's sewers, costing Thames Water £1 million a month to contain. Last year, a fatberg discovered under the streets of Whitechapel made the news when it was revealed that it weighed as much as a blue whale and stretched the length of 22 double-decker buses. Sewage workers (or 'flushers') spent nine weeks disposing of it.

One small shoebox-sized chunk of the 'berg was saved by the flushers and put on display at the Museum of London in February. Protected by Perspex, it continually changed shape and colour throughout the six months it was exhibited. It even spawned flies. And it proved hugely popular: more than twice the usual number of visitors to the museum flocked to see the *Fatberg!* exhibition, and they eagerly snapped up a range of

As well as being turned into a museum exhibit, the Whitechapel fatberg is getting its own musical. *Flushing Fatbergs!* is a comedy horror set in a world where people live in the sewers, their existence threatened by the fatberg.

'berg merchandise that the museum put on sale in its gift shop, ranging from 'DON'T FEED THE FATBERG' T-shirts, to tote bags, badges and bags of fudge called Fatberg Sludge.

Curators are now considering sending the fatberg on a world tour.

FILMS

For a cinematic jockstrap, *see* **Auctions**; for a film Chinese people appeared to enjoy, *see* **China**; for films that praying mantises appeared to enjoy, *see* **Eyewear**; for how hobbits helped terrorists, *see* **ISIS**; for how Steve McQueen helped criminals, *see* **Jails**; for a team who think *Cool Runnings* is not cool, *see* **Rebranding**; for a country who thought *The Emoji Movie* was 💩 *see* **Saudi Arabia**; and for why 'Hot Animal Action' is not so hot, *see* **XXX**.

FINGERNAILS

The man with the world's longest fingernails sold them to a museum for 'enough to retire on'.

Eighty-two-year-old Shridhar Chillal started growing his nails when he was 14 to prove his teacher wrong. Chillal, who had been messing around with a friend, had accidentally broken the teacher's long fingernail, been scolded and told that he couldn't possibly understand the effort needed to grow long nails. Sixty-eight years later, his fingernails had achieved a combined length of 9.096 metres, his thumbnail alone measuring 197.8 centimetres (that's 5 centimetres longer than the height of former wrestler and future president Dwayne 'the Rock' Johnson). In 2018, however, Chillal finally decided that enough was enough and clipped the nails, selling them to the *Ripley's Believe It or Not!* museum in New York City.

Chillal's nails were so long and heavy that for most of his life he was unable to use his left hand. But at least he never chewed them, unlike Luke Hanoman of Southport, who learned the hard way that the habit can have near-fatal consequences. Because the father-of-two regularly bit his nails, the skin around his finger became broken, and an infection entered his bloodstream. He ended up on a stretcher with a drip in his arm and just hours from death. Hanoman is now trying to raise awareness of the dangers of sepsis.

FIRE AND FURY

A book about the Second World War accidentally became a bestseller after people mistook it for a tell-all book about Donald Trump.

Michael Wolff's *Fire and Fury* became one of the fastest-selling non-fiction books of modern times when it was released in January. More than a million people placed orders within the first week. But Michael Wolff wasn't the only beneficiary of this buying frenzy. Randall Hansen, author of a book about the Allied bombing of Germany during the Second World War also titled *Fire and Fury*, similarly saw his book become a

bestseller on Amazon. It was, however, very definitely
Wolff's book that Iran's supreme leader Ayatollah Ali
Khamenei was photographed reading at a Tehran book
fair (he later posted the photo on his Instagram page).
And it was definitely pirated versions of Wolff's book
that hackers used to spread malware and gain access
to readers' computers.

Wolff's record as a truth-teller is not a wholly unblem-
ished one: when working as an Internet entrepreneur,
he attempted to keep bankers at bay by lying about his
father-in-law having open-heart surgery. 'How many
fairly grievous lies had I told?' he later wrote. 'How
many moral lapses had I committed? How many ethical
breaches had I fallen into? . . . Like many another financial conniver, I was in a short-term mode.' Whether or
not this still applied when he wrote *Fire and Fury*, the
book provided plenty of fuel for the Trump-haters. Wolff
wrote that press baron Rupert Murdoch called Trump a
'f*cking idiot'; he disclosed that Trump has three televi-
sions in his bedroom and added his own lock so that the

Secret Service couldn't enter; and we also learned that Trump's main aim during his campaign was to become 'the most famous man in the world'.

He certainly managed the last of these. Whether his presidency ends in fire and fury is yet to be seen. But one thing is for sure: some of his businesses almost have. Trump Tower in New York managed to catch fire twice within the first four months of 2018.

FLAT-EARTHERS

The UK's first ever Flat Earth Convention took place, less than two months after another one on the other side of the globe.

There were about 200 attendees at the three-day conference, which was held at the Jurys Inn hotel in Birmingham. It came two months after another convention in Australia, a place (according to anyone who's fallen for the government line) on the other side of the Earth. Sadly, owing to arguments between the organisers, the Aussie convention proved something of a damp squib. In the end only three people turned up: two delegates and one jour-nalist who was writing about the event.

One of the speakers at the Birmingham event explained that 'continuous east–west travel is a reality', and that we only think the Earth is round because celestial bodies teleport from one side of the Earth to the other, due to what he called the 'Pac-Man effect'. But while those present were agreed on what shape the world isn't, they couldn't settle on what shape it actually is: suggestions included that it's diamond-shaped; that it has a domed roof; or that it's made up of a series of linked rings. Other theories aired included the ideas that the Moon is a projection; that the universe is a giant egg; and that the Earth is a pond carved out of a massive crust of ice. While many may scoff at all this, one fact that *is* true is that searches for the phrase 'flat Earth' have risen tenfold in the last five years.

Meanwhile, one flat-Earther put his money where his mouth was and fired himself a purported 580 metres into the air above the Mojave Desert. 'Mad' Mike Hughes' journey was just a preparatory trip for a planned 110-kilometre ascent designed to prove his personal theory that the planet is shaped like a Frisbee. He landed unharmed except for a slightly sore back (although he could have saved a lot of effort by going up in a commercial flight, which would have got him 17 times as high for much less money). 'Do I believe the Earth is shaped like a Frisbee?' he said in an interview with Associated Press. 'I believe it is. Do I know for sure? No. That's why I want to go up in space.' His next plan is to go up in a 'rockoon' – a rocket carried into the atmosphere by a balloon. Flat-Earthers around (or across) the world are counting on him to succeed.

FOOTBALL FANS

Nigerian fans were told not to bring their lucky chickens to World Cup matches.

According to one of Russia's regional culture and tourism ministers, Andrei Yermak, 'fans from Nigeria asked if it's possible to go to the stadium with a chicken, it's their symbol. We told them bringing a live chicken is not possible.' For many Nigerians this was crushing news. Back home, bringing a chicken to a football match is traditional. They are viewed as lucky charms. Some fans even dye their poultry green and white to match their team's national colours. And many were forced to miss seeing their team play at the 2010 World Cup in South Africa because they couldn't bear to abandon their lucky chickens. Yermak was able to offer a slight compromise to Nigerian fans, though: he was quoted as saying, 'We will of course advise them on places where you can buy a chicken. We are ready to accommodate the most eccentric requests.'

Another set of fans to make the news was Japan's, who cleaned up the stadium after each one of their team's matches. Even after they were dramatically knocked out of the World Cup when they lost to Belgium in injury time, they still made sure to collect every bit of litter, packing it all away in blue rubbish bags. The Japanese team shared their fans' impeccable manners. After the Belgium match they cleaned their changing room to perfection – and left a 'thank you' note behind, too.

England fans, conversely, celebrated their World Cup win against Sweden by making an absolute mess in IKEA stores, attacking furniture, jumping on beds and kicking over tables. Before the match, in a more peaceful mood, pranksters in Gateshead hung up signs in their local IKEA for a product called 'Football ETSKÖMMÅNHJÖME' with a pricetag of £19.66.

A group of Mexican football fans took a cardboard cut-out of a friend to the World Cup after learning that his girlfriend wouldn't let him go. The Russian embassy tweeted that his friends were the 'real heroes' of the World Cup.

FOR YOUR EYES ONLY

For a movie made for one, *see* **Advertising**; and for a movie made for Un, *see* **Singapore Summit**.

FORTNITE

American sports teams are refusing to sign players who are addicted to video games.

The *Guardian* reported that a number of parents in America were paying private tutors to improve their children's *Fortnite* skills, in order to stop them from being picked on at school.

This detail came to light in an article about the Washington Capitals ice hockey team, who, it turns out, ask potential picks if they are addicted to the hugely popular multiplayer online game *Fortnite*. It's a sensible thing to ask: the game has been blamed for ruining the career of at least one (unnamed) high-profile American football player. And when Boston Red Sox pitcher David Price missed a match against his team's hated rivals, the New York Yankees, *Fortnite* was suspected. Price denied the game was to blame for the numbness in his hands that caused him to miss the match, though he had previously said he played it so much that he sometimes forgot to eat.

Soccer players also love the game. Tottenham Hotspur's Dele Alli celebrated his FA Cup semi-final goal by performing the 'Flossing' dance, a move from the game; Jesse Lingard did the 'Shoot' dance after scoring in England's 6–1 win over Panama; and France's Antoine Griezmann performed a *Fortnite* dance after scoring in the World Cup final: his 'Take the L' dance consists of making a 'loser' L-sign on one's forehead and kicking one's legs out in a kind of deformed cancan.

It's not just sportspeople who have become obsessed. At any given time, 3 million people across the globe are estimated to be playing *Fortnite* – and while the game itself is free to play, paid-for extras such as costumes and dance moves generated more than $300 million a month this summer. The World Health Organization has included 'gaming disorder' in its draft for next year's diagnostic manual of mental health issues; and one gamer's girlfriend launched a petition on Change.org to get *Fortnite* banned because it was becoming so detrimental to their relationship. Even though she was joking, the petition still managed to attract more than 8,000 signatories.

In which we learn . . .
What smells worse than the G7, why your data needs
Jehovah's Witness protection, what links Kim Jong Un
and Elt-on John, why Xi didn't get his gee-gee, and the
secret ingredient in space Marmite.

G7

Canadian farmers were asked not to spread manure on their fields before the G7 summit, so it didn't smell of bullshit when the politicians arrived.

Quebec's Agricultural Ministry sent a letter to the farming association in the Charlevoix region asking that they hold off on manure-spreading until after the summit because they didn't want 'unpleasant odors' drifting from the fields to the G7 venue.

In the event, 'unpleasant odors' were the least of the G7's worries. The summit was awkward from the start. Donald Trump pitted the US against the other member nations (Canada, France, UK, Germany, Japan and Italy). He caused controversy when at one point he threw some Starburst sweets on to the table in front of Angela Merkel, with the words: 'Here, Angela, don't say I never give you anything.' He also arrived late to a Gender Equality Advisory Council breakfast. (They started without him, meaning Canadian Prime Minister Justin Trudeau had to repeat his opening speech when the US president finally arrived.) And his premature departure

Protesters were kept well away from the summit, but were allowed to voice their disapproval 2 kilometres away in a car park, ironically dubbed the 'official free speech zone'.

to meet North Korea's leader in Singapore meant he missed meetings on how to protect the oceans and tackle climate change.

Trump–Trudeau relations were especially strained. The president interrupted the Canadian premier at a joint press conference with the words 'No, he's not happy' when Trudeau was asked whether he minded Trump leaving the summit early to meet Kim Jong Un. And there was an ugly spat over Trump's tariff policy. Trump had endorsed the G7's official communiqué as he left for Singapore, saying, 'they fully understand where I'm coming from . . . free and fair trade will happen', and declaring relations with Trudeau, Merkel and Macron were 10/10. But by the time he'd disembarked at the other end and heard that Trudeau had said in a speech that Canada would stick to retaliatory tariffs against the US, Trump proceeded to tweet a retraction and effectively un-sign the agreement (the first time in the history of the G7 that this has happened). Trump's trade advisor announced there was 'a special place in hell' for Trudeau. Trudeau's former policy advisor responded by calling Trump a 'pathetic little man-child'.

GDPR ▶

Priests stopped praying for people in case they breached new data protection laws.

The laws in question are the new General Data Protection Regulations (GDPR), which came into force in May in the form of the Data Protection Act. Designed to protect people's privacy, they have had some unexpected side effects. Marcus Walker, the rector of Great St Bartholomew in the City of London, for example, tweeted: 'We've been told we can't pray for anyone who hasn't given their personal consent, which is just ridiculous.' Jehovah's Witnesses, for their part, have been told they now have to ask express permission before collecting personal data on the doorstep.

One element of the Act had to be changed at the last moment because, as originally drafted, it would have left those policing online security open to prosecution. The problem was this: a researcher seeking to prove that a company is not adequately safeguarding people's anonymity can only do so by demonstrating how easy it is to discover their identities; but the very process of discovering their identities would have been illegal if the legislation had been passed as written. It was eventually amended to make an exception for these researchers.

GENDER PAY GAP

The industry with the fairest pay for women is sewerage.

In April, all UK companies employing more than 250 people were compelled by the government to make public how their male and female employees' pay compared. It emerged that, nationally, the disparity was 14.5 per cent in favour of men. But in the sewerage, waste management and water sector the disparity was a modest 5.5 per cent. Bywaters, the waste management company that removes all rubbish from the Houses of Parliament, emerged from a list of over 10,000 organisations as the one whose wage structure was most favourable to women – by some 30 per cent.

Many companies struggled with government guidelines on how to calculate their wage gaps and ended up publishing statistically impossible figures. Millwall FC, for example, announced their gender pay gap to be 159 per cent, a figure that would suggest that women employed at the club were actually handing over money to work there. Other businesses changed their figures

Bucking the usual state of affairs in media, Channel 5 actually paid its female employees more than its male workers. Channel 4, on the other hand, reported a 29 per cent gap in favour of men, though Carol Vorderman did reveal that the only argument she and *Countdown* co-host Richard Whiteley ever had was when he found out she was paid three times more than him.

numerous times as they attempted to master the maths. Skincare brand Elemis initially published a gender gap of 111.4 per cent, then changed this to 0.9 per cent.

But perhaps the biggest gender pay gap story of the year emerged during the Potato Carrying Race in Robertson, New South Wales. Here prize money for men was AU$1,000, but for women it was just AU$200. Defenders of the status quo pointed out that women only have to carry a 12.5-kilogram sack of potatoes, while men are loaded down with 50 kilograms. Critics argued that the women's race is just as entertaining as the men's and draws the same size of crowd. The organisers promised to review the prize structure in time for next year.

GIFTS, DIPLOMATIC ▶

The government of Burundi looked a gift donkey in the mouth.

When the French government donated an aid package to a remote village in the African country of Burundi, including 10 donkeys that would be used to help fetch water, Burundian politicians reacted with fury. One of them objected on Twitter that the French were 'taking us for donkeys'. The French hastily pointed out that the animals had been paid for by a project that had originally been suggested by a Burundian organisation. But then the argument probably wasn't solely about donkeys. Burundi was annoyed that France had criticised a recent, controversial referendum in the country.

Other world leaders dished out animals with happier results. Narendra Modi, the Indian prime minister, gave a village in Rwanda 200 cows. Nepal sent China two endangered one-horned rhinos as a gesture of goodwill. China gave Japan two crested ibises. And when France's President Macron visited China in January, he was inspired by China's 'panda diplomacy' – where pandas are given as gifts to curry favour – to present the best France had to offer: a horse called Vésuve de Brekka (Vesuvius of Brekka). Unfortunately, the horse had to be quarantined during the visit, so in the short term President Xi had to make do with a saddle, a sword and a photo of Vésuve de Brekka. Incidentally, Macron's name when translated into Chinese – 'Ma-ke-long' – means 'the horse vanquishes the dragon' – an arguably provocative statement to make to a nation that identifies itself with dragons. It is not yet known whether Xi will mount Vesuvius.

At the bargain basement end of diplomatic presents, Donald Trump risked Kim Jong Un's wrath by suggesting he'd be giving him an Elton John CD, featuring 'Rocket Man' – Trump's insulting nickname for Kim. Trump himself received a football from President Putin, which had to be immediately put through a security scanner. And on her visit to China in February, Theresa May gave President Xi Jinping a DVD box-set of *Blue Planet* worth approximately £20.

One of the most impressive diplomatic gifts of the year was a jeep given by Israeli Prime Minister Benjamin Netanyahu to his Indian counterpart Narendra Modi. The GalMobile vehicle also works as a desalination plant. It is able to turn up to 20,000 litres of seawater a day into drinking water as it drives around.

GLASS

For glass walls, *see* **Offices**; for glass ceilings, *see* **Gender Pay Gap**.

GOO

Astronomers have concluded there's enough grease in the Milky Way to fill 40 trillion, trillion, trillion packs of butter.

Their study recreated the conditions of outer space in a lab, measured how much of the carbon became what they term 'space grease', and discovered it was far more than expected. The author of the report described the substance as being like 'greasy soot' that would make everything around it dirty; also that it was probably toxic and was 'not the kind of thing you'd want to spread on a slice of toast'.

Greasy carbon isn't the only slimy stuff astronauts might find in outer space in future. Scientists this year developed a way of turning human faeces into a 'Marmite-like' food source that those on long trips into space might one day be able to eat. It's high in protein and fat, although researchers appetisingly added that technically what the astronauts would be eating is 'a smear of microbial goo'.

One substance that people shouldn't really be eating is slime, the goopy mixture that has become a global craze over the last year. Multiple countries began to panic about the potential adverse health effects of slime-based toys, which usually contain borax. Borax can cause irritation to throats and eyes; however, unless children are eating large amounts of it for many weeks, it is unlikely to cause kidney toxicity, cerebral oedema, gastroenteritis, infertility, or any of the other horrors claimed by tabloid newspapers. This didn't stop the country of Jordan banning the import, manufacturing, sale or possession of it; nor did it stop the governments of France, Finland and Dubai from issuing official warnings against it. Norway also banned some slime products, but specifically the ones that contained lead and arsenic, which seems fair enough.

GUN CONTROL

Google tried to stop people buying guns but instead blocked people buying water guns, music by Guns N' Roses, and the film Anchorman: The Legend of Ron Burgundy.

Google Shopping prohibits the buying of firearms on its site, but its block on searches for guns has proved rather too heavy-handed. Burgundy wine and references to the Arsenal Football Club mascot Gunnersaurus are just two in a long list of innocent search terms to be blocked. Would-be gun owners would have been better off making their purchases offline, in Florida, where it emerged that no background checks had been carried out for an entire year because the guy who was supposed to make them had forgotten his login details.

If that seems irresponsible, it's nothing compared with what some actual gun handlers have been up to recently. A Californian teacher, for instance, accidentally fired a gun in class during the middle of a lesson on advanced public safety. Nobody was seriously injured, although bits of the ceiling fell on the floor. And an FBI agent dancing in a club in Denver lost his gun halfway through a backflip, causing it to go off as he went to retrieve it, injuring another customer in the leg. The agent faced an assault charge, while the victim was offered free drinks for life, though presumably he won't be asking for any more shots.

Tammy Duckworth, a Senator from Illinois, was criticised for accepting money from an employee registered to the National Restaurant Association. Online commentators, who had failed to do their research, argued it was hypocritical for a major voice for gun reform laws in America to be accepting money from the NRA.

In which we learn . . .
Why hackers love hawking expensive cheese,
what Hawking had to say about holograms,
which holograms are hosting their own concerts,
why a concert-goer's life was saved by a guitarist's
spit, and how a Belgian footballer caused a spat
on the other side of the world.

HACKING

The US State Department spent $0 fighting Russian hacking despite having a budget of $120 million to do so.

Because of the zero spend, no new employees were hired to fight Russian hacking. But then, none of the 23 analysts working in the department's Global Engagement Center, tasked with countering Moscow's disinformation campaign, speaks Russian anyway. The reason for this, according to Rex Tillerson, the US Secretary of State who was fired in March, was that his department wouldn't have been able to do much to stop Russia, whatever their budget was. 'If it's their intention to interfere,' he said, 'they're going to find ways to do that.'

Despite global clampdowns, it has been estimated that in 2017, hackers stole $120 billion, from as many as 978 million people, in 20 countries. A report also revealed that more than 90 per cent of attempts to log into online shops come from hackers. For airline bookings it's 60 per cent and for banks it's 58 per cent. The report also noted that a popular item hackers like to buy with cash they've stolen is expensive cheese, which they then sell on to retailers for cash.

The *Guardian* reported that during his stay in the Ecuadorian embassy, WikiLeaks founder Julian Assange was spied on by Ecuador's intelligence agency, Senain. At the same time, Assange was hacking into the embassy's computer network and reading staff emails.

HAITI

Belgian footballer Kevin De Bruyne inadvertently toppled the Haitian government.

Ever since Haiti was devastated by an earthquake in 2010, the Haitian government has subsidised the country's fuel. However, in return for $100 million in grants and loans from the International Monetary Fund, it agreed it would remove the subsidy. (The IMF believes that cheap fuel helps richer people and wants the money previously earmarked for fuel subsidies to be spent on social welfare.)

All the government had to decide was when they would make the announcement, and they came up with a genius plan. Haiti's football team is pretty terrible, ranked 104th in the world, so most people in the country support Brazil. The government's idea was to make the announcement during Brazil's World Cup quarter-final with Belgium, in the hope that people would be celebrating too much to notice the increase in prices.

However, when Kevin De Bruyne put Belgium 2–0 up, the mood in Haiti began to change, and by the time Brazil had lost 2–1, the protests had already started. Three days later, with things turning ugly, the government backed down on the fuel price increases; and less than a week after De Bruyne's decisive strike, the government had fallen.

HAWKING, STEPHEN

The world lost the physicist who bitterly regretted never having run over Margaret Thatcher's toes.

Stephen Hawking (1942–2018) was a professor of mathematics at Cambridge University, as well as a pioneering theoretical physicist, and the author of record-breaking, bestselling book *A Brief History of Time*. Diagnosed with a rare form of motor neurone disease in 1964 when he was 21, he was given just a few years to live, yet continued to work and lecture until his death this year at the age of 76. He spent 49 years in a wheelchair and was, according to colleagues, a reckless driver who forced Cambridge scientists to leap out of the way as he sped past them, and would drive out into the road whether or not there were other cars present.

His memorial, which took place at Westminster Abbey, was attended by family, friends and celebrities. But, unfortunately, no time travellers. When tickets to the event were made available to the public via an online ballot, many noticed, while filling in the application form, that the date of birth menu went up to 31 December 2038. Asked about this, a spokesman said: 'We cannot exclude the possibility of time travel as it has not been disproven to our satisfaction.' It wasn't the first time Hawking had attempted to attract people from the future. In 2009, he threw a cocktail party exclusively for them, sending out invitations only after the evening was over. (Nobody turned up.)

While Hawking's ashes were interred between the graves of Charles Darwin and Sir Isaac Newton, a European Space Agency (ESA) satellite dish in Spain beamed a song featuring Hawking's voice towards the nearest black hole. 'It's fascinating,' said Professor Günther Hasinger, ESA's Director of Science, 'and at the same time moving to imagine that Stephen Hawking's voice . . . will reach the black hole in about 3500 years, where it will be frozen in [time] by the event horizon.'*

*According to the latest theories, if you were to see a clock falling into a black hole, it would appear to run slower and slower until it came to a complete stop, frozen in time, at the edge of the massive failed star.

Throughout his adult life, Hawking's wheelchair had proved a useful weapon, allowing him (so it was rumoured) to run over the feet of people who annoyed him. According to his biographer, Kitty Ferguson, 'One of Hawking's regrets in life was not having an opportunity to run over Margaret Thatcher's toes.' Hawking himself denied the claims, saying it was all 'A malicious rumour . . . I'll run over anyone who repeats it.'

HEATWAVES

During this summer's heatwave, archaeologists discovered multiple sites without digging a single hole.

———— ▼ ————

This summer, Sweden's second-highest point became its highest, after the glacier at the top of the previous highest melted. The mountain that's now the second highest is expected to become the highest again in the winter.

In what was described as a 'gold rush' for archaeologists, the record-breaking hot and dry weather in June and July revealed previously unknown historic settlements. Wherever there was once a foundation, the top layer of soil is deeper, so the grass above it remains green during a dry spell, while all around it turns brown. Wherever there was a wall, the soil is shallower and contains less nutrients, making these parts turn especially brown. Hence, during the drought, ancient sites outlined in green and brown became clearly visible from the air.

Among these sites were a Roman villa in Glamorgan; multiple Stone Age forts; a 'drowned village' that was flooded and submerged in 1898; a 19th-century Italianate garden in Lancashire; and, in Ireland, a perfectly circular, 200-metre-wide henge dating back to 3000 BC. Precise outlines of air raid shelters appeared on school sports fields just in time, a teacher tweeted, for her to teach a module about the Second World War.

As the heatwave continued, railway lines reached temperatures of 50 degrees Celsius, forcing trains to

stick to lower speed limits to prevent tracks buckling, and the London Underground was 5 degrees hotter than the legal maximum for transporting cattle. The Environment Agency evacuated more than 130 trout and salmon from the River Teme before it dried up, and asked the public to look out for and report fish 'gasping' (a sign of lower oxygen levels in water caused by the heat). And the roof of the Glasgow Science Centre began to melt and drip black goo.

Heatwaves were even more extreme in other parts of the world. In Algeria, thermometers hit 51.3 degrees – Africa's hottest-ever recorded temperature. Scotland also registered its highest-ever temperature, though this was later declared invalid when it emerged that the thermometer that recorded it had been positioned next to a vehicle that had its engine running.

Headlines, from the Sublime . . .

'Doncaster psychic evening cancelled due to "unforeseen circumstances"'
Doncaster Free Press, 11 July 2018

'Cured Bacon'
Metro, 20 July 2018 (After TV presenter Richard Bacon was cured of a mystery lung disease)

'Galileo figure row'
Sun, 25 May 2018 (After Britain and the EU disagreed over the amount that would have to be paid for the Galileo satellite system after Brexit)

'Burglar left DNA on cheese as he tried to get a whey'
The Times, 9 August 2018

'Man who jumped out of freezer and died was cold-case suspect'
Associated Press, 6 August 2018

'A huge "30ft" deep hole has opened up on a street in Salford and police are looking into it'
Manchester Evening News, 23 July 2018

'Gareth Southgate on the Lions, the pitch and his wardrobe'
ITV News, 30 August 2018

'Crash, Bang, Scallop'
Financial Times, 29 August 2018 (After British and French fishermen clashed over scallop-fishing rights)

'Xi sells Seychelles by India's seashore'
Quartz India, 21 June 2018

... to the Ridiculous

'Holly Willoughby turns to psychic banana to determine gender of royal baby'
Evening Standard, 23 April 2018

'Monster 4.7-metre saltwater crocodile thought to be largest ever removed from Katherine'
ABC (Australia), 10 July 2018 (Katherine is a town in Australia's Northern Territory)

'Parrot tells firefighters to f**k off after being stuck on a roof for three days'
Daily Mirror, 14 August 2018

'Titanic historian warns the ship "has never been in more danger than she is now"'
Belfast Live, 1 August 2018

'Topiarist "sickened" by drunk people simulating sex with his woman-shaped hedge'
Independent, 26 July 2018

'How does your self-control fare against great tits'?'
Gizmodo, 31 July 2018 (Scientists discovered this year that despite being birds, great tits have more self-control than chimpanzees)

'Zafar the sexually-frustrated dolphin shuts down beach in France'
LiveScience, 27 August 2018

'Cardi B's real name is not "Cardigan Backyardigan"'
CapitalFM, 30 August 2018 (After rumours of the rapper's 'real name' appeared online)

Walmart refused to sell a heavy metal album by a Christian band for being too satanic.

—————— ▼ ——————

Arizona metal band *Okilly Dokilly,* inspired by *The Simpsons* character Ned Flanders, announced their first UK tour. The band will be touring with a virtually all-new line-up, replacing Bled Ned, Red Ned, Cred Ned and Dead Ned with Shred Ned, Dread Ned and Zed Ned. Their lead singer, however, remains Head Ned. Their debut album was titled *Howdilly Doodilly.*

This year the band Stryper released their 17th Christian rock album, *God Damn Evil.* With tracks such as 'Take It to the Cross' and 'The Devil Doesn't Live Here', the album's title expresses the hope that God condemns all wickedness. Walmart, however, didn't see it that way and refused to stock the record. 'Although we respect their decision and what's done is done,' the band responded, 'it's frustrating to see something that's meant for good get misinterpreted and misunderstood.' Meanwhile, Greek metal band Rotting Christ, who admittedly don't have quite the same pious credentials as Stryper, were arrested in Georgia on terrorism charges after locals who objected to their name claimed to the authorities that they were satanists.

But heavy metal definitely has a positive side, as a fan of Every Time I Die discovered when band guitarist Jordan Buckley spat beer in her eye. Fearing it might cause an infection, she went to a doctor, who consequently discovered she had a tumour that they were then able to treat in time. And a study in Australia found that the music helps people who would otherwise struggle with ostracism, bullying and loneliness to get through difficult periods of their life. Heavy *metals*, on the other hand, are not conducive to good mental health. That, at least, is the verdict of a University of Antwerp study that established that elements such as cadmium and lead make birds more depressed and less likely to leave their homes.

HOLOGRAMS

Abba will tour again as holograms, known as 'Abbatars'.

The band are all about 70 years old, but for their next tour they will look nearly as good as they did in 1979. In fact, they'll look *exactly* as good as they did in 1979: they have been recorded and digitally 'de-aged' by almost 40 years. These computer-generated versions will appear in a special TV show scheduled for late 2018, and will then go on tour in 2019 and 2020. To make sure they look realistic, the band have been scanned and measured from all possible angles and had to grimace in front of cameras. (While their bodies will have changed, their skulls won't: according to band member Björn Ulvaeus, 'a cranium doesn't change with age the way the rest of your body falls apart'.) The digital versions will be able to tour the world at almost no cost, and with zero artistic disagreements.

Scientists have now managed to create 3D holograms like the ones seen in *Star Wars*. The only drawbacks with them are, firstly, that because they're created by moving a single particle at a time, it's currently impossible to make them larger than a fingernail, and secondly, that if they're shown outside, they blow away.

Hologram appearances are becoming quite the thing. Roy Orbison is touring as a hologram this year, despite having been dead for 30 years. Japanese hologram pop star Hatsune Miku is touring America and Europe. (She has a four-piece backing band of real humans, but her fans have to use extra-dim glowsticks because if the lights from the audience are too bright, the artiste disappears.) And New Zealand Prime Minister Jacinda Ardern appeared on stage as a hologram at a technology event she was unable to attend in person.

Actually, there is a (slim) chance that you're a hologram, too, and so is everyone you know. Stephen Hawking's final theory, published after his death, is that the entire universe is a hologram, and that the apparently solid world is all projected from information stored on a flat 2D surface. If he's right, it means Abba have already spent years touring as holograms completely unnoticed.

HONEYBEES

Scientists discovered that honeybees know nothing.

Until recently, it was assumed that only humans, chimpanzees and monkeys can understand the concept of zero. Even humans don't really get it until they're about four years old. But scientists at the RMIT University in Melbourne, Australia, have now announced that honeybees also grasp the concept.

In the course of their experiment, the researchers set up two platforms, each with up to six shapes. One platform also housed a sweet liquid, the other a nasty-tasting quinine solution. Gradually, the honeybees learned to associate the platform with fewer shapes on it with the sweet reward (which they received if they got the answer right 80 per cent or more of the time). And they continued to get the answer right even when that platform had no shapes on it. This suggests that they can comprehend the abstract notion of nothingness and that the ability to understand zero may be more widespread among animals than previously thought.

In which we learn . . .
Who got to the World Cup thanks to his mummy,
who invented the smart nappy and the robo-bee,
where Mr Nobody swept to power, who shouldn't
have gone to Specsavers, and why crayfish
populations are going absolutely cray-cray.

INCAS ▶

Three 500-year-old Inca mummies helped Peru's biggest football star make it to the World Cup.

--- ▼ ---

A new study of over 800 skulls concluded that the Incas were very skilled surgeons – better, in fact, than American surgeons during the American Civil War.

In December 2017, FIFA announced that as a result of testing positive for benzoylecgonine, a substance found in cocaine, the Peruvian footballer Paolo Guerrero would be banned from the sport for a year, meaning he would miss the World Cup. Maintaining his innocence, Guerrero appealed against the ban, arguing that he must have unwittingly consumed a tea containing coca leaves while he was battling the flu. Fortunately for Guerrero, he wasn't the only person to have failed a test for benzoylecgonine. In 2013, three 500-year-old Inca mummies had as well.

Discovered on top of a 6,700-metre-tall volcano in Argentina, the mummies, whose bodies had been naturally preserved by the freezing temperatures, were found to have the chemical in their hair. Further analysis revealed that one of the mummies, known as the Llullaillaco Maiden, had been consuming coca during the last year of her life, proving that a person could theoretically test positive for cocaine without having consumed the illegal drug.

The appeals court didn't buy it. But months later, and with only two weeks to go before the World Cup's opening ceremony, a Swiss Federal Tribunal agreed to temporarily lift the ban for the duration of the tournament. In explaining their decision, they noted that FIFA did not 'categorically oppose' Guerrero's reinstatement.

INDIA ▶

For falling faeces, *see* **Blue Ice**; for immature diplomats, *see* **Doorbells**; for banning shoes and socks, *see* **Exams**; for dating ancient rocks, *see* **Oldest, Second**; for counting downward dogs, *see* **Records, Broken**; for celebrating a civil servant, *see* **Statues of the Year**; and for *not* celebrating a day of love, *see* **Valentine's Day**.

INSECT FARMS ▶

China has a robot-controlled farm containing 6 billion free-range cockroaches.

The farm is in the city of Xichang, and is almost entirely run by AI; humans rarely go in. Inside, it's warm, humid and dark, and the billions of cockroaches who live there have the run of the place. A computer system monitors the temperature and how much cockroach food is consumed, before the insects are eventually fed into machines to make a 'healing potion' that is popular in China. While officials worry it would be catastrophic for the surrounding area if the roaches escape, another possible fear – that they might evolve into super-cockroaches – was allayed by Professor Zhu Chaodong, an insect expert at the Institute of Zoology in Beijing. He said that cockroaches are already so well evolved that 'Every cockroach is a super-cockroach.'

While the healing benefits of cockroach-juice are unproven, there is extensive evidence that insects are an excellent source of protein. On top of that, because their larvae eat thrown-away food, they help to recycle what would otherwise be waste, producing as much as 1 kilogram of proteinous mass from 2 kilos of waste. So it should come as no surprise that in addition to the Xichang cockroach farm, there are now an increasing number of fly farms across the world. For animals farmed for food (particularly in Europe) they're a much more efficient source of protein than fishmeal or plants such as soya. And the flour you get from grinding insects up is high in protein, too, so there's talk of selling it to bodybuilders.

INVASIVE SPECIES

A Californian man was trapped in his home for two hours by a plague of tumbleweed.

When heavy winds sent the weeds tumbling into the town of Victorville, residents called 911, and emergency services found themselves having to clear the plants from more than 100 doors. 'It looked like a war of tumbleweeds, like we were being invaded,' said one victim. Tumbleweeds became a problem after they were introduced to America from Russia in the 19th century. They're a nuisance at the best of times, but in dry conditions they can also be a severe fire risk.

Europe had its own problems with invasive species this year, notably a species of crayfish whose existence we didn't even know of until 1995. Marbled crayfish were initially kept as pets, but because they can clone themselves, their owners invariably ended up with more than

Inventions

The biggest companies in the world filed patents for the inventions of tomorrow, including:

Amazon – a wrist buzzer: Amazon patented a wrist bracelet that can track a worker's hand and that buzzes if they reach for the wrong shelf.

Google – a smart nappy: Verily, the life science unit of Google's parent company, Alphabet, invented a 'smart diaper' that can work out when a baby's nappy is full, decide what it's full of, and notify the baby's parent of the problem via an app.

Uber – a drunk detector: Uber patented a system to measure whether prospective passengers are likely to be drunk. It considers an approaching customer's walking speed, their location, the time of day and any errors they make while typing their address, and is able to conclude (for example) that someone walking slowly near a pub, late at night, and typing badly, is probably drunk.

Apple – a crumb-proof keyboard: To stop snack crumbs from getting into the keyboard, Apple has designed a keyboard that puffs out a jet of air whenever a key is pressed.

Walmart – a robo-bee: Walmart wants to make robotic bees that can pollinate crops. They use sensors and cameras to work out where they are. The company has also patented a robo-hive where the bees can dock when they're not out pollinating.

Nike – shoes with built-in treadmills: The shoe is designed for people who struggle to put shoes on – as you put your foot in, a little internal treadmill rolls your toes all the way to the end.

they wanted, and took to dumping any they didn't want into rivers. Now there are cloned crayfish all over the place – in Spain, Croatia, Japan, Madagascar . . . there's a danger they could end up taking over the world. In Berlin, where the invasion is particularly bad, eels have been introduced into the rivers to eat them, and locals have been given licences to catch the crayfish and sell them to local restaurants. They've proved quite a trendy menu item and have become known as 'Berlin lobsters'.

The UK has its own invasive species to worry about: Asian hornets. They attack bumblebees on the wing, pull them limb from limb, and then carry them to their nests to feed them to their larvae. To counter them, scientists are putting tiny electronic trackers on the backs of hornets so they can track down their nests. Although that may not be much consolation to the poor dismembered bees.

IRONY

The world was awash with ironic news stories this year:

▶ A Specsavers-branded company car crashed into a lamp post in Liverpool. The council, using the hashtag #shouldvegoneto, tweeted that they were 'on sight' to fix it.

▶ Chancellor Philip Hammond delivered a Spring State-ment on the economy, in which he claimed there was 'light at the end of the tunnel'. Just before he deliv-ered it there was a power cut throughout Parliament.

▶ King's College London shut down a lecture about the importance of free speech due to concerns that the subject matter was too controversial.

▶ Todd Heatherton, author of *Losing Control: How and Why People Fail at Self-Regulation*, retired from his role at Dartmouth College after being accused of sexual misconduct. He admitted to acting unprofessionally while intoxicated.

▶ The US navy was accused of piracy after it was found to have installed virtual reality software on 558,000 of its computers, but only paid the licence 38 times.

▶ Vancouver's 'Car Free Day', a festival during which the city centre is pedestrianised and everyone celebrates the lack of cars, was blighted by a lack of parking spaces because so many people drove to it in order to attend.

▶ A hotel in Canada made entirely of ice caught fire.

ISIS ▶

Oxford University magazine The Isis *keeps getting messages from aspiring terrorists.*

Owing to the unfortunate similarity between the names of terror group ISIS and arts and culture magazine *The Isis*,* the magazine frequently receives emails and Facebook messages from people keen to find out how they can help bring down the West. The magazine's student staff have been reporting them to the police, and its editor, Emily Lawford, suspects the magazine's outbox is being monitored by the Home Office.

The magazine gets its name from the fact that 'The Isis' is an alternative name for the River Thames as it runs through Oxford.

ISIS forged another link with Oxford this year when they started promoting themselves via the work of former Oxford academic J. R. R. Tolkien. They did so by inserting a short clip from a battle scene in the third *Lord of the Rings* film, *The Return of the King*, into one of their propaganda videos. This suggests that in addition to facing various murder and terror charges, the group could now also be in serious trouble over copyright infringement.

While ISIS were using a movie to promote themselves, a film-maker was using ISIS to promote his movie. The Iranian film director Ebrahim Hatamikia staged an ISIS-themed stunt to advertise his new film, getting actors wielding guns and riding horses to storm a shopping mall in Tehran. Understandably, a number of shoppers became quite distressed. In his subsequent apology, the director said he had no idea the stunt was going to involve horses or a mall invasion.

ITALY

The mayor of Genoa asked the Queen for 250 years of back payments for her use of the St George's flag.

A ubiquitous symbol of English football fans this summer, the St George's Cross was initially adopted by England as a deterrent to her enemies. In the 13th century, the city-state of Genoa, one of the most feared naval forces in the world, licensed the use of its St George's flag to the English monarch in return for an annual fee, so that English traders in the Mediterranean could display the banner to let others know they were protected by the Genoese. At some point in the

130

18th century, however, England stopped paying, leading Marco Bucci, Genoa's current mayor, to ask for the arrears to be paid. 'Your Majesty,' he wrote, 'I regret to inform you that from my books [it] looks like you didn't pay for the last 247 years.'

Bucci became mayor in 2017 as the head of a coalition of right-wing parties, and his victory was echoed this year in the national elections, where the right stormed to victory. The populist Five Star Movement (which was co-founded by comedian Beppe Grillo) won 32 per cent of the vote, and the far-right League Party won 18 per cent, allowing them to form a coalition government with the relatively unknown Giuseppe Conte, whom neither party objected to, as a compromise president. So Conte, who was known in the press as 'Mr Nobody', was not directly voted into power by the Italian people. He is Italy's fifth unelected prime minister in a row.

Conte's official CV has come in for quite a bit of scrutiny, and a lot of mockery. It claims that he studied or taught at New York University, the Sorbonne, the University of Malta and the Internationales Kulturinstitut of Vienna, but either the institutions in question had no record of him, or the courses he claimed to have taken didn't exist. He also said that he 'studied at Girton College, Cambridge, in September 2001, conducting scientific research'. Journalists concluded that this must be a reference to the time he visited his girlfriend, who was studying there.

This year an Italian man was acquitted of stealing an aubergine, nine years after being charged. The Italian courts have a backlog of over 100,000 cases, one of which involves a man suing his daughter for serving him shop-bought instead of homemade pasta.

IVORY

Peers argued in favour of banning ivory, while competing over which of them had the best ivory.

Despite attempts to clamp down on the ivory trade, 20,000 elephants a year are still being slaughtered for their tusks, so the measures now being taken to combat it are becoming ever more draconian. China and Hong Kong, the two biggest markets for it, are banning all trade in ivory, while the UK, where sales of new ivory have long been illegal, has now passed a law that bans the sale even of old pieces. When the proposed legislation was being debated in the House of Lords, members had first to declare any personal interest, and this seems to have turned the debate into something of an ivory-owners' bragging match.

Lord de Mauley, for example, in thanking the government for exempting portrait miniatures more than 100 years old from the ban, mentioned that he happens to have a collection of them. Lord Inglewood declared he owns an ivory-keyed Broadwood piano 'almost identical to the one owned by Beethoven'. And Lord Lingfield humbly admitted to having a 19th-century ivory paper knife of 'little artistic merit', before adding: 'It belonged to Benjamin Disraeli and is one of the few Disraeli treasures outside the ownership of the National Trust at Hughenden. It has letters of provenance from his niece, Mrs Coningsby Disraeli, attesting that it was always on the great man's desk, and family tradition had it that it was given to her Prime Minister by Queen Victoria herself when she was created Empress of India.'

Lingfield quickly went on to say he entirely condemns the practice of killing elephants for their ivory.

In which we learn . . .
Where to find the world's loveliest prison,
where not to apply to become a ninja, which country
named a roundabout after Donald Trump, and what
links Boris Johnson to a syphilitic mummy.

JAILS

Greenland opened the world's most beautiful prison, but couldn't convince convicts to move in.

Two prisoners escaped from a maximum-security jail in Bogotá by getting a guard drunk and convincing him to let them go out to buy more alcohol.

Until now, Greenland's prisoners have ended up in one of two places: low-risk criminals are kept in an open prison in Greenland where they can go and do what they want during the day and have to come back at night; high-risk ones are sent to Denmark. The Danish solution is not great, however – not least because most of the prisoners don't speak Danish. Hence the reason for the new jail.

And it has to be said that the new 'humane' prison is amazing. It has views of the sea and the mountains, and is designed like a village, with residential blocks, workplaces, education and sports facilities, a library, a health centre and a church. For some reason, though, when asked if they wanted to move in, only 5 of the 27 Greenlandic inmates currently in Denmark expressed an interest in relocating.

One prisoner who had a definite interest in relocating this year was famed French criminal Rédoine Faïd, who managed to break out of Paris's Réau prison. Faïd is a huge fan of caper films, especially those starring Steve McQueen and Robert De Niro, and is well known for employing escape methods that he has seen in the movies. In his latest prison break, his group reconnoitred the prison with drones ahead of landing a helicopter in the one place in the compound hidden from the guards' view, and then used smoke bombs to mask their escape. At the time of writing, he is yet to be caught.

134

JAPAN

Japan ran low on ninjas and sumo wrestlers.

In July, American radio network NPR broadcast a report that Iga, the birthplace of ninjas, was running low on ninja performers (which it is) and that ninjas could earn a salary of $85,000 a year (which they can). Newspapers around the world picked up on the story, but added the detail that Iga wanted people to apply to become ninjas – which they definitely did not.

Within days, puzzled city officials had received more than 100 CVs from 23 countries, and the city's mayor was forced to hold a press conference to deny that vacancies existed and to warn people to 'be careful of fake news'. The government website, though, did point out that anyone visiting the town was very welcome to hire a ninja costume for the day.

As if a dearth of ninjas wasn't enough, Japan's also grappling with a distinct lack of sumo wrestlers. This year, for only the second time in its history, the Japan Sumo Association (JSA) was forced to cancel a test for new recruits because no one applied. The JSA believes this may have something to do with various recent scandals. In January, for example, a referee was fired for sexual harassment, and in March a popular wrestler was forced to retire after getting into a car accident – driving is strictly banned under sumo rules. Worse still, he was driving without a licence, which is strictly banned under anyone's rules.

———— ▼ ————

A Japanese priest went viral after losing his temper online with tourists who posted bad reviews for the guesthouse at his temple. When one Western visitor said the meals were 'strange', priest Daniel Shimura replied, 'Yeah, it's Japanese monastic cuisine you uneducated f***.' He said he'd tone his language down in future.

JERUSALEM ▶

A Palestinian couple protested against the new US embassy in Jerusalem by naming their new triplets Jerusalem, Capital and Palestine.

In acknowledgement of the fact that Jerusalem is disputed between Israel and Palestine, Tel Aviv has long been the preferred location for foreign embassies. This year, however, Donald Trump decided that America would move its diplomats to Jerusalem, the city that Israel claims as its capital and that is known in Arabic as Al-Quds.

While Palestinians were furious, and protested accordingly, the move was celebrated throughout much of Israel. A roundabout in Jerusalem was named in honour of Trump; a park was named after him in the northern town of Kiryat Yam; and Israeli Premier League football team Beitar renamed themselves as Beitar Trump Jerusalem Football Club. The change of name didn't help their results, though. In their first competitive game with the new name, Beitar Trump were knocked out of the UEFA Cup by Chikhura Sachkhere, a Georgian team whose own stadium isn't big enough to host European matches, and who therefore have to play 150 kilometres away from home.

The cost of the new embassy was another cause for controversy for Trump, who underestimated the price by 10,000 per cent. He boasted that the initial figure he'd been quoted for the building upgrades in Jerusalem was $1 billion, but that he'd brought the cost down to $250,000. However, when the contract came to light, it was revealed that the State Department had actually agreed to pay $21.2 million for the building work.

JOBS

For an eight-month-old government official, *see* **Babies**; for where not to apply to become a terrorist, *see* **ISIS**; for where not to apply to become a ninja, *see* **Japan**; and for an unemployed android, *see* **Robots**.

JOHNSON, BORIS

Boris Johnson's daddy's mummy's mummy's daddy's daddy's daddy's mummy's mummy is a syphilitic mummy.

The mummy in question was discovered in Basle in 1975, buried in front of a church altar. Judging by her clothes and burial position, in life she had clearly been wealthy, but it was only thanks to newly discovered archives and up-to-the-minute genetic analysis of DNA from her big toe, and then comparison of the DNA with that of potential descendants, that we were able to learn her identity. Anna Catharina Bischoff was the great-great-great-great-great-great grandmother of former Foreign Secretary Boris Johnson, related to him through his paternal grandmother, whom he always called 'Granny Butter'. Since her bones were full of mercury, a one-time cure for syphilis, there's a strong suspicion that she herself suffered from the disease.

Boris may have viewed the discovery of this long-dead relative as a relative bright spot in an otherwise difficult year. Not only did he feel the need to resign over Theresa May's Brexit plans (which he described as like 'polishing a turd'), but none of the various ambitious transport plans he proposed while foreign secretary came to fruition. His suggestion that the government build a bridge between Britain and France was swiftly dismissed by the UK Chamber of Shipping, who said

Although he's generally considered a Leaver, Boris decided to remain in the £20 million, taxpayer-funded mansion reserved for the foreign secretary for a few extra weeks after resigning, despite his successor, Jeremy Hunt, holding official functions there.

it was unrealistic; by the French government, which declared it pointless; by Theresa May, who said it wasn't being considered; and by an architect who pointed out that 'It would really be cheaper to move France closer.' Then there was the silence that greeted his idea that a bridge should be built between the British mainland and Northern Ireland. This was then followed by mockery of his plea for his own, official plane that could jet him around the world while he promoted Brexit. The one he was supposed to use, he complained, had to be shared with the PM, other Cabinet members and the royal family, and 'never seems to be available'.

JUDO ▶

The finalists in the Düsseldorf World Judo Grand Prix fought so badly that they both came second.

'Our team deemed this contest unacceptable,' said the head referee, bemoaning the competitors' passiveness: 'There was no intention to fight from either.' At the subsequent medal ceremony both players had to stand on the second-place position on the podium, and neither national anthem was played. Lack of activity seems to have become a general problem in judo in recent years – hence the reason why new scoring guidelines were adopted in January to encourage competitors to attack more.

One person who would have fallen foul of judo laws old and new was Spanish footballer Sergio Ramos. When the Real Madrid midfielder tackled Liverpool's Mo Salah, seriously injuring the Egyptian player's shoulder and forcing him out of the Champions League Final, the European Judo Union issued a statement that the hold would have been illegal even in their sport. The tackle, which looked a lot like a judo throw, made waves all over the world: a Syrian law school exam included a question about the event,* and an Egyptian lawyer took out a £873 million lawsuit against Ramos for the emotional pain he inflicted on the country of Egypt.

*The question read: 'Sergio Ramos injured Mohamed Salah in the 2018 European Champions League final. Naturally, Ramos cannot be held to account for this action from a criminal law perspective due to four conditions that make the use of violence justified in sports. State these conditions.'

In which we learn . . .
Why KFC fell fowl of a chicken crisis, what a
French town had to kiss goodbye to, who needs
to use protection against condoms, which country
finally decided to pick up the phone, and which
museum turned out to be mostly phoney.

KEAS

Ornithologists tried to save endangered birds by building them roadside gyms.

The kea is a curious, olive-green species of parrot that lives on New Zealand's South Island and is the world's only alpine parrot. According to recent studies, it is also the 'first non-mammal species to demonstrate infectious laughter' and outscores gibbons in intelligence tests. Yet despite these advantages, there are as few as 3,000 remaining in the wild.

The problem is that while keas might be clever, they are not doing much to help themselves: they have a tendency to fly into the road to play with construction equipment or perhaps beg drivers for food. As a result, dozens are accidentally killed every year. To try to distract them and keep them out of danger, researchers from the University of Canterbury decided to build kea gyms, featuring ladders, spinning flotation devices, swings and climbing frames. The gyms, it was hoped, would also enable conservationists to film the birds, analyse their behaviour and develop new ways of interacting with them. Unfortunately, just as the new facilities were launched, the keas decided to move to another forest for the summer.

KENYA

Kenya's opposition leader lost the election but held an inauguration ceremony anyway.

Raila Odinga officially lost the 2017 Kenyan presidential election, but rejected the result, alleging widespread vote rigging. So in January thousands of his supporters gathered in Nairobi's biggest park to watch him be inaugurated as the 'people's president'. Officiating at the ceremony was an ally wearing a white wig and black robe in imitation of the uniform the chief justice wore at the real inauguration, and Odinga swore an oath on the Bible to protect the nation.

The real president, Uhuru Kenyatta, ordered all the major TV stations not to broadcast the event, and when they disobeyed he had the three main channels (which account for two thirds of the country's TV viewership) shut down. The channels returned to air after about a week, and a few months later Odinga and Kenyatta were publicly reconciled, shaking hands and calling each other 'brothers'. The timing was suspicious, though: it was just before US Secretary of State Rex Tillerson was due to visit the country, prompting speculation that the two men were faking their new-found goodwill in order not to get scolded by America.

Kenyatta and Odinga might not get on, but their fathers were once allies. Indeed, Odinga's father, Jaramogi Oginga Odinga, secured the release of Kenyatta's father, Jomo, during his negotiations with Britain for Kenya's independence. When Jomo became president, he briefly made Odinga his vice president, although he later put him in prison, which somewhat soured relations, and the rivalry was passed on to the two men's sons.

KFC ▶

British police asked people to stop calling 999 to report chicken shortages.

Police in Whitefield, Manchester, tweeted, 'For those who contacted the Police about KFC being out of chicken . . . please STOP', while Tower Hamlets officers said that the lack of KFC chicken was 'not a police matter'. In fact, it was a matter of logistics: KFC had recently moved over to a single distributor, the firm

DHL, and a single distribution site, so when the new system encountered teething problems, the entire restaurant chain was affected. 'To put it simply,' KFC tweeted, 'we've got the chicken, we've got the restaurants, but we've just had issues getting them together.' They apologised through adverts published in various newspapers that featured an image of their iconic buckets and read, 'FCK. We're sorry'.

As a result, by mid-February fewer than 90 of the company's 900 restaurants were able to open. Fortunately, 97 per cent of outlets had reopened within a couple of weeks. Unfortunately, KFC's problems didn't end there. A few days later, many of their restaurants ran out of gravy.

KFC unveiled its first-ever female Colonel Sanders. It was only a partial victory for feminism, though, as the company insisted that she wear a fake moustache.

KISSING, FRENCH ▶

A French council had kissing cancelled.

Aude Picard-Wolff, the mayor of the French village of Morette, emailed all 73 of her colleagues on the local council to say she no longer wished to kiss each and every one of them before council meetings. She admitted that she frequently arrived late to meetings on purpose to avoid kissing 73 people, and that she'd actually welcomed having a cold on one occasion because it meant she'd had an excuse not to kiss. From now on, she said, she wanted to shake hands, like men do, and that she would be keeping her kisses for people she actually liked.

This prompted a huge debate about the practice of 'la bise', as it's called in France – especially as it came just a month after railway staff in Metz had been told that while at work they should not kiss anyone who didn't work for the rail company. (The directive had been issued partly to cut down on sexual harassment cases, even though there hadn't actually been reports of any.) One newspaper, *Le Populaire du Centre*, timed a young journalist at the start of the working day and found it took her five minutes to get round the office kissing everyone. They also calculated that even in regions of France which indulge in just two kisses per recipient (elsewhere anything from one to four kisses is the norm), that schedule would involve spending three working days a year kissing one's colleagues.

While the French were debating how much kissing to do, an American athlete managed to get out of trouble thanks to an energetic kiss. Sprinter Gil Roberts claimed the reason he had failed a drug test during the 2016 Olympics was that it came immediately after he had passionately kissed his girlfriend, and that her sinus medication must have entered his system. The authorities accepted his explanation.

KITES ▶

Egypt warned Hamas to stop flying kites.

The Palestinian fundamentalist organisation has come up with a new, low-fi way of attacking Israel – by attaching incendiary devices to kites, balloons and even condoms filled with helium with the aim of setting fire to Israeli crops. Egypt, which has been acting as a peacekeeper in the conflict, implored Hamas to stop, saying that Israel might use the kites as an excuse to launch attacks on Palestinian-held land in Gaza.

At least 3,000 hectares of farmland and parkland have been incinerated by the kites and balloons, and 570 hectares of wheat was lost, so Israel banned condoms, kites and birthday balloons from crossing the border. Hamas then improvised further – according to Israeli reports, they began sending falcons with burning materials attached to their legs.

KNOCK-OFFS

A French museum found out that over half its exhibits were forgeries.

The Terrus museum in the south of France has over 100 works by the artist Étienne Terrus and this year bought some new paintings as well as enlisting art historian Eric Forcada to help reorganise the collection. While doing so, Forcada spotted a strange-looking signature on one particular painting, gently brushed it with his glove, and found it wiped off easily to reveal a completely different signature beneath it. He went on to examine the others, and eventually came to the conclusion that 82 paintings out of 140 were fakes.

It turned out that the museum had spent £140,000 on fraudulent paintings and drawings over the previous 20 years, and it had to close down temporarily while it weeded them out. The forged works contained some fairly obvious anachronisms, such as depictions of buildings constructed in the 1950s (Terrus himself died in 1922). The museum eventually reopened with 60 genuine works on display.

Meanwhile, in Genoa, a Modigliani show was investigated by police after 20 out of 21 paintings turned out to be fakes. And during a routine audit, the Czech Republic's National Museum in Prague discovered that at least half their rubies and lots of their diamonds were not the real thing but cheap imitations. They're now checking their whole collection – all 20 million artefacts.

One fake, on the other hand, turned out to be real. The Buffalo Museum of Science in New York, which had displayed what it believed to be a fake elephant bird egg for 80 years, found out that it was actually the real thing, and one of fewer than 40 intact elephant bird eggs owned by museums around the world.

The winner of the Wildlife Photographer of the Year award – who had submitted a shot of an anteater preying on a termite mound – was stripped of the prize, after an investigation concluded that the anteater in question was dead and stuffed, and had been carefully placed in shot.

KOKO

The world's most intelligent gorilla was mourned by 'nipples' all over the world.

For six months, Koko owned a pet cat she named 'All Ball' and with whom she had a love-hate relationship. Once, when Koko ripped a steel sink from a wall, she tried to pass the blame by signing to her carers, 'cat did it'.

Koko the gorilla (1971–2018), who died peacefully in her sleep aged 46, was an artist, photographer and interspecies communicator, famous for her supposed ability to communicate with humans (or 'nipples', as she would often refer to us). She was survived by her companion, Ndume the gorilla, who was 11 years her junior.

By the time Koko passed away it was claimed that she could understand 2,000 English words, and could communicate over 1,000 by using what Koko's handler Francesca Patterson called 'Gorilla Sign Language' (GSL).

Using GSL, Koko gave us an incredible insight into primate cognition. She managed to request a dentist when she had a toothache; discussed the artworks she had painted; and taught sign language to another gorilla called Michael, using unique signs with him that she did not use with her handlers.

But her life wasn't without controversy. Some scientists suggested her ability to communicate was largely down to her handler, who prompted Koko to make certain signs and then interpreted them into sentences. As Patterson never allowed independent researchers near Koko, an impartial scientific study of her abilities was never conducted.

Koko's nipple fetish also caused problems. In 2005, two female handlers were fired, allegedly because they refused to expose their breasts to Koko. According to their testimony at the subsequent lawsuit, Patterson had tried to pressure them into complying, arguing that it would help them to bond with the gorilla, and saying, 'Koko, you see my nipples all the time. You are probably bored with my nipples. You need to see new nipples.' The suit was settled out of court.

Koko's funeral was held close to her home, so that as well as being attended by human friends and handlers, Ndume could see the whole ceremony from his enclosure.

KOREA

South Koreans finally got through to North Korea after two straight years of phoning.

The phone line across the Korean border in the village of Panmunjom once served as a kind of crisis hotline between the two states. But when tensions became particularly bad in 2016, contact between the two countries was broken off. In case the Northerners had a change of heart, the South kept to schedule: every weekday, an official would ring the North, once at 9 a.m. and again at 4 p.m.* But nobody on the North Korean side answered until January this year – when, with tensions slowly relaxing, the two sides finally started talking to each other again.

*Originally South Korea would call the North on odd dates whilst North Korea would call the South on even ones, and the calls were made twice a day. After a period of tension, South Korea had taken to calling every day, regardless of whether it was an odd or even date.

147

These calls were just the prelude to a substantial de-escalation of tensions on the Korean Peninsula, culminating in a summit between South Korea's president, Moon Jae-in, and the Northern Supreme Leader Kim Jong Un. Kim visited Moon in the South, where the leaders sat at a table specially constructed to look like two bridges merged into one. To mark the year, the pair sat exactly 2,018 millimetres apart, even though, according to the North Korean calendar, it's technically only the year 107.

At the summit, the two countries agreed to rid the peninsula of nuclear weapons, although they didn't say how they'd do it. And the thaw had a few other (albeit mostly symbolic) consequences. The two countries' table tennis teams joined forces rather than playing each other; in preparation for the summit, South Korea stopped playing pop music and propaganda speeches through loudspeakers on the border; and North Korea adjusted its time zone by half an hour so it matched that of the South.

Arguably, two victors emerged from the meeting of the two presidents. The first was Kim Jong Un himself: after the summit, trust in him on the part of people in the South rocketed from 10 per cent to about 80 per cent. The other victor was the noodle industry: after Kim mentioned a traditional North Korean cold noodle dish at the summit, he kick-started a craze in the South, and long queues formed outside the few restaurants that sold it.

In which we learn . . .
Who's firing lasers at legwear, who literally fell
on their own face, where it's illegal to feed a bear,
how the postal service took a liberty with their statues,
and why mathematicians love Love Island.

LANGUAGES

For a gorilla's sign language, *see* **Koko**; for gorilla-like body language, see **Macron, Emmanuel**.

LASERS

Levi started firing lasers at its jeans.

The company usually gives its jeans a worn look by having them manually distressed by workers who sand them down by hand. It's physically gruelling work that can take up to 30 minutes per pair of jeans and can lead to employees inhaling small particles and chemicals. But in the first real change to the way jeans have been made for over a century, Levi have announced that they're now going to use lasers instead. By firing them at the denim, they make it look faded or worn in as little as 90 seconds per pair. The hope is that by 2020 this new approach will have completely replaced the manual process in their factories.

The lasers can create over 1,000 different types of finish on the jeans. They can even set them on fire to create scuffs and holes. You can still generate the effect at home without lasers, though: Levi's website explains you can use a cheese grater, sandpaper or an old brick to give jeans a rugged and 'lived-in' look. The process is called 'whiskering'.

In other laser news:

▶ The Netherlands, which sends three truckloads of flowers to the Vatican every year as an Easter gift, had to guard them with lasers this time after marauding seagulls ruined the 2017 consignment. The lasers project green light over the plants, which is enough to scare the birds away.

- Shepherds in Scotland trialled a new system of scaring sea eagles away from their sheep by firing lasers on to the hillside.

- The US bought its first two 'laser cannon' weapons that, when fired at boats or missiles, will completely fry them upon impact. They will be operational by 2020.

- It was revealed that Thai men are paying £500 to have their penises whitened by lasers. A clinic in Bangkok reported that, having introduced the service six months earlier, it treats up to 100 patients a month.

LEAFLETS

A Labour Party candidate broke his ankle after slipping on his own flyer.

While campaigning in local elections, Liverpool councillor Stuart Fordham said he literally 'fell on his face' after losing his footing on one of his own leaflets, that included a photo of him. He continued the rest of his campaign on crutches and sadly ended up losing to Green Party candidate Tom Crone.

At least his leaflet was otherwise inoffensive, which is more than can be said for the Conservative election leaflet in Dudley that claimed the Labour Party had brought hepatitis to that part of the West Midlands; or the Labour leaflet in Batley that listed one of the Tory Party's priorities as 'shitting on us'. And then there was the circular sent to OAPs in south London, asking for donations to the Conservative Party, that was addressed with a default name input by a joker at Tory HQ rather than with people's actual names. As a result, various people received letters addressed to Mr Youmustbe Fuckingjoking.

Laws

The following were all finally made illegal in 2018:

In the UK: Riding a lawn-mower while on your phone

In Vietnam: Buying or selling bitcoin

In Saudi Arabia: Spying on your spouse's mobile phone

In Jersey: Feeding seagulls

In South Korea: Killing dogs for meat

In Indiana: Eyeball-tattooing

In Iceland: Paying men more than women

In Australia: Paying more than AU$10,000 cash for anything

In Ireland: Applying make-up while driving

In Minnesota: Groping a clothed buttock

In Ghana: Evangelising about your religious faith on public buses

In Vermont: Feeding a bear, even unintentionally

In Kansas: Having sex with someone you pulled over for speeding, if you're a traffic cop

LEAKS

A memo warning Apple employees to stop leaking information was leaked.

The memo bragged that last year the firm had 'caught 29 leakers' and that 12 had been arrested. It also pleaded with employees to consider all the work that goes into Apple products, said anti-leaking methods were getting better and better, and finished with a heartfelt message that 'Everyone comes to Apple to do the best work of their lives . . . The best way to honor those contributions is by not leaking'. It's not known whether Apple have yet tracked down whoever it was who leaked the memo.

In America, researchers studied the thousands of hacked accounts from Ashley Madison – a dating site for adulterers – that were leaked in 2015. They found Democrats are significantly less likely to cheat on their partners than Republicans (on the Ashley Madison site, anyway). Libertarians were the most adulterous.

And up in space, the International Space Station had a *real* leak. A Russian capsule docked onto the ISS got a tiny rip in its shell, just two millimetres wide. When it was discovered that oxygen was leaking out, astronaut Alexander Gerst temporarily plugged the hole by putting his finger over it.

▼

Donald Trump's national infrastructure plans, including maintenance plans for water supplies, were leaked.

LEGO

LEGO plants and bushes are now made out of actual plants.

Almost all LEGO bricks have traditionally been made from plastics derived from fossil fuels. This year, in an effort to improve their green credentials, LEGO

launched bricks made from sustainably sourced polyethylene – a plastic derived from a bioethanol that comes from sugar cane crops. Pleasingly, the first bricks to be properly green were the green ones – most were LEGO trees and bushes (although LEGO car wash brushes and LEGO dragon wings are now also plant-based). Due to current costs, the new bricks will only replace 1 or 2 per cent of the firm's plastics, and at the moment, there's no economically viable replacement for ABS, a petrol-based substance responsible for up to 80 per cent of building blocks – but the firm aims to be completely planet-friendly by 2030.

LIBERIA

The first sportsperson to become a head of state was inaugurated in a sports stadium.

In August, Weah bestowed his country's highest honour on his former coach Arsène Wenger. Wenger was invited to attend a ceremony at which he would be inducted into Liberia's Order of Distinction and gain the title Knight Grand Commander of the Humane Order of African Redemption – the country's most prestigious title.

The only African ever to be named the world's best footballer, George Weah, became president of Liberia in the first peaceful, democratic transfer of power in the West African country for more than 70 years.

Weah grew up in the Liberian slums, before playing football in nearby Cameroon as a teenager. Here he was spotted by then Monaco manager Arsène Wenger, who signed him on the spot for $12,000. A long career in Europe followed, during which he played for Manchester City and Chelsea, as well as for the Liberian national team – a team that he ended up bankrolling since the country's civil war had so financially weakened it. Weah also served as a UNICEF ambassador, working on schemes to re-educate the country's child soldiers.

After his football career ended, Weah went into politics. In 2005, he fought his first presidential campaign, losing to Ellen Johnson Sirleaf, the first elected female head of state in Africa, and a future Nobel Prize winner. In that election, Weah was ridiculed for the fact that he had dropped out of high school, so he went back to the classroom and got a master's degree in business management. This year, he finally achieved his ambition, and was confirmed as president of Liberia in a lavish ceremony at the SKD Sports Complex in Monrovia. People queued for miles to attend the inauguration, singing and dancing as they did so; others present included politicians from across Africa and football stars Samuel Eto'o and Didier Drogba.

Ahead of the ceremony, Weah took part in one final football match, scoring the opening goal in a 2–1 win over the Liberian army. Somewhat worryingly, the army took quite a lot of shots during the match, but continually struggled to hit the target.

LIBERTY, STATUE OF ▶

The US Postal Service had to pay $3.5 million because one of their stamps was too sexy.

In December 2010, the US Postal Service (USPS) released a stamp featuring the Statue of Liberty's face as part of their 'Forever Stamps' collection. Four months and 3 billion stamps later, a collector noticed a problem – they had used the wrong statue.

The face printed on the stamp didn't belong to New York's Statue of Liberty, but a copy in Las Vegas, built in 1996 by sculptor Robert Davidson. The USPS nevertheless continued to sell the collection even after they had been informed of their mistake, and by the time the stamp was discontinued in 2014, 4.9 billion had been sold. In the meantime, Davidson filed a lawsuit for copyright infringement.

During the subsequent trial, the USPS argued that as the original statue was in the public domain, any replicas must be as well. Davidson counter-argued that his version wasn't a replica at all. He said his updated Lady Liberty was 'sultrier', 'sexier' and largely based on his mother-in-law.

The court agreed with Davidson, ruling, 'A comparison of the two faces unmistakably shows that they are different . . . We agree that Mr Davidson's statue evokes a softer and more feminine appeal. The eyes are different, the jaw line is less massive and the whole face is more rounded.'

LICENCE PLATES

To get his hands on a rare licence plate, the boss of an accident claims firm claimed to have had an accident.

Miles Savory, a director at the Bristol firm Accident Claims Handlers, wanted to buy the number plate W1 DOW for his car. He knew it existed. What he didn't know was who owned it or where they lived. So he wrote to the authorities claiming that he had been in an accident with a car bearing that registration number, and that the other vehicle had failed to stop. The DVLA therefore agreed to reveal the details of the car's owner to Savory. But it also contacted the owner of the W1 DOW plate about the supposed accident, so alerting him to the fact that things were amiss (he lived in Yorkshire, hadn't been in an accident, and had never been to Bristol). Consequently, when Savory contacted him with an offer to buy the plate, he smelled a rat. Savory's scheme collapsed, and he was fined £700 for breaching the Data Protection Act.

In other licence plate news:

▸ The licence plate 'F1' was put on sale for £14.4 million by an entrepreneur. The previous owner, Essex County Council, had sold it for £440,000 in 2008.

▸ North Carolina rejected, then allowed, a woman's request for the licence plate LSBNSNLV (signifying 'lesbians in love'). She explained that it was her way of celebrating her love for her wife.

▸ A Kentucky atheist sued the authorities over his right to use the licence plate 'IM GOD'. It hadn't caused him any problems during the decade he had used it in Ohio, but when he moved to Kentucky he was told it could be viewed as 'vulgar or obscene'.

▸ A man with the licence plate DIRTBAG was arrested for punching a police officer after a minor traffic incident.

LIECHTENSTEIN

All emergency phone lines in Liechtenstein crashed for a day. Luckily, there were no emergencies.

An error made in the course of modernising the country's communications networks caused all of Liechtenstein's fixed landlines, most mobile phones and the whole of the Internet to crash on one Sunday in March. Worried that people would be unable to contact emergency services, the authorities set up a special number in Switzerland, and ordered that police patrols should be stepped up so that people could reach out if they got into trouble. As it turned out, given that it was Liechtenstein and a Sunday, nothing actually happened that required emergency services, and everything was back to normal by the Monday.

LIONS

Britain's last lion tamer lost his licence because he couldn't provide itineraries for his lions.

Thomas Chipperfield comes from a 300-year-long line of circus animal trainers, being a direct descendant of one James Chipperfield, who displayed his menagerie in 1684 at the frost fair on the frozen River Thames. But this year he was told he wouldn't be allowed to tour the UK with his two lions and one tiger, both because he hadn't provided written itineraries for them, and because it was felt that he had not drawn up a suitable care plan. He's still committed to his career, though, saying, 'There's still a demand for this as entertainment, if there wasn't there wouldn't be any of us left.' Although admittedly, there is only *one* of him left.

In the US, an Oregon woman called Lauren Taylor who found a mountain lion in her sitting room claimed she persuaded it to leave using telepathy. She said she 'elevated the energy field' to calm it down, then psychically sent it the route out of her house. By her account, it managed to read her mind, see the route she was willing it to take (which mainly involved exiting through an open door), and follow it. She did have to wait while it took a six-hour nap behind her sofa first, though.

While Taylor was speaking telepathically to real lions, a couple in Canada spoke gibberish to a fake one. The pair were fighting a custody case for the right to live with their child, whom social services had taken away. They refused legal aid on the grounds that they had Jesus Christ as their witness and judge – in the form of a stuffed lion. During the trial, they spoke in unintelligible words to the lion and conveyed its thoughts, purportedly coming directly from God, to the court. The judge decided against returning the child to their care.

LITERARY PRIZES

The world's most lucrative literary award presented its €100,000 prize to a book that is one sentence long.

The International DUBLIN Literary Award is the only major book prize in the world to take nominations exclusively from public libraries. This year judges whittled down a long list of over 150 novels submitted by librarians from 37 countries, ultimately opting to give the award to Mike McCormack for his book *Solar Bones*, a one-sentence novel, narrated by a ghost, which runs for 272 pages.

On receiving the award, McCormack explained: 'A ghost would have no business with a full stop. It might fatally falter and dissipate.' When asked what he was going to do with the prize money, he said, 'I have a very modest plan: I'm going to buy a chair . . . The chair I was writing in collapsed under me last night.'

Another literary prize to make the news was the Bollinger Everyman Wodehouse Prize for comic fiction. This year, the judges decided that none of the 62 novels submitted was funny enough and decided not to award the usual prize of a case of champagne and a rare-breed pig. Organisers have promised that, assuming the standard is higher next year, the winner will receive a methuselah of champagne and a particularly large pig.

———— ♥ ————

The writer Ian McEwan revealed that he tutored his own son on an essay about an Ian McEwan novel. His son was awarded a C+.

LOVE ISLAND

Every female Love Island *contestant had their own personal chaperone reminding them to take their contraceptive pill.*

Love Island was the most talked-about TV show of the year in Britain, providing ITV2 with its highest-ever viewing figures. According to a spokesperson,

For instance: the rules of Love Island *dictate that if you are in a couple at a certain point, you're unlikely to be kicked off the show. When a new, particularly attractive man arrives on the island, female contestants have to choose whether to stay with their current partner or swap to the new man. If they swap, they might end up in a better relationship, but they also face the risk that if a new woman arrives the next week they could be dumped in favour of her. If they stay in their current relationship, they are probably safe from elimination, but things will be less interesting for them, and they also have to be absolutely sure they can trust their partner. This is a version of the 'prisoner's dilemma', one of the most famous thought experiments in game theory – only with more bikinis and fake tan.*

it assumed such universal popularity that between June and the end of 2018 it would be possible to see it somewhere around the world every single day.

Something many viewers didn't realise was that every contestant was given their own personal chaperone, who followed them around, offering advice, support and instructions. Former *Love Island* winner Cara de la Hoyde explained that the chaperones are never filmed, but are always there. They remind the competitor they're responsible for things like taking contraception and wearing make-up. They also make sure the contestants don't have any juicy conversations off camera. If they start gossiping or arguing while not being recorded, the chaperone interrupts and makes them save it all for when they're on camera, so the public can see.

At least twice as many people applied to be on the show as applied for Oxbridge, and *Love Island* was statistically harder to get into. And those who survived for eight weeks or more could expect to earn more over the course of their lives than the average Oxbridge graduate. Merely appearing on the show is not nearly as lucrative, though. Participants received £200 a week, or, assuming a 40-hour working week, roughly £5 an hour (in fact, the poor contestants grafted away for considerably longer than that).

Some commentators remained hopeful that the series provided some sort of education. According to Oxford economics professor Alex Teytelboym, the complex social dynamics that it involves offer a good example of game theory at work.*

In which we learn . . .
Who's been grooming the French president, why you
shouldn't squeeze a rubber duck, what Russia failed to
outlaw, who Prince Harry welcomed as in-laws, how
Sweden lost its balls and tried to get them back, and
when a flamethrower is definitely not a flamethrower.

MACARENA ▶

According to a new study, CPR is best performed while humming the 'Macarena'.

The research, which was presented at the European Anaesthesia Congress 2018 in Denmark, involved splitting 164 medical students into three groups, and getting each group to test a different way of timing their chest compressions. One was given a smartphone metronome app, another was told to hum the 'Macarena' in their heads, and a third was given no guidance at all. The 'Macarena' was selected because, according to one of the researchers, it's 'the most famous song in Spain, and probably one of the most well known in the world, and the beat of the chorus of the song is 103 bpm, a correct rhythm for performing the rate of compressions'.

The 'Macarena' group achieved a correct CPR tempo 74 per cent of the time, while the group with no guidance only managed 24 per cent. The most effective method was the smartphone app, which worked 91 per cent of the time – but researchers noted that in real life smartphones are much more fiddly: unlocking the phone and opening the app can lose precious seconds. For those unfamiliar with the 'Macarena', an alternative 103 bpm song recommended by doctors is the Bee Gees' hit 'Stayin' Alive'. An earlier study found that the song 'Achy Breaky Heart' does not work at all.

MACRON, EMMANUEL ▶

The French president was ritually groomed by Donald Trump.

French President Emmanuel Macron met Donald Trump in April on a state visit to the USA. At their joint press briefing in the Oval Office, Trump leaned over and brushed Macron's shoulder, saying, 'I'll get that little piece of dandruff off . . . We have to make him perfect. He is perfect.' A body language expert later claimed this was 'primate grooming', expressing the message, 'We have an intimate relationship, but I'm dominant, I'm the alpha gorilla.'

Macron and Trump's bromance got off to a good start. A French newspaper revealed that Donald Trump enjoyed cutting out and sending Macron positive newspaper clippings about their relationship or the French economy, with little comments in the margin like 'it's true' or 'good job'. Indeed, Macron's apparent understanding of the way the American president ticked earned him the nickname 'the Trump Whisperer'. The high point came during Macron's visit, when the pair used golden shovels to plant an oak sapling together in the White House garden. But it all went sour after Macron criticised Trump's tariffs in June and the two men had a 'terrible' phone call. Meanwhile, the tree had disappeared: government officials explained it had been dug up to be put in quarantine.

As it turned out, the falling-out might have done Macron good on the domestic front: all this bonhomie had made him very unpopular with his colleagues. An opposition MP said France had 'prostituted itself' by sucking up to Trump, and French social media users said it was 'sycophantic' and 'painful'. But at least Macron had avoided the sort of gaffe he made when he visited the Australian PM and complimented him on his 'delicious wife'.

———— ▼ ————

Late last year, it was revealed the French president spent €26,000 on make-up in three months. This year, after a backlash, M. and Mme Macron started paying their own living expenses, including government flights, clothes and dog food. However, just a few weeks later, it was discovered that he was spending thousands of euros of taxpayers' money installing a swimming pool at his private presidential retreat, and had spent €500,000 on a new dinner set.

MALAYSIA ▶

The world's oldest leader came to power thanks to the youth vote.

Malaysia introduced laws to combat the circulation of fake news. Those breaking them can receive a prison sentence of up to six years.

Prime Minister Mahathir Mohamad, who turned 93 in July this year, became the oldest leader in the world (overtaking Queen Elizabeth II, who is a spring chicken at 92) when he won a bruising election against the incumbent, Najib Razak. His victory marked the first change of government in Malaysia since its independence in 1957. It also marked the first time in Malaysian history that young people had been galvanised into participating – those aged 40 and under accounted for 41 per cent of the vote. After his victory, Mahathir promised to stand aside for former opposition leader Anwar Ibrahim, who had been in prison on and off since the late 1990s – but not quite yet: he said he intended to stay in power at least into his 95th year.

While he was being investigated for graft, the ousted PM, Najib Razak, complained that police searching his home had stolen chocolate from his fridge. This resulted in a great deal of mockery from the Malaysian public, who proceeded to send the police chocolate, arguing that they must be in need of treats if they were having to steal them from the former PM.

The most memorable exchanges of the election involved food. Supporters of Mahathir accused Najib Razak of extravagance for eating quinoa rather than rice.* He hit back by saying that the amount Mahathir spent on horse feed every month would keep him in quinoa for three years. And then the British TV show *Masterchef* got involved. When Malaysian-born contestant Zaleha Kadir Olpin was kicked off the programme, partly due to her chicken rendang not having crispy skin, both sides in the election cried fowl – Malaysian rendang is absolutely *not* supposed to have crispy skin, they said. Malaysia's foreign minister, Datuk Seri Anifah Aman, went further, telling the show's hosts that 'You have succeeded in a way that many of us politicians could not, i.e. to unite Malaysians in the most divisive of times.'

MANDELA, WINNIE

The world lost South Africa's first black social worker –
who went on to marry Nelson Mandela.

South Africa's first black professional social worker had
been in the job for just a couple of years when she met
Nelson Mandela at a bus stop in 1957. He was immediately attracted to her, and on an early date drove her
to the gym so that – as she later recalled – she could
'watch him sweat'. Their marriage lasted 38 years, but
they rarely saw each other, largely because for 27 of
those years Nelson was in prison. In fact, any kind of
communication was difficult: the first letter Winnie sent
to Nelson after he was jailed was so heavily censored
that only the greeting and farewell were visible. Winnie
herself was repeatedly put on trial and imprisoned,
making her birth name, Nomzamo, meaning 'she who
must endure trials', surprisingly apt.

In her decades-long campaign against apartheid,
Winnie was always passionate. Once, when policemen
raided her house, she knocked one of them to the ground.
But by the 1980s she had become genuinely dangerous,
advocating violence as a means of protest. Her gang
of bodyguards, MUFC (Mandela United Football Club),
were linked to kidnappings and killings, and Winnie
herself was convicted of kidnapping 14-year-old Stompie
Seipei, who was later found murdered. For a while Nelson
seemed to turn a blind eye, but eventually he fired her
from government and divorced her. However, even when
he announced their separation, he said his love for her
remained undiminished.

Although a controversial figure, Winnie had an enormous following. Her funeral had to be moved from South
Africa's largest Catholic church to the 37,000-capacity
Orlando Stadium to accommodate the mourners. One of
the people there was the mother of Stompie Seipei, who

———— ▼ ————

Nelson Mandela wore
Winnie's glasses for his
first speech after leaving
prison. He needed them
to read from his notes,
since he had left his own
in his prison cell.

165

says she has forgiven her. The sermon was cut short by loud claps of thunder.

Winnie Mandela never remarried, and was close friends with Nelson again by the end of his life. She was at his bedside when he died, along with his third wife. A week before her own death, Winnie was chatting to her granddaughter, who wanted to find her a boyfriend and wondered what sort of partner she'd like. Winnie replied, 'Darling, just look at your grandfather. That's my type.'

MARKLES, THE

Prince Harry's nephew-in-law created a strain of marijuana guaranteed to 'blow your crown off'.

When Prince Harry announced that the 'Royals are the family that Meghan never had', Meghan's father was reportedly very hurt. Even though only one member of her family was present at the wedding (*see* **Royal Wedding**), Harry actually has plenty of new in-laws:

Nephew-in-law Tyler Dooley: Tyler grows marijuana in Oregon, USA. He created a special hybrid strain this year specifically to honour Meghan's wedding, calling it 'Markle's Sparkle'. Tyler described it as 'unique and classy like my aunt' and said that it will 'blow your crown off'. Neither Tyler nor his mother were invited to the wedding, but they flew to the UK nevertheless. Hours after the ceremony, Tyler was given a warning by police for attempting to bring a knife into a London nightclub. He had reportedly brought it over from the US because President Trump had warned Americans that London wasn't safe.

Brother-in-law Thomas Markle Jr: Meghan's half-brother is a window fitter. He and Harry haven't met yet, but Thomas contacted Harry earlier in the year via an open letter published in *In Touch* magazine. In it he warned the prince that it was becoming 'very clear' that the coming event would be the 'biggest mistake in royal wedding history'. He added that Meghan was a 'jaded, shallow, conceited woman that will make a joke of you and the royal family heritage'.

Sister-in-law Samantha Markle: Meghan's half-sister is a former model who has gained a reputation for constantly criticising Meghan in the press. However, in a TV interview with *Good Morning Britain* she claimed she had been misquoted and that Meghan is actually 'lovely'. She used the same interview to confirm she is writing a tell-all book about Meghan titled *The Diary of Princess Pushy's Sister.**

She has since renamed the book A Tale of Two Sisters, arguing that the original title had been misrepresented.

Ex-husband-in-law Trevor Engelson: Meghan's ex-husband is a Hollywood producer. His current projects include a new TV sitcom pilot, with a script by the writers of *Modern Family*, about a man whose ex-wife starts dating a British prince.

MARS

NASA is sending robo-bees to Mars.

The bumblebee-sized robots, known as 'marsbees', have giant cicada-sized wings, and will map Mars and search for signs of life. The idea (still in its early stages) is that the bees will replace the bulkier rovers we have been sending for the last 20 years. The bot bugs were selected by NASA as one of 25 projects they'll be funding as part of their Innovative Advanced Concepts scheme. Other projects picked from that scheme include a flying amphibious robot called Shapeshifter and a steam-powered jumping robot named Sparrow that will explore Saturn's moon Titan.

Robot bees aren't the only flying machines NASA want to send to Mars. They are also planning to send a helicopter. Travelling to Mars as part of NASA's 2020 Rover Mission, the helicopter will be humankind's first-ever attempt to fly a heavier-than-air vehicle on another planet.

Flying the helicopter on Mars won't be easy. The Red Planet's atmosphere is 1 per cent of the thickness of the Earth's, which means that when the chopper is sitting on the Martian surface, it will already be at the Earth equivalent of 30,000 metres in the air. Since the current altitude record for a helicopter is 12,000 metres, that will be quite a challenge. In order to fly in the incredibly thin Mars atmosphere, the blades will have to spin at a rate of 3,000 times a minute, 10 times faster than those of the average Earth helicopter.

One other way in which a Mars helicopter will differ from an Earth one is that it will be roughly the size of a cricket ball.

MARX, KARL ▶

History's most famous critic of capitalism turned 200,
and his home town really cashed in.

To celebrate the bicentenary of the economist's birth,
the German city of Trier sold Karl Marx bicycle bells,
Marx-shaped cookie cutters, and sets of rubber ducks
holding *Das Kapital*. 'Zero euro' banknotes were also on
offer: they had no monetary value, but cost €3 for a pack
of five. In addition, the city installed a set of traffic lights
in Marx's likeness and unveiled a statue that had been
donated by China. At exactly 5.5 metres in height, the
statue was a lot taller than the man himself: the measurement was selected to signify Marx's birthday, 5 May.

China itself embarked on a week-long propaganda
push to persuade its youth of Marxism's contemporary
relevance, which included a primetime TV show called
Marx Got It Right. In Britain, meanwhile, Marxists celebrated by visiting his grave in Highgate Cemetery – but
they had to pay £4 to do so.

MAY, THERESA ▶

The most powerful woman in the UK failed to make it on to Vogue's *list of Most Powerful Women in the UK.*

After being filmed dancing on a trip to Africa, Theresa May's moves were (rather unfairly) compared to: a baby robot giraffe (*Politico.eu*); a very well-meaning wardrobe being shifted up a staircase (*i*); your ironing board strutting its way into your hallway (*NME*); and a villain in a 1960s children's movie creeping up on a child who is about to go missing (*Vice*).

To add insult to injury for the prime minister, Ruth Davidson, leader of the Scottish Conservatives, did make it on. *Vogue* explained their decision by saying that Theresa May's 'authority remains too precarious' for her to be included.

It hasn't been the best of years for the prime minister. Back in January, for example, in the course of a Cabinet reshuffle, she accidentally made Transport Secretary Chris Grayling party chairman. The tweeted appointment lasted 37 seconds, until a new tweet was sent from the PM's account which announced that it was actually Brandon Lewis who was to be chairman and Minister without Portfolio (or 'Porfolio', as the tweet put it).

May did manage to get a mention at the prestigious Ivor Novello music awards, but this was only because the winner of Best Contemporary Song, 'Question Time', was a direct attack on her (it opens: 'A question for the new prime minister, / How'd you have a heart so sinister?'). And in the week that the PM got special permission to jump the 26-year-long waiting list for entry to the Marylebone Cricket Club, which owns Lord's Cricket Ground, the England team were utterly thrashed by Pakistan at Lord's.

MEATBALLS ▶

Sweden admitted the Swedish national dish is not from Sweden, and then immediately changed its mind.

The country's official Twitter account announced that the traditional Swedish meatball was actually based on a recipe King Charles XII brought home from Turkey

Measurements

This year, the following things have been measured:

The happiness of dolphins: It turns out they're happier when interacting with a human.

The pressure in the middle of a proton: It's a billion, billion, billion times the pressure at the bottom of the Mariana Trench, the deepest part of the Pacific Ocean.

The largest wave ever in the southern hemisphere: It was the height of six double-decker buses.

The cleanliness of chimpanzee beds: They have fewer bacteria than human beds.

The cleanliness of rubber ducks: They have up to 75 million bacteria per square centimetre on their insides. But it's probably only a problem if children squeeze the ducks so hard the sludge inside hits their faces.

The temperature of people's noses: Your nose cools down when you're thinking, because blood is rushing to your brain.

The length of a New Zealand councillor's penis: After he was accused of rubbing it against a colleague. The measurement was not announced in court.

The speed of death: At a cellular level the body dies at a speed of 2 millimetres per day. Luckily, for most of your life, your cells regenerate just as quickly.

in the 18th century. A Swedish food historian called Richard Tellström angrily denounced the claim, arguing it was 'fake news . . . You make something up for a political or a commercial purpose, and you spread the news without doing proper research.' Linguistically, he argued, meatballs were likelier to be French or Italian.* The Swedish national account then posted an apologetic tweet, saying, 'We should have looked deeper into the origins and history of Swedish meatballs before tweeting.' It was too late: the Turkish media had already happily claimed credit for the dish.

IKEA, who sell 2 million meatballs every single day, announced their test kitchen has created two prototypes for new varieties of 'Neatball'. One is made from crushed mealworms, and the other – which is expected to be more popular – is made with vegetables. Neither will be on sale any time soon. Other prototype dishes included a salad grown without soil, a Bug Burger, and the Dogless Hotdog – an algae-based bun stuffed with vegetables.

———— ▼ ————

A Pennsylvania man who stole a pot of meatballs was tracked down and arrested thanks to one vital clue: he was spotted with tomato sauce all over his face.

In Pennsylvania, a whole court case hinged on the meaning of 'meatballs'. During the trial of Mayor Ed Pawlowski – who was charged with fraud, bribery and conspiracy – phone calls were played back in which the mayor's finance director and political consultant could be heard saying things like 'You're going to get your meatballs' and 'You don't want to lose your meatballs, you know?' The prosecution argued that 'meatballs' was a code word for dirty money. The jury clearly agreed: Pawlowski was found guilty on most charges.

MESSAGING, INSTANT

The Russian government tried to stop people from using an instant messaging service, only to block their own website instead.

Telegram is the most popular instant messaging service in Russia. But because it is heavily encrypted, and therefore completely private, it is used by terrorists, drug dealers and – perhaps most worryingly for the Kremlin – opponents of the Putin regime. Because of this, Roskomnadzor, the federal service for monitoring Internet communications in Russia, tried to close Telegram down by blocking key IP addresses (the label given to devices that allows them to communicate). It was an extremely ham-fisted effort. In the process of attempting to block Telegram, they also blocked and crashed MasterCard, Google, Amazon, Volvo, Gett Taxi, Nintendo, Spotify, popular Russian search engine Yandex,* and, most embarrassingly of all, Roskomnadzor's own website. Telegram's servers remained open.

Iran, which had originally embraced Telegram on the grounds that it is one of the few messaging systems to be non-American in origin, also has concerns about it, notably a worry that it is reportedly being used by Islamic State. The app has now been banned there, and Iran is instead promoting its own instant messaging service, Soroush. It works just like any other system, but has additional features, such as an emoji of a woman clutching a picture of Supreme Leader Ali Khamenei, and placards demanding death to Israel, America and Freemasons.

*This year, Yandex launched Emoji Map, a feature that allows users to review locations simply by posting emojis. Within a week, they had to pull the 'poop' and 'toilet' symbols because they were being used too often.

MESSAGING, VERY MUCH NOT INSTANT ▶

A message in a bottle was found 132 years after it was sent.

It was one of thousands dropped in the late 19th century by the German Naval Observatory, which hoped to discover more about ocean currents by plotting where the bottles washed up. Each contained a note encouraging the finder to report the bottle's final location to scientists at the observatory. Until this year, only 662 had been reported, the last one in 1934.

The 663rd turned up when Kym and Tonya Illman were driving a four-wheel drive on the beach near Perth, Australia, and got bogged down. While stuck, Tonya decided to scan the beach for any flotsam she might be able to use to decorate their house. She spotted the bottle, which had no stopper and was full of sand, and took it home. Realising there was a message inside, but that it was too delicate to unroll, she put it in the oven to dry out, and then took it to experts at the West Australia Museum. It's not thought that the bottle washed up this year; rather, it probably landed on the beach 131 years ago, was covered by sand, and the wind and rain then uncovered it shortly before the Illmans walked by.

Messages in bottles may appear to be a harmless pursuit, but they add to the problem of littering in the sea, and as a result, perhaps the world's most prolific adherent of the hobby announced he would be retiring this year. Harold Hackett of Prince Edward Island in Canada, who has thrown an estimated 10,000 messages into the ocean over the last 22 years, has tossed his last bottle. He was told that he would be fined $5,000 if he continued the practice.

METAL DETECTORISTS

Two metal detector enthusiasts found a stash of Roman gold that was roughly one year old.

Metal detectorists Paul Adams and Andy Sampson found the hoard of 54 Roman gold coins in a field in Suffolk. Thinking that they could be worth £250,000, the two men ran home to show their detectorist neighbour, who instantly pointed out that they weren't real. They refused to believe him, until Mr Sampson's wife recalled that an episode of the TV sitcom *Detectorists* had been filmed in the same location a few months earlier, at which point they realised the coins were simply props and probably worth no more than £250. Mr Sampson said, 'After we found them I was paying off my mortgage and buying a sports car in my head. We thought we were looking at the real McCoy. Now I look at them and want to cry.'

Mackenzie Crook, who wrote, directed and starred in the series, said he'd intended to go back and look for any prop coins but the detectorists had beaten him to it. As it happens, he did actually find some Roman gold with his own metal detector last year.

A pie company in Wales put a chunk of metal into its own food to make sure its metal detectors were working. Unfortunately, they immediately lost track of it and it turned up in a customer's pie.

MIDTERMS

One candidate for the Texan House of Representatives got most of her donations in the form of deer semen.

In the American South, where a single 'straw' of deer semen can be worth around $1,000, some supporters of Democratic nominee Ana Lisa Garza opted to make their contributions via this unusual currency. The semen-filled straws were then auctioned, with the proceeds going to Garza's campaign.

Millennials

According to journalists, millennials hate sex, love house plants and think the Earth is flat:

'Fray Bentos to change iconic pie tins because millennials "failed to open them"'
Daily Express, 14 May 2018

'Sainsbury's to launch touch-free packaging for millennials "scared of touching raw meat"'
Independent, 16 April 2018

'One in eight 26-year-olds are virgins because millennials are scared of intimacy'
Metro, 6 May 2018

'A third of millennials think the Earth is flat, shocking survey reveals'
Mirror, 10 April 2018

'Millennials drink at home because it is "too much effort" to go out'
Daily Mail, 11 June 2018

'Millennials worry more about bad breath than bank balance'
Belfast Live, 26 April 2018

'Millennials are killing the TV Licence'
City AM, 6 April 2018

'Are millennials killing Club 18-30 holidays?'
Metro, 14 May 2018

'Why millennials love house plants'
Huffington Post, 19 March 2018

Another unusual donation went to the opponent of Republican candidate Kevin Nicholson in Wisconsin – from Nicholson's own parents. In an interview with CNN, he explained their decision to donate the maximum amount they were allowed to Democratic Senator Tammy Baldwin with the words: 'My parents have a different worldview than I do.'

Things were also tense in Virginia's 5th Congressional District: Democrat Leslie Cockburn accused Republican Denver Riggleman of being 'a devotee of Bigfoot erotica', citing as her evidence Instagram posts by Riggleman where he discussed Bigfoot penises.* Riggleman claimed the posts were a joke, and said he didn't believe in Bigfoot, though he did admit to having written a non-erotic book: *Bigfoot Exterminators, Inc.: The Partially Cautionary, Mostly True Tale of Monster Hunt 2006.*

You know what they say about Bigfeet . . .

MUMMIES

For a cocaine-addled mummy, *see* **Incas**; for a syphilitic mummy, *see* **Johnson, Boris**; for a tattooed mummy, *see* **Oldest**; and for drinking mummy juice, *see* **Sarcophagus**.

MUSIC

For a band performing 400 km above Earth, *see* **Astronauts**; for a prime minister's fifth pop song, *see* **Chan-o-cha, Prayuth**; for the finance minister who failed to duck out of trouble, *see* **Drake**; for what the writer of Sell Drugsz sold, *see* **Drugs**; for a singer with a newt problem, *see* **Ed Sheeran vs Nature**; for music that makes you move your foetus, *see* **Experiments**; for a band who were accidentally banned, *see* **Gun Control**; for a musical star, *see* **Hawking, Stephen**; for a hellishly bad pun, *see* **Heavy Metal**; for pop-aganda, *see* **Korea**; for pop for when they drop, *see* **Macarena**; for pop goes the pissweasel, *see* **Nigels of the Year**; for songs to shower to, *see* **Water, Water**; and for songs to be inaugurated to, *see* Yorkshire.

MUSK, ELON

Elon Musk released a product that could throw flames up to 3 metres. He called it 'not a flamethrower'.

The *Wall Street Journal* reported that when Elon Musk visited a Tesla factory in the spring, he became so annoyed with a safety sensor pausing the assembly line that he headbutted a car.

The branding was deemed necessary as some customs agencies refuse to allow the shipment of anything called a 'flamethrower'. Even then, Musk still couldn't find anyone prepared to deliver the propane-powered devices, so many customers had to pick up their purchases themselves; the rest were delivered by SpaceX staff in trucks borrowed from Musk's Boring Company.

In the end Musk managed to sell 20,000 flamethrowers. His website also offered a fire extinguisher that could be bought separately for 'exorbitant amounts of money'. 'You can definitely buy one for less elsewhere,' the website stated, 'but this one comes with a cool sticker.'

It wasn't the only out-of-the-ordinary product Musk was associated with this year (*see also* **X, Space**). He also sold cinder blocks made from ground excavated by his giant boring machines, and continued his research into self-driving cars. Two days after Tesla acknowledged that its autopilot function was involved in a fatal crash, Musk sent out a series of April Fool tweets saying that his company had gone bankrupt. He wrote: 'There are many chapters of bankruptcy and, as critics so rightly pointed out, Tesla has them *all*, including Chapter 14 and a half (the worst one).' The company's shares dropped by over 8 per cent the next day.

Musk also made the gossip pages this year when it emerged that he and Canadian singer/artist Grimes (real name Claire Boucher) had begun dating. With his encouragement, Grimes said she would be changing her name to 'c', the symbol for the speed of light, explaining that she didn't much like the name Claire: '[it] has been the bane of my existence since i became sentient . . . i can barely say it w[ith] my speech impediment,' c tweeted, though she did add: 'c is technically worse 4 lisp.'

In which we learn . . .
What the A stands for in Anas A. Anas, how to tell
a Navy dolphin from a Navy SEAL, what the Prince
of Belgium can't have, where the Prince of Bel Air
can't go, and why the French went nuts over Nutella.

NAMES, FROM THE SUBLIME . . .

Appropriate names from this year's news included:

▶ A woman called Crystal Methvin was arrested for possessing crystal meth.

▶ Stan Wawrinka was knocked out of the Australian Open by Tennys Sandgren: a man called Tennys who plays tennis and comes from Tennessee.

▶ Footballer Jason Puncheon was given community service after attacking someone outside a nightclub (technically he wasn't Puncheon anyone – he actually hit them with his belt).

▶ A man in Iowa named Mr Beer pleaded guilty to drink-driving.

▶ After a fire in California which burned over 7,000 hectares of forest, the man arrested and charged with arson was called Forrest.

▶ The ex-wife of billionaire Bill Gross says that he put balls of human hair in drawers, let off fart spray and left dead fish in air vents.

▶ Two job losses at a Canadian TV station were announced by the station's news director, Les Staff.

Some of the year's names had the opposite problem: the woman who came first in the women's mountain biking at the Commonwealth Games was called Annie Last.

They weren't the only sublime names of the year. For why birds are singing the praises of Mr Song, *see* **Songs**; for Professor Call's thoughts on cetacean calls, *see* **Whales**; for Professor Rein's thoughts on artificial rain, *see* **Wildfires**; for why Mr Blind is no longer a referee, *see* **World Cup, Non-FIFA**; and for why Mr Valentine is unlucky with love, *see* **Zoos**.

NAMES, ... TO THE RIDICULOUS ▶

Unfortunate names that cropped up in the news this year included:

▶ In a scientific breakthrough, researchers created a pair of monkey clones. The team responsible included one Dr Mu-ming Poo.

▶ A massive football corruption scandal in Ghana, which ultimately led the country to shut down its football association, was exposed by journalist Anas A. Anas (the A stands for Arameyaw, not Anas).

▶ The first Russian to win a medal at the Winter Olympics in South Korea was speed skater Semen Elistratov.

▶ A study finding students rate teachers higher if they are given biscuits during class was authored by Dr Manuel Wenk.

They weren't the only ridiculous names of the year. For Lucas Skywalker Scott, *see* **Babies**; for Quim Torra, *see* **Catalonia**; for Meow-Ludo Disco Gamma Meow-Meow, *see* **Cyborgs**; for Lord de Mauley and Mrs Coningsby Disraeli, *see* **Ivory**; for 'c', *see* **Musk, Elon**; for the Most Reverend Dr Michael Jackson, *see* **Saints**; for Superintendent Randy Brown, *see* **Schoolchildren**; for Mr Handsome, *see* **Spain**; for New Dirty Bastard, *see* **Trademarks**; for Pineapple Featonby, *see* **Valentine's Day**; for Jacob 'I laugh at you as I destroy you' Zuma, *see* **Zexit**; and for Welshman Ncube, *see* **Zimbabwe**.

NAUGHTY

The Belgian parliament voted to cut their prince's pocket money.

Prince Laurent of Belgium, the King's brother and a former navy captain, got into hot water when he turned up, without official permission, at a Chinese embassy reception dressed in full naval regalia. He'd been repeatedly warned to stop having unapproved meetings with foreign dignitaries, so it was probably unwise to tweet a picture of himself at the event. When his superiors spotted the picture, his annual government allowance was cut by €46,000 to a paltry €261,000, which the misbehaving royal argued was a violation of his human rights.

On a less princely, but equally naughty, scale, a boy who stole one loaf of bread from his school in Kenya was suspended and told that to be allowed back he would have to bring 1,000 times what he'd stolen. That would have been enough bread to feed the entire school. The punishment was withdrawn after news of it went viral on social media. Instead, the boy was offered counselling to teach him not to steal in future.

A child in the UK faced a similarly harsh punishment when he misbehaved in the car on a motorway and was made to take 'time out' on the hard shoulder. A traffic officer spotted the disgraced boy walking alongside the M4 and issued a warning to parents not to use the hard shoulder as a 'naughty step'. A director from Highways England said that the official advice is not to stop unless it's genuinely an emergency. This wasn't.

One thing both these misbehaving children have in common is that they are more likely to be politically left-wing as adults. According to a study published this year, which analysed data from 16,000 participants, kids who are naughty between the ages of five and seven will probably turn out to be less conservative and to be more economically and politically discontented when they are in their thirties.

NAVIES

The US navy's newest ship had to be left on ice for the winter.

USS *Little Rock* (LCS-9) went into active service in New York on 16 December 2017, but got stuck in ice in port at Montreal eight days later, on Christmas Eve. It remained stranded there for over three months, during which time it had to be equipped with 16 emergency de-icers. It was also fitted with extra soundproofing after Montreal residents complained about the constant sound of its generators. The crew, who were provided with cold-weather clothes, made use of their time there by volunteering in the local food bank until the ice finally thawed and released them on 31 March.

In Navy SEAL news, it was revealed that the special operations force would have two new stealth motorbikes built for them. They're called Silent Hawk and Nightmare, they're almost completely silent, and they can run partly on olive oil.

And in navy *dolphin* news, Ukraine announced that its military dolphins had gone on hunger strike after being captured by Russia. The creatures, whose combat role involved them being deployed from helicopters to find underwater mines, had been taught to respond to whistles from their trainers. In 2014 they were seized by Russia during its annexation of Crimea, but according to a Ukrainian government official they refused to react to whistles operated by Russians. When it then emerged this year that most had died, the Ukrainian

It was revealed that US Navy SEALs are protected by Christmas trees. Apparently, people donate their used trees to the Navy, who then plant them around the SEAL training area so that their roots will reinforce the soil and prevent the ground collapsing.

New Species

Species discovered this year include:

Colobopsis explodens: a species of exploding ants, which blow their own heads up with yellow goo to defend their nest against predators.

Paguropsis gigas: the largest known species of blanket hermit crab. Instead of having a shell, it lets a sea anemone live on its back and, if threatened, can pull the anemone's body over its head.

Dendrocerus scutellaris: a type of parasitic wasp that has a saw-like spine it uses to break out of its host's body.

Apheloria polychrome: the world's most colourful millipede – it's also covered in cyanide.

Odontonia bagginsi: a hobbit shrimp with hairy feet discovered living inside a hole in a sea squirt.

Megapropodiphora arnoldi: a 'big-armed fly' named after Arnold Schwarzenegger. It's the smallest known fly. If Arnie had arms proportionately as long as the fly's front legs, they would be 1.25 metres in length.

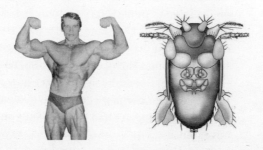

government announced they'd done so patriotically, having protested against their capture by going on hunger strike. A spokesman said, 'Many Ukrainian soldiers took their oath and loyalty much less seriously than these dolphins.'

NEW YEAR

Snapchat threw a New Year's party where Snapchat was banned.

The photo app company placed what one site called a 'digital cone of silence' over the venue where the party was happening. Employees were told not to put anything on social media and the company actively blocked anyone from posting public Snapchat pictures from the party. Guests responded by uploading photos to the rival app Instagram.

The island of Bali, meanwhile, shut off its entire mobile Internet for New Year in order to encourage people to reflect. The Balinese New Year (which takes place in March) is meant to be a day of silence for the mostly Hindu population. The official responsible for the island's communications explained that vital services would still have Wi-Fi.

Over in New Zealand, a group of friends built a fake island for New Year in order to get around a local ban on drinking in public places. It was constructed at low tide out of sand, and fitted with a picnic table and a cooler of beer. Attendees then sat on the table as the sea rose around them, claiming (somewhat dubiously) that they were actually in international waters. Local police commander Inspector John Kelly said, 'That's creative thinking: if I had known that I probably would have joined them.'

If they had the best New Year, the worst was probably had by a Norwegian man who, after a night in
Copenhagen, drunkenly got a taxi all the way through
Sweden, and then across the border into Norway to his
home in Oslo. By the time he got there he'd clocked up
a £1,640 bill, which he refused to pay until the police
called on him the following day.

NFL ▶

*Ahead of the Philadelphia Eagles' Super Bowl
appearance, rival fans banned Philadelphia cream
cheese from their businesses.*

When the New England Patriots, an American football
team based in Boston, were due to play the Philadelphia
Eagles in this year's Super Bowl, the decision was made
by Boston's Esplanade Association to ban all 'Philadelphia-
themed products' at their 26-hectare waterfront park.
The ban included not only the spreadable cheese, but
also cheesesteak sandwiches, soft pretzels and the
actor Will Smith (who is West Philadelphia-born and
raised).

Philadelphia, meanwhile, prepared for the game
by greasing the city's lamp posts, in order to stop
celebrating fans from climbing up them. It didn't do
much good. After the Eagles won the game, cars were
smashed, two police horses were stolen – and the lamp
posts were pulled down.

The Eagles' victory should have earned them a trip
to the White House, but Donald Trump decided to
cancel the event, claiming that they had been disrespectful to the national anthem. To illustrate the story,
Fox News showed photos of what they claimed were
the team kneeling during the anthem – in fact no Eagles

▼

American Football got
its first ever one-handed
player: Shaquem
Griffin, who joined the
Seattle Seahawks as a
linebacker (a defen-
sive player whose role
is to stop runners and
throws). In trials, Griffin
ran the fastest sprint
that any linebacker had
managed for more than
10 years.

player had ever done so. Fox then had to apologise, and explain that the images were actually of the players praying.

NIGELS OF THE YEAR

The world's loneliest bird died, with only his concrete girlfriend for company.

Nigel the gannet (?–2018), a seabird who became famous for spending the last four years of his life alone, courting a concrete model of a female gannet, died this year. Nigel's 'girlfriend' was one of 80 fake birds designed to lure actual gannets to Mana, the New Zealand island on which he lived. Other tactics included broadcasting noises of gannet calls and painting fake guano on the ground. Nigel arrived alone in 2015 and stayed – he was the only bird to be actually fooled by the concrete ones, building his 'mate' a nest, grooming her feathers and chattering away to her. Scientists named him Nigel because he had no mates.

Last year, another gannet arrived – but sadly for Nigel, he was a male, who was promptly given the name Norman. Tragically, soon before Nigel died, three more actual real birds joined the colony, including breeding females, but Nigel ignored them, choosing to stay loyal to his concrete girlfriend. The conservation ranger on the island, Chris Bell (who also lives there alone), said, 'Whether or not he was lonely, he certainly never got anything back, and that must have been a very strange experience . . . I think we all have a lot of empathy for him.'

Even so, Nigel had a positive effect – his presence probably helped to get a colony going. Bell said the three new birds were 'Nigel's legacy'.

In other Nigel news:

▶ Nigel Lawson, who was one of the heads of the Vote Leave campaign on Brexit, revealed that he was applying for an official French residency card.

▶ During an England–Scotland rugby match at which referee Nigel Owens was officiating, the BBC's automatic subtitling software incorrectly translated the phrase 'Nigel Owens is saying' as 'Nigel Owens is a gay'. As it happens, Owens *is* gay. He responded, 'Bloody hell, this voice recognition is good.'

▶ Nigel Farage decided to call his new politics podcast *Farage Against the Machine*. The band Rage Against the Machine responded by saying, 'Failed right-wing British politician Nigel Farage has called his podcast "Farage Against the Machine". This pissweasel IS the machine . . .'

NIGERIA ▶

A British couple genuinely received £1 million from a wealthy Nigerian prince.

Prince Arthur Eze, an oil billionaire, had offered the Conway family £5 million for their house in north London, but then pulled out. They ended up having to sell for less, sued the prince for compensation – and won.

Back in Nigeria, the problem of corruption kept rearing its head. During an investigation into a missing £70,000-worth of state funds, an official at the Nigerian exam board, Philomena Chieshe, claimed it had been eaten by a snake that had repeatedly sneaked into the vault where the money was kept. A whistleblowing Nigerian politician revealed that senators get expenses of 13.5 million naira (£27,000) every month to spend as they like with almost no accountability (the national

———— ▼ ————

In a victory against corruption, it was announced that about £228 million looted by Nigeria's former corrupt leader, Sani Abacha, will be distributed amongst 300,000 poor households. Critics have said these funds could end up being used corruptly to influence next year's election.

minimum wage in Nigeria is about £38 a month). And worst of all, two Nigerian civil servants appeared in court accused of embezzling funds earmarked for International Anti-Corruption Day.

In an effort to combat corruption, the country has become the latest to make its own version of the global hit TV programme *Integrity Idol*, a reality show in which civil servants in corrupt countries compete to show how honest they are. It has become extremely popular: 10 million Nigerians watched the show, and 400,000 voted for their favourites. Though the nomination period for candidates did have to be extended because the producers couldn't find enough non-corrupt candidates. One policeman who was contacted by the producers after being nominated said he shouldn't have been, as he was involved in dodgy deals.

NIPPLES

For a nipple law, *see* **Rugby**; and for a nipple lawsuit, *see* **Koko**.

NOBEL PRIZES

The Swedish Academy lost so many members it didn't have enough members to elect new members.

The Academy, which awards the Nobel Prize in Literature, was rocked by a major scandal this year after one of its members' husbands was accused of sexual assault, as well as leaking winners' names. Eight people withdrew as a result, which left the Academy in a catch-22 situation. It needed to elect more members. But since the rules state that at least 12 current members are required before a vote can take place, and only 10 were now left, it couldn't.

It looked, therefore, as though the Academy would gradually die out, powerless to elect anyone new. Fortunately the King of Sweden stepped in to change its founding statutes. (He himself was indirectly involved in the affair, because the member's husband at the centre of it was also accused of having groped the heir to the Swedish throne in 2006.) However, not even the King could save the Literature Prize from being temporarily suspended: it was considered to be so mired by the scandal that it won't be revived until 2019, when it's hoped some public trust in the institution will have been restored.

In protest at the Nobel Prize, a group of Swedish writers, actors and cultural figures formed the 'New Academy', their plan being to make their own literary award. Once that's happened, the Academy will dissolve itself.

While Swedish police investigated one set of Nobel allegations, Norwegian police were busy with another as evidence emerged that Donald Trump's Nobel Peace Prize nomination had been forged for the second year running. The secretary of the Norwegian Nobel Committee, Olav Njølstad, said that when they contacted the supposed nominator, that person confirmed they'd had nothing to do with it. The committee suspect that the same person may have been behind both nominations.

Trump may be in with a genuine chance next year, though, as a committee of Republican lawmakers later said they have now legitimately nominated him for the 2019 prize for his 'tireless work to bring peace to the world'.

NOVICHOK ▶

A British distillery apologised for selling Novichok-branded vodka.

The joke would have been of questionable taste at the best of times, but the timing could hardly have been worse, as it was released a day before Salisbury resident

191

Dawn Sturgess was tragically killed by the nerve agent. The Bristol Dry Gin micro-distillery admitted they may have 'lacked sensitivity'.

The nerve agent was widely accepted to have been brought to the UK by Russia's Federal Security Service. Until that point, the only actual deaths attributed to the Novichok had been a cat and two guinea pigs at the home of Russian double agent Sergei Skripal, who, along with his daughter Yulia, had fallen victim to the poison some weeks earlier. Because police found the highest concentration of the poison on Sergei Skripal's front door, they sealed off the entire house for several days, which meant that by the time the pets were eventually recovered, they were so dehydrated that the guinea pigs had died and the cat had to be put down.

There aren't many tried-and-tested ways of dealing with Novichok poisoning, since only three previous cases in medical history have been recorded. Nonetheless, authorities tried their best. Public Health England advised people in the Salisbury area to clean their phones and handbags with baby wipes, and wash jewellery and specs with warm water and detergent. And at Zizzi, the restaurant where the victims ate before collapsing, the table at which they had sat was burned, along with the uniforms of all the staff working that day.

The British distillery wasn't the only one to attempt to cash in on the Novichok name: beer, coffee and even sunflower oil with the name were available in Russia after the attack, where the official government line was that Putin's regime was absolutely not to blame. According to the British government, Russian state media put forward over 30 different theories as to who was responsible for the poisoning. One suggestion was that Yulia's prospective mother-in-law was to blame. Another was that it might have been revenge for England's alleged poisoning of Ivan the Terrible in 1584.

NUTELLA ▶

Nutella riots spread all over France.

The French are the world's biggest consumers of Nutella, so when a French supermarket chain, Intermarché, offered a 70 per cent discount, charging just €1.40 for almost a whole kilo, customers started fighting and scuffling for the cheap jars. One customer told *Le Progrès* newspaper that 'They were going for each other like animals. A woman had her hair pulled, an elderly lady took a box on her head, another had a bloody hand. It was horrible.' An employee at one shop got a black eye, and another had to call in the police. A woman who witnessed a crowd of 200 people scrabbling for cheap Nutella said, 'Today, I have definitely stopped believing in human beings and their supposed intelligence.'

The manufacturers, Ferrero, hastily issued a statement blaming the supermarket for the furore: 'We want to clarify that the decision for the special offer was taken unilaterally by Intermarché . . . We regret the consequences of this operation, which created confusion and disappointment in the consumers' minds.' The minister for the economy, Bruno Le Maire, called the head of the supermarket in and told him that 'we can't have scenes like this every few days in France'. The firm apologised, but within a week had launched similar promotions on other products, at one point prompting a series of nappy brawls. A law has since been proposed that would create a maximum discount of 34 per cent.

In which we learn . . .
Why you shouldn't throw stones in the new Apple office,
why it was an ill wind that blew no Olympian any
good, why there's no place like home for the Penn State
University Outing Club, and for whom the bell tolled.

OFFICES

Apple built a new office made of glass. On the first day, seven employees injured themselves by walking into walls.

The design of Apple's new campus in California was intended to encourage an open working environment. Instead, it encouraged employees to keep walking into the walls. After a number of injuries, workers started putting Post-it notes on the walls so they could see where they were, but Apple bosses kept removing them, concerned that they detracted from the look of the building. The building is the fifth most expensive in the world and the company claims it possesses the largest piece of curved glass in existence. *The Times* was the first to state the obvious truth: that it left workers in 'a world of pane'.

Meanwhile, Amazon announced it would be choosing a city for its new offices by the end of 2018, and that it would generate $5 billion investment and 50,000 jobs for the city selected. Everyone was therefore keen to get involved. Tucson, Arizona, gifted the company a 6-metre-tall cactus, which Amazon politely rejected; Birmingham, Alabama, built huge Amazon-themed buttons around the city which, when pressed, sent out one of 600 automated tweets including 'Amazon, we got a 100 per cent match on Bumble. Wanna go on a date?'; and Sly James, the mayor of Kansas City, Missouri, bought 1,000 Amazon products in order to leave reviews that merged into not-especially-subtle advertisements for the city. When reviewing a baby's train engineer costume, for instance, he reported that 'The mere sight of this surprisingly authentic [costume] makes me wish I was at the helm of a 200-ton steam locomotive riding the rails into the nation's #1 railroad hub by volume: Kansas City, Missouri.'

All of these cities failed to even make it to the shortlist.

A new study revealed that open-plan offices reduce face-to-face interactions by about 75 per cent. Part of the reason for this is that because it's much harder to have a private conversation when others are around, people tend to resort to email instead. Another study found that open-plan spaces make people more active – perhaps because they're having to walk a long way to find any privacy.

Obituaries

This year we said goodbye to:

Boxing trainer Brendan Ingle, 77: He trained four world champions and taught his boxers to 'dance' in the ring by inviting drunks from Yorkshire working men's clubs to try to hit them.

Cookery writer Barbara Kafka, 84: She enjoyed upsetting the culinary world by, for instance, publishing *Microwave Gourmet*, in which she controversially recommended using a microwave for deep fat frying, and *Roasting: A Simple Art*, in which she advocated turning on the oven as high as possible, opening the kitchen windows and disabling the smoke alarm.

Pioneer of the Internet Pål Spilling, 83: In 1988 Spilling helped save Norway's internet (known then as ARPANET) from an online bug spreading from America, by cutting the country's network off from the rest of the world. He was able to do this by unplugging one single cable.

'The Sherlock Holmes of the mountaineering world', Elizabeth Hawley, 94: For 50 years Elizabeth Hawley authenticated successful ascents of Mount Everest. She kept her meticulous records of climbs from 1963 onwards in a database that covered 9,600 expedition teams. To ensure the records were accurate she drove around Kathmandu interrogating people who claimed to have reached the summit.

Actress Dorothy Barrett, 101: She proudly boasted of being in three of the biggest Hollywood movies of 1939: *The Wizard of Oz*, *Gone with the Wind* and *The Women*.

However, her roles could hardly be described as memorable. In two of the films she was uncredited, and in the third she played a mannequin.

Inventor Trevor Baylis, 80: Famous for creating the wind-up radio, he was much less famous for inventing electric shoes, which he used to walk 100 miles across the Namib Desert. He is also credited with inventing over 200 devices for the disabled, including the one-handed tin opener and the foot-operated scissors.

'The Grand Dame of Cowboy Poetry', Elizabeth Ebert, 93: She wrote poetry in secret until she was in her sixties, and is recognised for opening up the field of cowboy poetry to women. In 2012 she was the first recipient of the Badger, an award for excellence in cowboy poetry. Her method of writing was to start with a rhyme; 'then you have to fill in all this other garbage,' she said.

Political prankster Dick Tuck, 94: Dick Tuck was a political operative and taunter of Richard Nixon. When Nixon was renominated as vice president, for instance, Tuck arranged for rubbish trucks to drive past him and his supporters bearing huge signs that read 'Dump Nixon'. He also used to hire pregnant women to wander around Nixon rallies in T-shirts bearing his campaign slogan: 'Nixon's the One'.

Sumo commentator Doreen Simmons, 85: She was a Nottingham teacher before she became the English voice of sumo, commentating for Japan's national public broadcaster NHK for 25 years. Doreen was also an amateur singer, an amateur adventurer, and an amateur actor whose roles included those of 'soccer hooligan', 'transvestite geisha' and 'dying rhinoceros'.

OLDEST ▶

The world's oldest tree is having a growth spurt.

The standard way to age trees – by taking a sample of wood and checking for growth rings – didn't work for an ancient pine that was discovered this year in Italy, because most of the middle of the tree had turned to dust. So a team from the University of Tuscia instead cross-referenced the information they could gather from the trunk with rings found in the roots to come up with an estimate that the tree is 1,230 years old – around 150 years older than the previous record holder. The newer, outer trunk rings were visible, and wider than expected, so it is believed that the tree is now growing more quickly than before: surprising as the growth of most trees in the Mediterranean is slowing.

In other oldest news:

▶ **Tattoo art:** Discovered on a 5,000-year-old mummy that has been on display in the British Museum for the last hundred years. The tattoo is of a sheep. It was spotted by Daniel Antoine, who is in charge of all the museum's human remains, and is the oldest African tattoo yet found by some 1,000 years.

▶ **Dandruff:** Discovered in China, the 125-million-year-old skin flakes were found on three different species of dinosaur and one early bird, known as *Confuciusornis*. It's the first fossilised dandruff ever found.

▶ **Footprints:** Also discovered in China, they are 540 million years old, and predate the era when experts previously thought feet evolved by 10 million years. Until this find was made, there had been no evidence that limbed animals existed before the Cambrian Explosion (a period on Earth around 510 to 540 million years ago when life suddenly became abundant and diverse). Scientists still don't know which creature made the footprints, but from studying its gait, they believe that whatever it was, it was clumsy.

OLDEST, SECOND

The world's second-oldest banyan tree was put on a drip.

The tree, which grows in the southern state of Telangana, sprawls over 3 acres and is thought to be 700 years old. In order to fight a termite infestation it was dosed with insecticide, but initial attempts to apply it via holes drilled in the bark simply resulted in the liquid leaking out. Scientists therefore gave the tree an intravenous drip. Termites aren't the only problem for the banyan – it is also under threat from tourists who keep bending its ancient branches downwards to use as swings.

Also in India, and even more excitingly, scientists revealed they had discovered the world's second-oldest rock. Estimated to be 4,240 million years old, the rock misses out on being the oldest by a mere 160 million years. Though it was found in Champua, a small town in the state of Odisha, it's worth noting that when the rock came into existence, there was not only no Champua and no Odisha, but also no India, as none of today's continents yet had their current form.

OLYMPICS, WINTER

It was so windy during the Women's Slopestyle Olympic final that every single one of the competitors was blown off her snowboard.

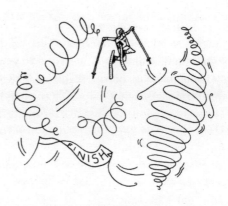

Norway accidentally ordered 15,000 eggs to their hotel instead of the intended 1,500 – enough for 8 eggs a day for every member of the team for the entire tournament.

Slopestyle is a sport in which snowboarders career down a course and perform aerial tricks. It's difficult enough at the best of times, but with 70-kilometre-per-hour gale force winds crossing the piste, the 25 athletes who had spent four years preparing for the event found themselves tossed around, with arms flying and bodies flailing, and landing on their faces as often as they landed on their boards. Norwegian Silje Norendal said, 'All I wanted to do was sit up top and cry' . . . and she was the athlete who finished fourth.

Ecuador, Eritrea, Malaysia, Nigeria, Kosovo and Singapore all took part in the Winter Olympics for the first time, and the Russian Federation was banned for doping, though they were allowed to send clean athletes under a neutral 'Olympic flag'. More than 160 Russians made the journey to South Korea, meaning that despite the ban, they were the third-largest nationality taking part. The largest representation came from the US: in fact they were the largest team in Winter Olympic history with 242 athletes. And it wasn't just athletes: due to increased tensions around the time of the Olympics, America also sent 15 bombers, an aircraft carrier, a cruiser, two destroyers, a nuclear submarine and lots of marines and fighter planes to the Korean Peninsula.

Tensions between the two Koreas were, however, thawing; and so North Korea decided to send some athletes to the Games. Indeed, a joint Korean women's ice hockey team, made up of North and South Korean players, was formed. But they struggled to train for their matches because the South uses English words for most sporting terms, whereas the North has coined special North Korean terms for each manoeuvre. The only North Korean athletes to qualify on merit were figure skaters Ryom Tae-ok and Kim Ju-sik. 'Right now, to be realistic, the goal is to make it into the top 12,' their Canadian coach Bruno Marcotte told reporters. In the event they finished 13th.

OUTDOORS, THE GREAT

The Penn State University Outing Club is no longer allowed to go out.

The 98-year-old club has been told by Penn State University that a recent risk assessment has found their typical activities of organised hiking, walking and backpacking trips to be too risky. And so they will have to conduct all future outdoor adventures indoors.

Only two more of the university's 79 clubs were restricted to indoor activities: the caving club and the scuba diving club. The other 76, which include an archery club, a martial arts club, an alpine skiing club and a rifle club, were told they could carry on as usual.

The outing club decided to fight the university's decision, and in a statement said that support for the club 'is not going anywhere'. Much like the club itself.

OVERWORKED ▶

Russian men are now expected to work longer than they're expected to live.

——— ▼ ———

French MPs have been complaining that since workaholic Emmanuel Macron took power, they're having to work 80-hour weeks and aren't getting weekends off.

On the day that the rest of the country was distracted by Russia's 5–0 World Cup victory over Saudi Arabia, Prime Minister Dmitry Medvedev announced an increase in the pensionable age for men from 60 to 65 and for women from 55 to 63. This means that, according to some estimates of Russian life expectancy, a Russian male born this year is not expected to live to retirement age – the Chukchi indigenous people of North East Russia, for instance, have an estimated life expectancy for men of just 60 years and 4 months.

But at least work–life balance is improving – in one or two countries, anyway. South Korea, for example, made it illegal for people to have to work more than 52 hours a week (the previous maximum was 68 hours). The hope is that less work will mean more babies for a country whose birth rate has been falling in recent years. Less dramatically, a law passed in Israel cut the working week from 43 hours to 42 hours; and less dramatically still, Irish civil servants demanded a 27-minute decrease to their working week.

In similar vein, Japan brought in a new law aimed at reducing *karoshi*, or 'death from overwork'. Overtime is now capped at 45 hours per month and 360 hours per year, with bosses who ignore the law facing six months in prison. Among those who must be relieved by this reform is a Buddhist monk who felt so overworked

by his temple that he decided to sue them. He claimed
that he had become depressed after being forced to
perform his duties for up to 64 days in a row without
a day off.

OXBRIDGE

For the magazine that attracted terrorists, *see* **ISIS**;
and for a more attractive life choice, *see* **Love Island**.

In which we learn . . .
Whose pants were on fire, where to go to find MILFs,
what the hell the Pope was thinking, how dog poo can
light up your life, and why IKEA is taking the piss.

PAKISTAN ▶

*The second sportsperson to become a head of
state was inaugurated in front of the 1992 Pakistan
cricket team.*

Imran Khan became prime minister of Pakistan in
August, having been narrowly beaten to the honour of
being the world's first sporting leader by George Weah
(*see* **Liberia**). But while the Liberian inauguration was
extremely lavish, Khan made do with a relatively small
ceremony at which just a few hundred officials were
present, along with many of Khan's teammates from the
1992 Cricket World Cup. Pakistan won that event, and
Khan, who was the captain, became a national hero.

The modest inauguration was indicative of Khan's new
image as a serious, religiously devout nationalist, and
apparently reformed character, far removed from his
past as a notorious womaniser in 1980s London. This
year, he married his spiritual advisor, Bushra Maneka,
who is never seen without a full veil (indeed Khan
did not see his new wife's face until after they were
married).

As well as religion, Khan's party, the Pakistan Tehreek-
e-Insaf (PTI), embraced technology. They created a
phone app which proved especially useful in getting
supporters to the polls. When the government's own
telephone information service crashed, failing to give
out polling place locations on election day, the PTI
were alone in being able to mobilise the troops.

The election was not without controversy. Opposition
parties claimed the results were rigged, and when,
during hustings, Khan called the supporters of his
opponent Nawaz Sharif 'donkeys', an animal charity
reported that Khan's followers had beaten a donkey
to death. And the BBC were forced to apologise when

———— ▼ ————

Imran Khan's dogs
were given their own
Wikipedia page after
his victory. Their names
translate as 'Lion',
'Lioness', 'Fatty', 'Tiny'
and 'Largest'.

Newsnight managed to show a photo of the wrong cricketer, Khan's former teammate Wasim Akram, during a report on the election. Akram was probably not too worried: he's a big supporter of Khan and was one of the first to congratulate his former cricket captain when he won the presidency.

PANTS ▶

The president of the Czech Republic set his pants on fire.

President Miloš Zeman held a press conference during which he set light to a giant pair of red underpants in front of the assembled journalists. The pants were the same ones that a group of artists had installed on Zeman's palace flagpole in 2015 in protest against him. Quite why the president burned them is not clear. One radio station said it was a metaphor for ending 'the era of dirty laundry in politics'. Another theory is that, since the pants have become a symbol of opposition to Zeman, burning them was meant to make people forget about the 2015 stunt (in which case, it definitely didn't work).

Or perhaps the 73-year-old Zeman was just celebrating his re-election in January, which he achieved despite widespread worries about his health: he's a chain-smoker, and in 2013 boasted he drinks six glasses of wine a day (plus plum brandy on top). His victory came thanks to an anti-immigration platform: Zeman is a pro-Putin right-winger who calls himself 'the Czech Trump'. As the pants burned, he said, 'The time for underwear in politics is over,' and told reporters, 'I'm sorry to make you look like little idiots.'

Pants also made the headlines in Uruguay, where the racing driver Lucas di Grassi was fined €10,000 by the FIA and given three penalty points for not wearing the correct fireproof underpants. Stewards decided that they were too short. Di Grassi had chosen them because the Uruguayan heat had made all his other pants uncomfortable. Later in the year, two more drivers were fined for similar pants-based infractions.

PASSPORTS

Britain's post-EU passports will be made in the EU.

Franco-Dutch company Gemalto won the contract to make Britain's new blue passports that will come into effect after the country leaves the European bloc. It beat the British (although oddly un-British-sounding) firm De La Rue, which manufactures them at the moment. In a rare good deal for Britain, the documents will be £120 million cheaper than if they were made in the UK.

The colour might not be the only upcoming change to passports. Fourteen years after we were all told not to smile in passport photos, research published in the *British Journal of Psychology* found that smiling actually decreases the chances of identity fraud. Apparently people can more easily match one photo to a different

In Taiwan, 200,000 passports had to be destroyed after someone on Facebook noticed they featured an image of Washington Dulles International Airport in the USA instead of Taiwan's own Taoyuan International.

photo of the same person if they're smiling, and we can more easily tell two different people apart in pictures if they're both smiling.

PHILIPPINES

The MILFs found a new home.

Long an enemy of the government of the Philippines, the Moro Islamic Liberation Front, or MILF, has found favour with President Rodrigo Duterte since it started to take on ISIS in recent years. As a result, a new law called the Bangsamoro Basic Law has been passed to give the Islamic group their own self-governing area of the country.

While the MILFs were allowed into one part of the country, foreign tourists were banned from another. The island of Boracay is home to some of the world's most beautiful beaches, but as over 85 per cent of the island's businesses and properties have no proper way of dealing with sewage, and dump it straight into the sea, it has become, in Duterte's view, a 'cesspool'. The president therefore ruled that no tourists should be allowed there for six months, while improvements were carried out (a decision that temporarily put 30,000 people out of a job). It wasn't just tourists that Duterte decided he wanted to keep away. He also said that if UN investigators came to the Philippines to investigate his war on drugs, he would feed them to the crocodiles.

A 58-year-old Filipino man who has been nailed to a crucifix every Easter for the past 32 years, as part of a small village re-enactment of Jesus Christ's crucifixion, says he no longer feels any pain from the wounds. 'In the past, I went home injured and limping, but this year I feel so great,' he said.

PINEAPPLES

For a pineapple ring, *see* **Smuggling**; and for Pineapple's ring, *see* **Valentine's Day**.

PLASTIC ▶

Chepstow celebrated becoming 'plastic-free' by unveiling a massive banner made of plastic.

A former mayor of the Welsh town described it as being 'beyond irony' and said the council should remove it. Others argued that the banner was justified because 'plastic-free' referred to single-use plastic, not all plastic – though it's hard to see how a huge banner reading 'PLASTIC FREE CHEPSTOW' could have a second use. Chepstow residents weren't the only ones adding to plastic pollution: the Pope's elite personal army, the Swiss Guard, traded in their metal helmets for 3D-printed plastic ones on the grounds that they're cheaper, lighter and cooler (temperature-wise, not style-wise).

Gary Barlow was criticised for using plastic confetti during an eco-friendly concert at the Eden Project in Cornwall.

Laws that clamp down on plastic use are certainly working – thanks to the charge now levied on plastic bags, for example, the number pulled from British seas has halved since 2010. Volunteers in India removed 12,000 tons of plastic from a beach, in no small part thanks to diggers donated by Bollywood stars; scientists at Swansea University worked out how to make face washes using leftover whelk shells in place of plastic microbeads; and even the Queen got involved, banning plastic straws and bottles from all royal estates after talking to David Attenborough. And in further good news, scientists accidentally created a mutant enzyme that eats plastic, which they hope will reduce plastic levels in the environment in future.

But it's still a big problem, illustrated by the discovery by divers of a plastic bag 11,000 metres underwater, at the bottom of the Mariana Trench. As for the famous Great Pacific Garbage Patch, 99.9 per cent of which is made of plastic, this has now been found to be 16 times larger than previously thought, though in terms of mass, researchers note, most of it is discarded fishing equipment.

POO, DOG

A small corner of Britain is now dog-poo-powered.

Australian Labor MP Emma Husar took personal leave after being caught making her staff perform tasks that were deemed inappropriate, such as clearing up her dog's poo.

Inventor and gas-lamp enthusiast Brian Harper was so annoyed at finding dog poo bags left around his home in the Malvern Hills that he spent three years creating a device that could both deal with the problem and light the road. Now, dog walkers can drop their dog poo into a machine at the street light's base and turn a handle to move it into a biodigester. Over the course of a few days biogas is produced which is stored and then burned when the lamp switches on at dusk. Ten bags of dog poo can light the lamp for two hours.

Harper is developing more lamps, but it's unclear whether his invention will catch on. The residents of nearby Frome recently had the chance to invest in a dog-poo-powered light, but (understandably) voted to spend the money on a town orchard instead.

In Cambridgeshire, a woman in Wimblington set up Doodoowatch, a scheme whereby residents can map all the locations where dog poo has been found and publish their findings with smiley poo emojis, in the hope of shaming people into picking up after their dogs. Over 60 local councils promptly requested information on how to set up their own poo programmes. And in Cornwall, a mysterious poo vigilante started planting little Union Jacks in piles of dog poo in the town of Lostwithiel. One local paper reported that it might be 'a Cornish nationalist "happening"', 'an ironic comment on Brexit Britain' – or possibly just someone trying to draw attention to the problem.

POPE, THE ▶

The Pope denied the existence of hell, only for the Vatican to deny he'd denied it.

According to Eugenio Scalfari, the 93-year-old journalist who interviewed him, the Pope said that the souls of the unrepentant 'disappear' rather than go to a lake of fire and that 'a "hell" does not exist: what exists is the disappearance of sinful souls'. The Vatican quickly corrected the alleged statement, because if that is what he said, it would have made him a heretic. The journalist must have misheard him, the Vatican added, pointing out that he didn't take any notes. The Pope is very much on record for his belief in hell. In the past, he's preached about it, threatened gangsters with it, and explained it to a Girl Scout.

This isn't the first time Scalfari has got the Pope in trouble. On four previous occasions the Vatican's press office has had to issue a press release denying a comment attributed to His Holiness by the journalist. In 2014 he reported that Pope Francis considered celibacy in the Church a 'problem' and that he had said, 'There are solutions and I will find them.'

Pope Francis faced much more serious problems during his trip to Ireland in August, the first papal visit to the

———— ▼ ————

At a meeting with Italian astronauts, Francis was given an official International Space Station suit. It has his name embroidered on it, as well as the Argentinian flag. Also, as he is pope, it comes with a cape.

country for 40 years. He visited survivors of child abuse inflicted by Catholic officials, and begged forgiveness on behalf of members of the hierarchy who had failed to deal with the problem. The controversy led to a much smaller attendance at his mass in Dublin's Phoenix Park than expected: as many as a million had been antici-pated, but only 130,000 turned up. Those who did wish to celebrate His Holiness's visit, though, were certainly well-catered for: retailers sold Pope-themed keyrings, fridge magnets and bags for life, as well as a cardboard chair adorned with Francis's face, and even papal candy dubbed 'lollipopes'.

POST ▶

A postman admitted hoarding 17,000 pieces of mail, but said he'd only done it so he could focus on delivering the important ones.

The New York postie had been employed to deliver mail for 16 years, and had been failing to do so for at least 13. He said he'd been so overwhelmed by the amount of post he had to deal with that he had stockpiled most of it in his home and car, but he also insisted he made sure the important packages always reached their destination.

He wasn't the year's only mail chauvinist. Italian police arrested a man after finding the largest haul of undelivered mail ever – 570 kilograms of post dating back to 2010 stashed in his garage. The Vicenza postal service said they'd make sure it all got delivered now, even if it's eight years late. Almost exactly the same thing happened again in Italy a few months later, when 400 kilograms of mail dating back three years was found in a man's house in Turin. This particular indi-vidual said he'd stopped delivering any post because he wasn't being paid enough. And a postman in Scotland was found guilty of stealing dozens of greetings cards in case they contained money. He was caught after two fake birthday cards were put in the system by suspicious bosses and then tracked.

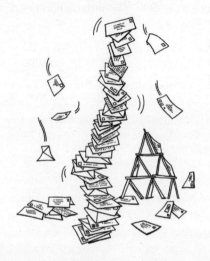

One Chicago mail thief was more ingenious, successfully changing the corporate address of the shipping company UPS to the address of his own apartment. When he was caught, investigators found more than 3,000 items of mail at his home as well as UPS cheque deposits totalling $58,000.

PRANKS

Boris Johnson, Donald Trump and the president of the European Commission were all victims of prank calls.

The first to be caught was Boris Johnson, who spent 18 minutes discussing international relations with a Russian caller pretending to be the new Armenian prime minister, Nikol Pashinyan. He managed to convince

Johnson to talk about the Novichok attack, Russian oligarchs and his own poetry (specifically, a poem he wrote in 2016 about the Turkish president having sex with a goat), before the foreign secretary became suspicious. Nonetheless, the callers described Johnson as seeming like 'a smart diplomat, an intellect' on the phone.

Later in the year, the two men behind the hoax, Vladimir 'Vovan' Kuznetsov and Alexei 'Lexus' Stolyarov, set their sights on the other side of the Brexit divide, pranking EU chief Jean-Claude Juncker. Again pretending to be Pashinyan, the pranksters managed to get Juncker to admit that Vladimir Putin was 'a personal friend'.*

Kuznetsov and Stolyarov have a long history of pranking, and once convinced Elton John he was speaking to President Putin. When the incident became public the real Putin called Elton, but struggled to get through because staff were convinced it was another trick.

Speaking of personal friends of Putin, Donald Trump also fell victim to a prank call – in his case, from comedian and podcaster John Melendez. In a call to Trump on Air Force One, Melendez, better known as 'Stuttering John', posed as Senator Bob Menendez, and proceeded to discuss the president's pick for the Supreme Court. He could easily have been caught out, though: 'All they had to ask me is what party affiliation is Senator Menendez, or what state is he a senator of, and I would not have known. But they didn't ask me any of this,' Melendez later said.

PREGNANCY

IKEA encouraged women to urinate on their adverts.

The company published an ad in the Swedish magazine *Amelia* that featured a pregnancy test strip. If the reader urinated on it and it detected she was pregnant, it would reveal a discount code that would get her 50 per cent off a cot. Reassuringly, the advertising company responsible stressed that expectant mothers wouldn't have to bring the wee-soaked voucher with them to the shop.

Those looking for a cot bargain in Sweden might also want to consider upping their consumption of seafood. According to one study, couples who eat seafood more than twice a week have more sex and are more likely to conceive during intercourse. Meanwhile, another team of scientists discovered that pregnancy temporarily lowers women's voices. Pregnant women's and new mothers' voices are an average of two semitones lower, and are also more monotonous. It's a process known as 'vocal masculinising'. The effects only last for a year before normal pitch is resumed.

In Japan, some expectant mothers had to apologise to their bosses for not adhering to pregnancy timetables. Apparently, in order to avoid too many of their female employees taking maternity leave at the same time, some Japanese companies have schedules that set out when they are allowed to give birth. One 26-year-old was told she'd have to wait 10 years for her turn.

In which we learn . . .
What you can't write about the Queen's bra size,
what you can't write in the Queensland skies,
and 28 years of quiche-based lies.

QATAR

*Saudi Arabia announced plans to cut off Qatar. Literally.
By digging a big trench.*

Qatar is a tiny nation in the Arabian Gulf. Its only land border is a 65-kilometre one with Saudi Arabia. But in 2017 the Saudis alleged Qatar was funding terrorism, and decided (along with Egypt, Bahrain and the UAE) to cut the country off completely. They did so by blockading land, sea and air routes, cancelling trade agreements, and kicking out any Qataris living in Saudi Arabia, along with their herds of camels (as reported in *The Book of the Year 2017*).

Relations haven't got any easier. When the Arab League assembled late last year, Saudi and Qatari diplomats furiously accused each other of treachery and cruelty to camels, and called each other hurtful things like 'rabid dog'.

The restrictions haven't bothered Qatar much yet – the country has set up an entire dairy industry in a year, and recently announced a $200 billion spending programme – but things might get worse soon. Saudi Arabian media reported that the Saudi government is

In the few months after the opening of the new Qatari Children's National Library, every one of its 150,000 books was borrowed at least once.

planning to dig a 200-metre-wide ditch across the entire 65-kilometre land border, effectively turning the whole of Qatar into an island without its consent.

Some have said this is just psychological warfare on the part of the Saudis, but although the Saudi government have not commented on the plan, reports have emerged that five companies which specialise in digging canals have been invited to bid for the project. It has also been reported that the channel will be multifunctional, with different parts of it holding a military base, a nuclear waste dumping site and a number of beach resorts.

QAZAQSTAN ▶

Kazakhstan's alphabet gained six new letters, then lost them again five months later.

After President Nursultan Nazarbayev switched his country's alphabet from Cyrillic to Latin and determined that Kazakhstan would be spelled Qazaqstan (as reported in *The Book of the Year 2017*), he swiftly encountered problems with other words, as many sounds in the Kazakh language can't be accurately written in the Latin alphabet. His solution was to represent these sounds with apostrophes. This went down extremely badly with his fellow countrymen. People on all sides protested that sentences would be littered with apostrophes – something, they argued, that would not only be ugly but inconvenient, as it takes extra time to type them.

Nazarbayev bowed to the pressure and changed the alphabet again, replacing apostrophes with accents. So, having been introduced in October 2017, the letters a', g', n', o', u' and y' were abandoned the following February. Most welcomed this, although some

----- ▼ -----

In this year's national 'Miss Virtual Kazakhstan' beauty contest, which involves people voting on pictures posted online, one finalist, crowned 'Miss Virtual Shymkent' (capital of the South Kazakhstan Region), was immediately disqualified when it turned out that 'she' was a man.

sign-makers complained that they'd have to scrap their newly made, apostrophe-laden signposts.

To prioritise his native language, Nazarbayev also tried to ban members of parliament from speaking Russian. Debates usually alternate between the two, depending on which one an individual MP speaks best. The president changed his mind within a week, possibly because many members of his parliament (along with more than a third of the population) aren't fluent in Kazakh.

QUAKERS ▶

Nottingham's Quakers released a podcast consisting of 30 minutes of silence.

The Society of Friends, also known as the Quakers, is a Christian denomination famous for having meetings where nobody says anything unless God inspires them to. So, in order to get people interested in their form of worship, Nottingham's Quakers released a podcast of a completely silent meeting. The 30-minute episode opened with a brief introduction, followed by almost no noise at all, apart from the ambient sounds of a clock ticking, some book pages turning, and rain. According to its online credits, a host, an audio editor and a script editor were involved in putting the podcast together.

The host, Jessica Hubbard-Bailey, said the podcast had piqued interest, although she also admitted that 'We've also had some people saying, "Oh, I'm not sure about this, seems like a bit of a waste of time." ' The episode got over 1,000 listens – which, said Hubbard-Bailey, 'makes it the biggest Quaker meeting this year technically'. At the time of writing, it had received no comments.

QUEEN, THE

The Queen changed her bra manufacturer after A Storm in a D-Cup.

◆

It has been revealed this year that the Queen's cows sleep on water-beds, and are milked by robots. Some of the cows can trace their bloodline back to the time of Queen Victoria.

Rigby & Peller lost their royal warrant after their owner, June Kenton, published *A Storm in a D-Cup*, a 'tell-all' memoir that included details about the Queen's bust. It was actually quite tame stuff, simply revealing that the Queen would discuss the weather as she was being measured, and that she would be 'half-dressed' at the time – which is surely a prerequisite for having your bra fitted – but it was enough for Kenton to receive a letter saying that the warrant originally granted in 1960 had been cancelled.

Another company that lost its official status as supplier to the Queen this year was shoemakers Anello & Davide. They were not too worried as they hadn't had an order from the Queen for five years. 'I think the Queen has got to a point in her life when she doesn't need any more shoes,' said their chief executive.

Rigby & Peller still make bras for Theresa May and Kim Kardashian, and have a robotic breast measurer which, according to reports, 'is able to scan a woman's physique to calculate her perfect bra size – without the need of a stylist'. It also has the advantage of not being able to write memoirs.

QUEENSLAND

Queensland's weather forecasters were asked to stop reporting bad weather.

It's discouraging day-trippers, argued the chief executive of the tourism board, Daniel Gschwind, who added: 'Rain in Queensland doesn't have the same implications as the Northern Hemisphere. I don't think it should be framed in a bad way.' He asked forecasters to change 'partly cloudy' and 'chance of rain' to 'mostly sunny' and 'likely sunshine', and requested that instead of 'showers', could they say 'cooling down rain' instead?

Queensland's sex workers have also fallen foul of the vocabulary police. Recent legislation put in place by the Queensland government's Prostitution Licensing Authority strictly limits the ways in which prostitutes can advertise themselves, banning, for example, all references to bodily fluids and unsafe sex. In addition, the words 'natural', 'tasty', 'sweet nectar' and 'Mistress Squirt A Lot' are explicitly forbidden, and false advertising has been outlawed, so a 'Spanish Beauty' is not allowed to promote herself as one unless she is definitely Spanish. The law does list words that are fine to use, including 'magic hands,' 'dominatrix' and 'exotic relaxation'. A further stipulation is that prostitutes are not allowed to use skywriting aeroplanes to advertise their services. The new rules were not popular: on 2 June – International Sex Workers' Day – protesters took to the streets to voice their opposition.

Queensland Health released a list that detailed the number of times that people had visited emergency rooms for non-emergencies: it included 13 people who had hiccups, 2,098 people who had a splinter, and two people who were suffering from nightmares.

QUEUING ▶

Amazon opened a new shop that promised to eliminate queues. On its first day, hundreds of people queued to get in.

The store, Amazon Go, which opened its first outlet in Seattle in January, charges customers automatically if they take items away. This, of course, removes the need for checkouts – as the company advertised, you 'never have to wait in line' once you are inside. Ironically, on launch day, hundreds queued up outside to get in and see what all the fuss was about. That wasn't the only hiccup: one journalist who visited in order to write a review realised she'd accidentally stolen from the shop as it had failed to charge her for an item she'd picked up.

Over in Europe, Geneva tried to teach its citizens to improve their queuing skills by encouraging them to follow the British example. It did this by employing actors to dress up as typical Brits and stand politely at bus and tram stops as living embodiments of the perfect queue. The 'quintessential' Brits included a man in a top hat and bow tie, another dressed as a Coldstream Guard, complete with bearskin hat, and a woman dressed as the Queen. Anyone who followed their example and queued properly was rewarded with After Eights.

The British fondness for queuing was exemplified in March when the Royal Mint released a coin dedicated to it. The 'Great British Coin Hunt' range comprised one for each letter of the alphabet, with Q devoted to Queueing. Others included E for English Breakfast, T for Teapots, L for Loch Ness Monster, and X for 'X Marks the Spot'.

The Home Office did look into giving Brits their own queue in UK airports after Brexit, so they could enjoy the 'visible demonstration to the public that we have left the EU'. The plan was cancelled when the government realised it would be too expensive, and that the British queues would actually be the slowest ones.

QUICHE

'Real men' began eating quiche.

Quiche replaced pork pies in the 'nation's shopping basket', a list of commonly bought products compiled by the Office for National Statistics to monitor inflation in the UK. To reflect Britain's changing buying habits, Edam cheese and 'bottles of lager in nightclubs' were also ditched in favour of items such as gym leggings and GoPros. According to the supermarket chain Waitrose, quiche is enjoying something of a revival. It became especially popular during the summer heatwave, with sales increasing by 11 per cent as more people opted to dine al fresco. This reverses a decline that began in the 1980s, with the publication of the popular book *Real Men Don't Eat Quiche*.

QUOKKAS

Davey the psychic quokka made some (quite bad) World Cup predictions.

Davey decided that Australia would top their group, ahead of France, Peru and Denmark. It was an optimistic call by the marsupial, and it started to look distinctly unlikely when, in their first game, Australia lost to France. By the third group match, Australia no longer stood a chance.

Psychic animals had a bad tournament in general. Mystic Marcus, a pig from Derbyshire, wrongly chose Argentina, Belgium, Nigeria and Uruguay as

———— ▼ ————

One successful psychic animal was Rabiot the psychic octopus, who managed to predict all of Japan's games correctly. As a reward he was chopped up and sold as food.

*As well as prestige,
airlines are battling
to save weight, and
therefore fuel – United
Airlines announced
that they'll save 643,000
litres of fuel a year
with their new plan:
switching to lighter
paper on their in-flight
magazine.

the semi-finalists; while Olivia the parrot from Japan predicted that her home country would lose their first game against Colombia which, against the odds, they won. Olivia must have been as sick as herself.

Davey the quokka is quite the celebrity in Australia. This year, he visited a new aeroplane named after his species, which then went on to beat the record for the fastest flight from Australia to London, making the trip in just 16 hours 35 minutes.*

In which we learn . . .
Who brought shaman the fashion world, how a
plastic bottle was re-re-re-re-re-re . . . re-cycled,
which orgy was a complete flop, why rhinos'
reproduction is totally screwed, and who sacked
a robot for being absolutely rubbish.

RAIN

Louis Vuitton tried to guarantee good weather at a fashion show by hiring a shaman.

━━━━━ ▼ ━━━━━

In Russia, a fire and rescue aircraft designed to drop water to put out forest fires missed its target during a practice session and instead 40 tons of water hit an undercover traffic cop who was trying to catch speeding motorists.

Vogue magazine reported that the Brazilian 'weather guru', who was hired to keep the rain off a show in the south of France, 'flies private only, sends information back to his fellow shaman wife in Brazil and together they command the winds'. Louis Vuitton declined to provide details, but several fashion websites reported that the shaman was briefly sacked, until, with a few days to go until their own show, a sudden rainstorm soaked an outdoor event near Paris – at which point he was hastily rehired. On the day at Saint-Paul de Vence, there were clouds overhead, but no rain, clearly proving he was earning his money.

The shaman had better hope he's not hired to work in Tibet. This year Chinese scientists announced plans to manufacture 10 billion tons of extra rain a year and drop it on the region. Five hundred fuel-burning 'rainmakers' have so far been installed, producing puffs of vapour and giving off exhaust laced with a chemical called silver iodide. This drifts into the atmosphere, mixes with clouds and helps vapour crystallise into droplets of rain. It's still awaiting final approval, but if signed off, Project Tianhe, or 'Sky River', will involve the building of tens of thousands of the burners to irrigate 1.6 million square kilometres of a plateau that is three times the size of Spain and currently one of the driest places on earth. It's the largest ever attempt to artificially alter the weather. It is also very controversial: if you make it rain over your country, it follows that you'll be robbing your neighbours of rain that would otherwise have fallen on them.

226

REBRANDING ▶

Swaziland changed its name to avoid confusion with Switzerland.

Due to its mountainous terrain, for many years Swaziland branded itself 'the Switzerland of Africa'. This year, however, King Mswati III decided that it was time to distance his country from the European one and he therefore renamed Swaziland 'eSwatini', which means 'home of the Swazi people'. Many worried that the rebrand would cost a fortune for what is a relatively poor country, but the official response was that people should not worry as the government would use up any 'Swaziland'-headed stationery before any new eSwatini letterheads were ordered.

In other rebranding news:

▶ Restaurants in the Houses of Parliament began calling the dessert spotted dick 'Spotted Richard'.

▶ Heinz decided to rename its salad cream 'sandwich cream' on the grounds that it's hardly ever used on salad.

▶ And the Jamaican bobsleigh team at PyeongChang rebranded itself to try to get away from the negative connotations of the 1993 Disney film *Cool Runnings*. Stuart Lang from the branding company WeLaunch explained: 'Whilst the movie was a great vehicle for allowing the world to know that there was, in fact, a Jamaican Bobsleigh Team, it was a comedy – and has meant that nobody outside the two sports [bobsleigh and skeleton] has taken the organisation seriously ever since.'

Records, Broken

This year, the following records were broken:

Fastest shed: A motorised shed broke its own record for the fastest land speed achieved by a shed, hitting 100 mph on a beach in Wales. The owner, a gardener, has spent £13,000 fitting it with a 400-brake-horsepower engine. It had previously broken a record at 80 mph, but had then blown up.

Most LEGO bricks trodden: In Virginia, Russell Cassevah walked barefoot along 120 feet of loose LEGO bricks to raise money for a charity that buys LEGO for children. There was a podiatrist on hand to inspect his feet (and his feat).

Fastest swimmer aged 100-104: George Corones, an Australian who turned 100 in April, swam 50 metres in 56.12 seconds – beating the previous record by 35 seconds. Corones gave up swimming when the Second World War broke out and only took it up again at the age of 80.

Fastest drive from John o' Groats to Land's End: The previous record was broken by Tommy Davies, who drove at an average of 90 mph, yet managed to avoid getting any speeding tickets. The head of the AA called him irresponsible and said he should be prosecuted.

Largest yoga lesson: In India, a lesson taught by yogi Baba Ramdev was attended by at least 105,000 students. Over 4,500 people were required just to adjudicate the record attempt.

Records, Unbroken

Not everyone trying to break a record achieved what they wanted, of course:

Failure #1: *Not the largest chihuahua gathering.* Cornwall tried to beat the record for most chihuahuas in a single place (270). Unfortunately, they could only gather 257. The organisers had been banned from holding the event in the town they wanted, due to a dachshund record attempt earlier this year, which left the whole town smelling of wee.

Failure #2: *Not quite the world's biggest oyster.* The oyster, named Jack, weighs more than 2 kilos, but at the Narooma Oyster Festival in Australia, Guinness World Records judged him 'too short' to be the champion. His human handler, Bernie Connell, said he was the heaviest, widest and deepest oyster, and that he deserved to have won.

Failure #3: *Not the biggest orgy in history.* Only 375 people took part in an orgy at the Sin City 8 adult weekend party in Las Vegas. This fell woefully short of the (unofficial) 2006 record in Japan, which involved 500 people. The organisers plan to try again next year. Guinness World Records have made it clear that they will not be officiating.

Failure #4: *Not quite the most dominoes.* After a team spent two weeks setting up 596,000 miniature dominoes in a gym in Germany, the huge chain was set off too early. The cause was a fly landing on one of the pieces.

RECYCLING

A man was accused of recycling the same bottle up to 4.8 million times.

Germany runs a scheme whereby if you insert a used bottle into a recycling machine, the machine shreds it and pays out 25 cents. The defendant, Artur K, allegedly dismantled the shredding mechanism in two machines, so that he could feed in bottles over and over again. He made €1.2 million, a sum that would have involved scanning a single bottle almost 5 million times. It's understood that he and the criminal gang he operated with mechanised the process, rather than inserting and retrieving a bottle by hand and thus ending up with extremely sore arms.

Bottles and cans, along with cardboard, plastics and textiles, that are put in recycling bins in Europe very often ended up in China, the world's leading importer of waste. About 15 per cent of the EU's paper recycling alone used to be sent there, and the country processed more than half the world's plastic rubbish. All this changed on 1 January when China banned the import of 24 different types of waste, causing it to accumulate across Europe. Scientists predict that by 2030, 111 million tonnes of plastic will have piled up, unprocessed, around the world. China's aim is to clean up their own country, and force others to deal efficiently with their own rubbish. It has been publicised as a campaign against 'foreign garbage'. In actual fact, the initial consequences were not especially positive, as the rubbish was often rerouted to neighbouring countries, which lack the infrastructure to deal with it.

Spanish football team Real Madrid unveiled their new football kit in August. It's made entirely from plastics retrieved from the world's beaches, and the shirt is coral-coloured to remind people of the plight of the world's oceans.

REFUGEES ▶

Rohingya refugees in Bangladesh built Ferris wheels for their children.

Many of the Rohingya people who fled persecution in Burma in 2017 ended up on the Bangladesh border at what became the world's largest refugee camp. Adding to the hardship of day-to-day life as a refugee, extreme monsoon rains struck the camp in June, causing destructive flooding and mudslides. But during a brief respite from the rain, the British Red Cross saw that at least six hand-operated Ferris wheels had sprung up. They couldn't determine exactly who built them, only that they were clearly made by the community. Children waited in line at each one as adults took turns to wind the hand cranks that spun them around.

Around the same time, Burma signed a deal with the UN whereby it agreed to repatriate the 700,000 Rohingya who had fled the country the previous year. Aung San Suu Kyi, de facto prime minister of Burma, said in an interview that this proved her government had fulfilled its duties towards the displaced population, and offered the text of the agreement as proof. However, since the wording of the agreement was kept secret from all but the Burmese and UN signatories, it was impossible for the Rohingya to be sure their safety would be guaranteed if they returned, hence the reason why a compound built to receive 4,800 of them back into the country remained empty. When journalists visited the camp, a refugee shouted through the fence on the other side of the border, 'We think it is not yet safe.'

Syrian refugees in Jordan also struggled against the odds to build livelihoods. Action Against Hunger paid them to collect rubbish from the streets and upcycle it into usable objects, such as handbags, lampshades, bowls and even tables. Other Syrian refugees in Jordan

▼

Figures from the UN Refugee Agency showed that just three countries – Turkey, Bangladesh and Uganda – take in more than half the world's refugees.

were busy buying groceries with their eyeballs. Experimenting with cutting-edge blockchain technology, the World Food Programme (WFP) compiled a database that will eventually contain the details of half a million people which it will then upload into scanners at the camp supermarket. Once in the system, refugees don't need any form of ID: they simply pick up supplies, and get their irises scanned on the way out.

RHINO, NORTHERN WHITE

The world lost its final male northern white rhino.

Sudan (1973–2018), who was suffering from lesions and bedsores and had lost the use of his back legs, was finally put down in his enclosure at Ole Pejeta Conservancy in Kenya. He was not the last of his species, but because the remaining two rhinos are female we have lost perhaps the most social of the world's large land mammals, barring a miracle that would make *Jurassic World* look like a school science experiment.

Zoologists did extract semen from Sudan before he died, but even putting aside the fact that one of the remaining females is Sudan's daughter and the other is his granddaughter, a viable birth seems incredibly unlikely. Both females are virtually infertile and must be chemically stimulated to ovulate, and even if eggs were available, it is practically impossible to get at them due to the rhinos' infirmity and their awkward, corkscrew-shaped vaginas. As a result, nobody has even come close to producing an embryo of a northern white rhino that might grow into a viable foetus.

So things don't look promising for the long-term survival of the northern white rhino. But there is one possible means of salvation. The rhino's sister subspecies, the southern white rhino, is not endangered, and so if the technological barriers can be overcome, healthy eggs could be taken from one of those animals and fertilised with Sudan's sperm. The resulting baby wouldn't be 100 per cent a northern white rhino, but experts say it would, at least, be better than no northern white rhino at all.

ROBOTS

Britain's first robot shop assistant was sacked after a week.

As part of an experiment filmed by the BBC, Fabio, aka 'Shopbot', was installed in the Scottish supermarket Margiotta to greet customers, high-five them and give them directions. But Fabio was useless. He often couldn't hear requests above background noise, and even when he could, he was vague: when asked where the beer was, he just said, 'It's in the alcohol section.' Fabio was demoted to a job offering samples of pulled pork, but customers didn't want to take pork from a robot, and found him so alarming they started to avoid him.

Fabio's sacking will have cheered Las Vegas's casino workers, who voted for a huge strike to protest against automation. One robot they were annoyed about was 'Tipsy Robot', a mechanical arm that mixes drinks at a bar where customers order via tablet computers. The only humans employed at the venue are 'Galactic Ambassadors' – i.e. human waitresses.

Elsewhere in America, a restaurant opened staffed by seven autonomous frying pans. The only humans present add garnish.

In other robot news:

▶ Singapore deployed five robots shaped like swans to measure water quality in reservoirs, in the Smart Water Assessment Network (or SWAN).

▶ Japanese engineers launched the Qoobo, a headless cat robot – or, as they put it, a 'tailed cushion' – designed to keep people company if they want a cat but can't be bothered to look after one.

▶ A Japanese firm started mass-producing a furry robot called the Super Monster Wolf to help farmers protect their crops from wild boar. The Super Monster Wolf has big fangs and flashing red eyes, and howls whenever anything approaches it. It was so successful, manufacturers couldn't keep up with demand.

▶ At the Winter Olympics in South Korea, 85 robots were on hand to clean venues and assist athletes. One fire rescue robot, HUBO, even carried the torch: it drove a car, punched through a wall and then passed the flame to its creator, Oh Jun-ho. The Games also hosted the world's first all-robot skiing competition, and mural-painting robots with 20-metre arms.

ROCKS

The earth contains enough diamonds for everyone in the UK to give an engagement ring to everyone else in the UK.

That would mean each person in Britain would end up with almost 70 million rings – and a lot of explaining to do to their partner. But before anyone gets excited or worried by the prospect, it's worth pointing out that the quadrillion tons of diamonds that were discovered this year are situated kilometres beneath our feet, in the earth's mantle, so we won't be extracting them any time soon. The discovery was made by geologists from the University of California who, while investigating the way earthquakes travel through the planet, found that they were moving faster than anticipated. They concluded that this is only possible if the mantle is made of rocks called peridotite and eclogite with a healthy sprinkling of diamonds.

Geologists also broke new ground in Australia when they found part of North America stuck on to the edge of Queensland. Researchers revealed that the rocks around Georgetown in the north-east of the state are very different to the rest of those found in the area – and very similar to some found in Canada. Their conclusion is that they were left behind when the two continents drifted apart around 1.7 billion years ago.

This was also the year when we officially entered a new geological age. Well, we actually entered it 4,200 years ago, but it was defined for the first time in 2018. The Meghalayan Age is defined by distinct lines that can be seen in rocks that were formed during a huge drought which devastated our ancestors in the Middle East, China and Africa.

———— ♦ ————

In very, very, very exciting news for geologists that barely made a ripple elsewhere, Russian scientists announced a new kind of rock, never seen before on earth. The structure is made of the chemicals vanadium and nitrogen and was found inside a meteor where it was formed in extreme heat, somewhere in the universe. It is known as uakitite.

ROUNDABOUTS ▶

The Norwegian government asked students to please, please stop having sex on roundabouts.

Every spring, Norway's graduating high school students like to party. A lot. Part of their *russefeiring*, or celebrations, involves setting each other ritual challenges, which frequently involve alcohol, nudity and sex. The celebrations often lead to traffic accidents, so this year the head of the Public Roads Administration made a statement headed '*Nei til sex I rundkjøringer*', or 'No to sex on roundabouts'. He also requested that students in Ringsaker should stop running naked across a 1. 4-kilometre-long bridge near the town, saying: 'Drivers can get too much of a surprise and completely forget that they are driving.'

A student representative from Ringsaker formally replied, acknowledging that roundabout sex could be a traffic hazard, agreeing to remove it from the list of challenges to graduates, and stating that they could have a good time without roundabouts anyway.

ROYAL WEDDING ▶

Before their wedding, Prince Harry took Meghan to Herefordshire to be kidnapped by the SAS.

Over the course of two days, Meghan was subjected to mock kidnappings to prepare her for the possibility that she might now be a terrorist target. According to SAS members, such exercises use real ammunition, and are 'devised to frighten the life out of anyone'. Harry's mother, Diana, had to undergo this training, too, when she was engaged to Charles. Unfortunately it didn't go that well for her – a stun grenade pellet set her head on fire.

Safety isn't the only thing Meghan has to say goodbye to now that she is a princess. She has also had to quit her career. Her final acting scene, in her TV series *Suits*, saw her getting married. Another thing she won't be allowed to do any more, according to royal protocol, is sign autographs. No royal is allowed to do that. Which is a shame, as Meghan has very nice handwriting. One of her jobs while she was still a struggling actress in Hollywood was professional calligrapher (she wrote out all the wedding invitations for 'Blurred Lines' singer Robin Thicke).

The wedding was eagerly anticipated in the UK. It also offered an opportunity for purveyors of unofficial memorabilia to cash in. Collectors of tat were offered bottles of Meghan's Windsor Knot Ale; commemorative condoms called Crown Jewels that were 'fit for a prince' and came in a box that played 'God Save the Queen' and 'The Star-Spangled Banner' as you opened it; and there was even commemorative marijuana released by members of Meghan's own family (*see* **Markles, The**).

The wedding itself took place on the 482nd anniversary of Henry VIII's execution of Anne Boleyn. Only one member of Meghan's family was present at the wedding – her mother. Her father had to pull out for health reasons, and because it had been alleged that he had staged paparazzi shots in the lead-up to the big day. Consequently Harry never met Meghan's father before marrying her. In fact, with the exception of her mother, Harry hadn't met any of Meghan's relatives. But at least one member of Harry's family had met one of Meghan's family. Henry VIII knew Meghan's direct ancestor Lord Hussey. He had him beheaded.

———— ▼ ————

The wedding veil worn by Meghan was 5 metres long. It was embroidered with images of plants representing each of the 53 countries of the Commonwealth, and the team making it had to wash their hands every half hour to ensure it stayed clean.

RUGBY ▶

Rugby Union introduced a new 'nipple law'.

World Rugby trialled a new rule in under-20 competitions whereby players were not allowed to tackle above the nipples. Previously an illegal tackle was one that hit above the shoulders. The hope is to reduce the risk of head injuries. Law 9.13 now reads as follows: 'Dangerous tackling includes, but is not limited to, tackling or attempting to tackle an opponent above the nipple line even if the tackle starts below the nipple line.' Coach of the Queensland Reds, Brad Thorn, was one of the most vocal opponents of the new rule: 'Soon it'll be the belly button . . . where's it going to go, where's it going to end?'

RUSSIA ▶

For how to pick up Russian women, *see* **Advice, Worse**; for how to avoid Russian assassination, *see* **Dead, Back from the**; for how to avoid uncovering Russian collusion, *see* **Hacking**; for when blocking backfired, *see* **Messaging, Instant**; for dolphins on hunger strike, *see* **Navies**; for tasteless vodka, *see* **Novichok**; for the team full of Russians that definitely wasn't Russia, *see* **Olympics, Winter**; for working longer and dying younger, *see* **Overworked**; for tricking Boris and duping Juncker, *see* **Pranks**; for Russians who may or may not be in New Zealand, *see* **Spies**; for dopey doping, *see* **Urine Trouble**; and for how to make sure the government gets your drift, *see* **Weather, Severe**.

RUSSIAN ELECTION ▶

Attempts to boost turnout in the Russian presidential election included semi-naked women, a selfie competition and discounts on tinned peas.

There was never any suggestion that Vladimir Putin would be beaten in the election, given his popularity in rural Russia (not to mention the shameless suppression of any realistic opposition). So the main worry for his regime was that nobody would bother voting – the worse the turnout, the less legitimate the government. The Kremlin therefore tried everything it could think of to get people to turn out.

An official print campaign was rolled out featuring semi-naked models posing in polling stations. In one, a woman refuses to sleep with a man unless he has voted. Another was captioned: 'What happens in the polling station, stays in the polling station.' Some districts provided clowns to entertain children while their parents voted. One local authority presented fish, eggs and peas to diligent voters, while another gave away iPhones to those judged to have taken the best polling station selfies.

Reuters did their own snapping in the polling stations, and in the process spotted 17 people who appeared to have voted twice in the election, at different locations. The *Guardian* looked into the matter and found that many of them were state employees. When electoral

———— ▼ ————

The Kremlin unironically accused the US of interfering in the Russian election, saying that sanctions imposed by Donald Trump had been timed to influence public opinion.

officials were asked about this, they said that perhaps those involved were twins, or just people who looked really similar to each other and happened to be wearing the same clothes.

State media (unsurprisingly) didn't talk about the multiple votes scandal. Instead it focused on a bet made between the Communist Party leader, Pavel Grudinin, who was the second-most-popular candidate in the election, and vlogger Yury Dud. Grudinin said that if he got less than 15 per cent of the votes he would shave off his signature Stalin-style moustache. In the event he won only 11.81 per cent of the vote, but nevertheless refused to shave. Eventually he bowed to huge public pressure and shaved off the 'tache. Democracy had triumphed – in this one small way, at least.

RWANDA ▸

Rwanda signed a £30 million sponsorship deal with Arsenal FC.

—— ▼ ——

DIY HIV-testing kits went on sale over the counter in Rwanda. They involve a gum swab, are even more reliable than pregnancy test kits and take 20 minutes to yield results.

The president, Paul Kagame, is an avid Arsenal fan, who tweets his disappointment when they lose and was among those who called for manager Arsène Wenger to resign. The £30 million contract – which is about half the amount Rwanda receives in aid from the UK each year – will pay for players' shirts to be adorned with the slogan 'Visit Rwanda' for three years. Kagame argues his country will make back the money via the tourism that the publicity brings.

The deal prompted a Twitter spat between Dutch and Rwandan MPs – the Netherlands donates tens of millions of euros to Rwanda in aid each year, and they saw the sponsorship deal as wasteful. A Dutch newspaper called for aid money to be withdrawn and a Dutch politician said the deal was outrageous.

The Rwandan state minister responded with a dig
at Dutch football teams, tweeting: 'Dear MPs from
The Netherlands. This is NONE of your business . . .
The day @AFCAjax or @Feyenoord_int get a similar
popularity worldwide like @Arsenal, then we will talk
business!'

In which we learn . . .
How to break a lock, how to use a clock,
what Mr Song managed to block,
and where to send a picture of your . . .

SAINTS

A group of Catholics tried to crowdfund a saint.

John Bradburne was a poet and missionary who was killed by guerrillas while working in a leper colony in what was then Rhodesia in 1979. Since then, his supporters say that he has miraculously cured a man with a brain tumour and that blood has been seen dripping from his coffin. If these events are confirmed by the Church, they would constitute the two miracles required to declare him a saint. The John Bradburne Memorial Society has therefore set up a JustGiving page to raise £20,000 to pay for an inquiry to look into his life and assess the 'miracles'. If the outcome is positive, Bradburne will become the first ever saint whose work mostly took place in Zimbabwe, and the only British saint to have been born since the 16th century.

Bradburne has one possible rival for the latter honour: the author G. K. Chesterton. According to the Bishop of Northampton, Peter John Haworth Doyle, numerous childless couples who have prayed to the writer of the Father Brown detective stories claim to have been blessed with 'miracle children'. However, opponents of this particular beatification have pointed to Chesterton's decidedly unsaintly anti-Semitic views.

A couple of well-established saints also made the headlines this year. In London, a waste company announced that when looking through a bin they'd found a fragment of bone believed to be a small piece of the fourth pope, St Clement of Rome (nobody knows how it got there).* And in Ireland, the heart of St Laurence O'Toole was returned to Christ Church Cathedral, six years after it had been stolen. Police found the relic in a heart-shaped box in the city's Phoenix Park but were unable to locate and arrest the culprit. The Most Reverend Dr Michael Jackson extended his 'deep thanks

*Their suspicions were aroused due to the fact that it was in a small case with the label 'ex oss. S. Clementis', meaning 'former bone of St Clementis'.

243

and warm appreciation' to the police. He passed no comment on the smooth criminal who managed to get away.

SARCOPHAGUS

More than 30,000 people signed a petition asking to be allowed to drink raw sewage.

A month after the sarcophagus was opened, archaeologists in Egypt found the world's oldest known cheese. Internet wags immediately suggested that it could be the perfect accompaniment to a nice glass of sarcophagus juice. Scientists pointed out that it actually contained a bacterium that can cause the deadly disease brucellosis.

When a mysterious black sarcophagus that had lain untouched for more than 2,000 years was discovered in Egypt this year, speculation was rife as to what might be inside. Some thought it might contain the body of Cleopatra, the pharaoh Rameses I, or even Greek leader Alexander the Great; others warned that it might house an ancient curse. When it was eventually opened, it was found to contain three skeletons and a liquid that smelled so foul that archaeologists had to flee the area after lifting the lid just 5 centimetres.

A few days later, a petition was posted on Change.org demanding the right 'to drink the red liquid from the cursed dark sarcophagus in the form of some sort of carbonated energy drink so we can assume its powers and finally die'. It attracted more than 30,000 signatories in less than a month. In fact, as Egypt's secretary-general of the Supreme Council of Antiquities, Dr Mostafa Waziri, pointed out, the mummy-juice was actually 'sewage which leaked through the grove in this area'.

The skeletons were sent to Alexandria's National Restoration Museum for analysis, and initial results suggest they may have been soldiers – one of the skeletons shows evidence that it was hit by an arrow. The elixir of life (or raw sewage, depending how you look at it) was poured away into the street.

SAUDI ARABIA ▶

*Saudi women were finally allowed to drive, despite
fears it would damage their ovaries, reduce the number
of virgins and lead to accidents, since women's brains
are only half the size of men's.*

These were some of the arguments put forward by
Saudi Arabian clerics opposed to the change, which
was spearheaded by Crown Prince Mohammed bin
Salman and implemented by his father, King Salman.
Saudi Arabia had been the only country where it was
illegal for women to drive. On 24 June, the day the law
passed, policemen handed out congratulatory bouquets
of flowers to female drivers, with safety messages
attached. Women were given free parking in many town
centres and shopping malls, and pink parking spaces
advertised as 'women only' appeared around the
country. Aseel Al-Hamad, the first female member of the
Saudi Arabian Motorsport Federation, marked the occasion by driving a supercar around the country's main
racetrack. Despite the fears expressed by clerics, not a
single traffic violation was recorded on the first day.

Celebrations were tempered by the fact that even
after 24 June, eight of the women who'd campaigned
to get the law passed remained in prison, facing long
sentences for previous civil disobedience. And women
in Saudi Arabia still can't travel, obtain passports, get
married or sign contracts without a male guardian's
permission; nor can they enter the men's entrance in
many buildings, eat with men in restaurants, or swim or
wear make-up in public. In fact, it's possible the motives
behind the law were less enlightened than they seemed.
Some argued the main reason the ban was lifted was
that the economy was suffering due to so many men
arriving late to work because they had to drop their
wives off first.

— ▼ —

A fashion show in Saudi
Arabia featured a
catwalk with no models
on it. Instead, Dolce &
Gabbana dresses were
flown down the catwalk
by drones to ensure the
show was 'Ramadan
appropriate'.

— ▼ —

At a Saudi Arabian pop
concert, the terms and
conditions for booking
tickets stipulated that
dancing and 'swaying'
were banned.

As well as driving, women can now run businesses, go jogging and attend football matches. King Salman also made cinema-going legal for them after a 35-year ban. The first film they were allowed to see, screened in a makeshift cinema, was the *Emoji Movie*, which gets 3.2/10 on IMDb and 8 per cent on Rotten Tomatoes and seems like an odd place to start.

SAUSAGES

A Devonshire butcher escaped his freezer by using a sausage as a battering ram.

Chris McCabe got trapped in a room at −20 degrees Celsius when the door of the freezer blew shut behind him and the release mechanism froze solid. To escape, he bashed it with a cylinder of frozen blood sausage, better known as black pudding. He said he'd tried beef and lamb, but found the beef too slippery and the lamb too big to wield.

Across the pond, a man working in a sausage factory in Wisconsin faced jail after he was caught allegedly inserting a cigarette paper and a wire connector into sausages on the production line, only to track them down and remove them later, and claim to bosses that he'd discovered them. His motivation remains unclear.

And research by a German company before the World Cup estimated that nearly 25,000 sausages would be eaten per match, producing a carbon footprint equivalent to the release of more than 3,000 kilograms of carbon dioxide. This in turn would represent a total sausage footprint of about 200,000 kilos of CO_2, requiring 45 football pitches' worth of Amazon rainforest to soak it up.

SCHOOLCHILDREN

Clocks were removed from English school halls because children can no longer tell the time.

The reason for this, according to Malcolm Trobe, deputy general secretary at the Association of School and College Leaders (ASCL), is that because most children only see the time displayed digitally these days, they can't read analogue clocks. And it's not just clocks. Delegates at the National Union of Teachers conference in Brighton were told that nursery school kids are so used to using iPads that when they pick up a library book they show a 'disturbing' tendency to 'swipe left'. Worse still, according to Sally Payne, the head paediatric occupational therapist at the Heart of England NHS Foundation Trust, many children are unable to hold pencils when they first go to school. She blamed touchscreens, suggesting that their overuse results in children's finger muscles not developing enough.

But while British teachers bemoaned new technology, schools in South Korea embraced it, as they did away with outdoor playtime and got children to play virtual sports instead. Owing to the terrible pollution in Seoul, indoor activities are seen as a healthier alternative.

An elementary school in Texas ended the traditional custom of 'birthday spankings'. The gentle spankings will be replaced with high-fives or hugs. There had been a few complaints about the celebrations, even though 'they are of course not actual spankings', according to the school district's superintendent, Randy Brown.

SCOTLAND

For exhausting temperatures, *see* **Heatwaves**; for shepherd vs eagle, *see* **Lasers**; for a surprisingly powerful Scotswoman, *see* **May, Theresa**; for a totally useless shop assistant, *see* **Robots**; for isolated islands, *see* **Shetland**; and for platonic pandas, *see* **Zoos**.

SELF-DRIVING CARS

Tesla worried its self-driving cars might get bullied.

A vessel called SB Met became the first self-driving boat ever to make it across the North Atlantic. More than 20 other boats have attempted the challenge since 2010, but they have either been lost, been picked up by passing ships, or got caught in fishing nets.

For safety reasons, a self-driving car will always give way to other vehicles. Human drivers, on the other hand, instinctively know that sometimes it makes sense to encourage other vehicles to yield. So Tesla's CEO, Elon Musk, said that his company's future models would come with a 'Mad Max' mode, with the aggressiveness ramped up. He joked that Tesla had thought of adding an 'LA Freeway' mode, but decided against it as Los Angeles drivers are so rage-filled that it would have been 'too loco'.

Self-driving technology took great leaps forward this year: some companies worked on systems where emoji-like pictures are shown on the front of the car to communicate with other road users, while others developed a 'more socially appropriate' honk to make up for the lack of human interaction between driver and pedestrian. Sweden opened the first ever electrified road, where electric cars can be recharged as they drive, and Singapore created an entire town to test self-driving cars, complete with a rain machine to see how the cars cope in bad weather, and fake skyscrapers that deliberately cause radio interference.

It wasn't just cars that began to self-drive. The Cheltenham Science Festival featured robotic traffic cones, which can drive themselves around motorways without human assistance, follow roadworks, and even replace themselves if they are knocked over or stolen by students.

SEND NUDES

Facebook asked users to send naked pictures of themselves to stop them ending up on the Internet.

In an attempt to tackle the growing problem of online 'revenge porn', Facebook created new software that aims to catch and block humiliating photos the very second they hit the Internet.

All users need to do is send their compromising photos to a team of five 'specially trained representatives' who will then create a 'fingerprint' of each photo, before deleting the originals. Should someone else then attempt to upload any of the images to Facebook, the company will know to block them. Facebook reassured people that once their employees have processed the nude photos, they won't be able to view them again.

Facebook weren't the only ones asking for nude photos. Missouri State University professor Alicia Walker hoped to get at least 3,600 men to send her pictures of their genitals for her study into the impact of the size of a man's penis on his overall physical health, sexual activity, condom usage and mental health. Potential volunteers were asked to fill in an online survey and submit photos of their penis (both flaccid and erect), but the study had to be abandoned after two weeks when men started uploading cartoon characters such as SpongeBob SquarePants instead of pictures of their genitals.

Honouring a vow he had made, Mark Williams, this year's World Snooker Champion, did his post-championship press conference in the nude. If he wins next year he promises to do the same, this time with added naked cartwheeling around the press table.

SHARKS ▶

Donald Trump helped protect sharks by saying he wanted them all dead.

Scientists discovered the first-known omnivorous shark. The bonnethead shark's diet is 60 per cent seagrass, which means it's the only shark that doesn't exclusively eat meat.

The president is terrified of sharks. This is according to porn star Stormy Daniels, who revealed in an interview that she and Trump spent a night together in his hotel room watching *Shark Week* on the Discovery Channel. The president reportedly told Daniels: 'I would never donate to any charity that helps sharks. I hope all the sharks die.'

The revelation was great news for shark charities, who often struggle to raise money for a species that many people fear. As a result of the president's comments, they saw a sudden spike in donations. Most contributions were from first-time donors and many were made in the name of Donald J. Trump.

Paul Watson, founder of the Sea Shepherd Conservation society, pointed out that the president shouldn't actually be afraid of sharks. The odds of being attacked by one are minuscule: Trump is more likely to be struck by lightning on one of his golf courses than he is to be bitten by a shark.

One person who defied the odds and *was* bitten by a shark this year was 20-year-old Dylan McWilliams, who was attacked while bodyboarding in Hawaii. It was the third time he had been bitten by an animal in the last three years. The other two bites were from a rattlesnake and from a bear who tried to eat his head. According to George Burgess, director emeritus of the Florida Program for Shark Research, the odds of one person being bitten by all three animals in as many years is 893.35 quadrillion to one.

SHETLAND ▶

*Maps in Scotland must now include an extra
250 kilometres of empty sea.*

The Shetland Islands are situated so far north of the
Scottish mainland that they have traditionally appeared
in an inset box on maps and in atlases. That way,
Ordnance Survey have argued, it has been possible to
avoid 'publishing maps which are mostly sea'.

Islanders, however, have long been unhappy with this
approach, arguing that it gives little idea of the challenges faced by those living in such a remote location.
The Islands (Scotland) Bill has therefore been passed,
which makes it illegal for public bodies to place the
Shetland Islands in a box, unless they can provide
written justification.

The downside of the new legislation is that in order to
draw the mainland, intervening sea and islands to scale,
they all have to be drawn smaller, reducing the detail
available by 40 per cent. On the other hand, as Scottish
Conservative MSP Jamie Greene said: 'nobody puts
Shetland in a box.'

SHOES ▶

For shoes handed out with desserts, *see* **Desserts,
Diplomatic**; for shoes full of crib sheets, *see* **Exams**;
for a shoe with its own treadmill, *see* **Inventions**; for a
shoe with its own generator, *see* **Obituaries**; for some-
body who doesn't need any new shoes, *see* **Queen, The**;
for shoes full of booze, *see* **Trademarks**; and for shoes
handing out just desserts, *see* **Upskirting**.

SHOPLIFTERS ▶

A suspected shoplifter was caught after leaving his fingerprints in some Play-Doh.

Even worse for the suspect who was arrested in Leicester, Massachusetts, he had brought the Play-Doh himself: he used it to cover up anti-theft devices on products in an unsuccessful attempt to neutralise them. He fled the scene, leaving his fingerprints behind, and was promptly arrested.

Shoplifting is rising sharply in the UK. The Association of Convenience Stores' 2018 Crime Report stated that offences have doubled in the last year, to 950,000, or 200 every hour. Retailers have blamed the government, suggesting the offence has been subject to 'effective decriminalisation' – if you steal less than £200-worth of goods, you are now dealt with by post and don't have to go to court or be interviewed by a police officer.*

*Even better news for thieves in Cornwall came when shop security guards were told that police will no longer attend shoplifting incidents, and that the best way to deal with young shoplifters is simply to ask them to return the stock and then call their parents.

Japan is looking to technology for the answer. A new system called AI Guardsman has been devised that is designed to scan live video streams in supermarkets. As soon as it spots a prospective thief acting suspiciously (checking their surroundings or looking for blind spots), it alerts the shop's staff with a mugshot. The designers admit it isn't perfect: it frequently flags up innocent customers and has even identified some staff restocking shelves as being shoplifters.

And so the crimes continue. In Indianapolis, a woman who shoplifted a video camera escaped by flinging a handful of her own faeces at the security guard; in Great Yarmouth, a shoplifter was caught after he was spotted wearing camouflage clothing, which ironically made him extremely conspicuous. Meanwhile, in Derby, a shop worker at Lidl chased a suspected shoplifter and then beat him over the head with a leg of pork. Lidl apologised.

[SIC]

White House aides deliberately insert grammatical errors into Donald Trump's tweets.

Donald Trump isn't solely to blame for all of the incoherent, rambling and grammatically incorrect tweets coming from his Twitter account. According to White House staff, many are drafted by his aides, who imitate his style by putting capital letters in places they don't belong and writing in fragmented sentences. The aides don't insert deliberate spelling mistakes, however. They leave that up to the president, who often edits the tweets provided before sending them.

While staffers have chosen to embrace the president's erratic written style, others have simply refused to put up with it. When retired high school teacher Yvonne Mason received a letter riddled with mistakes from the president, she immediately corrected it and sent it back to the White House. 'I have never, ever, received a letter with this many silly mistakes,' she stated. When asked what mark she would have given the president, Mason said, 'I would have handed it back without a grade on it and said, "I hope you left the real one at home."'

In fairness to Trump, it was probably his staff who wrote the letter – and they do have form when it comes to typos. In January they issued tickets inviting guests to join Trump at his first 'State of the Uniom' address. And in June when Trump signed an executive order that halted the separation of immigrant families, they had to get him to re-sign a revised document, because the first one they gave him was an executive order to stop families from being 'seperated'.

Addressing the constant mockery, Trump tweeted: 'After having written many best selling books, and somewhat priding myself on my ability to write, it should be noted

Ivanka Trump quoted what she thought was a Chinese proverb: 'Those who say it cannot be done, should not interrupt those doing it.' Nobody in China, however, had ever heard of it. It's not her first offence: in 2013, she claimed 'Choose a job you love, and you will never have to work a day in your life' was a quotation from Confucius. It isn't.

that the Fake News constantly likes to pour over my tweets looking for a mistake. I capitalize certain words only for emphasis, not b/c they should be capitalized!' He then deleted the tweet and reposted it with the correct spelling of 'pore' after being mocked some more.

SINGAPORE SUMMIT ▶

Kim Jong Un brought his own personal toilet to his meeting with Donald Trump.

Among the commemorative merchandise on offer was Kim 'n' Trump-themed cocktails, a 'Burger for World Peace', and Trump and Kim piñatas (from a Mexican restaurant).

The meeting of the year was the Trump–Kim summit in Singapore. It was first on, then off, then on again: in the build-up, Trump told reporters he'd received a 'very nice letter' from Kim and that it was 'very interesting'. Eight minutes later he admitted he hadn't read it yet.

The summit took place on Singapore's tourist island Sentosa, where security was tight. In preparation, police banned bullhorns, banners, drones and spray paint. Any kind of street demonstration – even a one-person one – required a police permit (one victim of the crackdown was Australian comedian and Kim look-alike Howard X, who was arrested almost immediately after arriving). Extra pot plants were placed outside Kim's expected accommodation to obstruct reporters' views. And Kim brought his own toilet so foreign spies couldn't use anything he left behind to analyse his health. His staff wiped everything he touched so he didn't leave any fingerprints either.

The pair spoke alone for 38 minutes. Trump wooed Kim with a four-minute movie trailer promoting peace, and praised him, saying, 'Anybody that takes over a situation like he did at 26 years of age' must be impressive. Eventually they signed an agreement, although Kim declined to use the Trump-branded pen he was offered. The last people to find out how it went were the North Korean population, who were not shown footage of the summit until the next day.

On the surface, it seemed to have been a successful summit. Donald Trump agreed to stop joint US–South Korea military exercises, and claimed he'd neutralised the Korean threat, as Kim Jong Un had committed to 'complete denuclearisation'. He also tweeted: 'There is no longer a Nuclear threat from North Korea.' When reporters asked why the joint statement didn't exactly define denuclearisation, Trump explained that it was 'because there's no time. I'm here one day.' More cautious observers noted that North Korea had previously promised to denuclearise in 1985, 1992, 1994, 2005, 2007, 2010, 2011, 2012 and 2016. Each time, they had then failed to do so.

SLOW

Villagers in Wales were so frustrated with their slow Internet connection that they made their own. They now have the fastest Internet in Wales.

Michaelston-y-Fedw is a small village situated between Cardiff and Newport. It has a population of around 300 and (until this year) an Internet speed of 4 Mbps. That's so slow, it took residents days to download a single movie.

So the village decided to do something about it. They raised £150,000 (as well as securing another £100,000 in government and EU money) and then spent a year digging 12 kilometres of trenches and laying fibre cable. Michaelston-y-Fedw now has the fastest Internet in Wales, with a speed of 1,000 Mbps. That's so fast the villagers can now download an entire series of *Game of Thrones* in one minute.

On another slow news day it was reported that seven adults and 12 children were left 5 metres in the air when Japan's 'slowest roller-coaster' derailed and stopped mid-ride. However, because the coaster travels so slowly, many of the passengers didn't actually notice it had stopped. It wasn't until the staff at the Tokyo amusement park started banging the back of the cars with hammers that the passengers realised what had happened.

SMARTPHONES ▷

Apple and Android encouraged people to stop using their phones.

A Polish charity racked up a phone bill in excess of £2,000 after they lost contact with a stork whose migration patterns they had been studying via a tracker they had placed on its back. While the bird was somewhere in the Sudan, someone found it, removed the SIM card from the tracker, put it in their own phone and then made 20 hours' worth of phone calls.

Apple's 'Digital Health' initiative is designed to help customers limit the amount of time they spend on their phones and tablets. Tim Cook, Apple's chief executive, said, 'I'm not a person that says we've achieved success if you're using it all the time.' Meanwhile, Google announced that the next Android phone will feature a dashboard showing you how long you have spent on it, so you can decide when to stop. And in America, phones were banned altogether from the White House, where Donald Trump made it clear that he didn't want aides using their personal phones in the workplace. (This did not stop Trump giving his own personal mobile number to Kim Jong Un.)

In a recent case in Florida, police attempted to access a smartphone via a dead man's finger. Linus Phillips was shot and killed by an officer in March, and investigating officers were keen to inspect his phone records. They therefore went to the funeral parlour where his body was being kept, and held his finger to the phone's sensor. The *Guardian* reported that: 'Legal experts mostly agree that what the detectives did was legal, but they question whether it was appropriate.' Either way, it didn't work.

The Catholic Church also came up with an unexpected use for smartphone technology this year when a speaker at the Vatican's annual exorcist training conference suggested that mobiles could be used in the casting out of demons. If you think you are possessed, he said, you can ring a priest, and ask him to read the prayers of exorcism down the line (although remote exorcism does mean that no one will be on hand to help if you find yourself thrashing about). Professor Giuseppe Ferrari, who helped to organise the conference, said that telephone exorcism is effective, but 'whether it is orthodox or correct, I couldn't say'.*

*Although exorcism may have moved on in some ways, it has a long way to go in another very significant one: it's currently an exclusively male pursuit. Women are only permitted to be 'auxiliary exorcists', offering moral support to the priest casting the Devil out.

SMELLS

For traces of Thai footballers, *see* **Cave Rescue**; for a fruity fragrance, *see* **Durian**; for the perfume of Play-Doh, *see* **Trademarks**; for eau de mummy, *see* **Sarcophagus**; and for the delicate bouquet of 10 million pounds of poo, *see* **Trains**.

SMUGGLING

Spanish and Portuguese police smashed a pineapple ring.

Anti-smuggling authorities in both countries worked together to seize 745 kilograms of cocaine hidden inside fresh pineapples, which were being smuggled from South America. The insides had been cut out, and the cocaine – wrapped in yellow wax – shoved in the middle. What happened to the middle of the pineapples was not reported.

Elsewhere:

▶ Chinese customs authorities seized 110,000 tonnes of smuggled rubbish. China has recently banned the importing of foreign rubbish for recycling (*see* **Recycling**) and so sneaking it in the country is a lucrative trade.

This sort of thing has happened before: two World Cups ago, Colombian police at Bogota Airport seized a replica trophy made entirely out of mouldable cocaine.

▶ Police in Colombia seized replica World Cup shirts that had been soaked in liquid cocaine, then dried for transport. They had so much cocaine in them that each shirt would have had a street value of about $35,000. Meanwhile, an Argentinian gang was caught smuggling cocaine, crack and cannabis in replica World Cup trophies.*

▶ In Spain two cars stopped by suspicious police were found to be completely full of oranges. Four tonnes were seized. The five people responsible boldly claimed the fruit had been legitimately purchased for personal consumption, which suggests that they were planning to consume a couple of thousand oranges each.

▶ The Portuguese police detained a man at Lisbon Airport who was wearing a false bottom over his bottom. The false bottom was filled with a kilo of cocaine.

Animals were victims, too: the authorities in Madagascar found 10,000 rare tortoises about to be smuggled out of the country; Japan announced a crime wave of otter smugglings, thanks to a craze for keeping them as pets; two Guyanese nationals were caught smuggling finches into New York in hair curlers, to enter them for singing contests; and a report found that for Asian crime networks, eel smuggling is now as lucrative as cocaine smuggling.

SONGS

A man called Song saved songbirds in Songyang.

A house in Songyang county, China, was due to be demolished and the resident human family were told they had to leave. But at the last minute, a family of swallows was found living there. Conservationist Song Shihe argued that the young birds couldn't be moved because if the scent of humans got on to the babies, their mother might abandon them. The demolition was postponed until the swallows grew up and left. It's the first time birds have halted a demolition in China.

SPACE EXPLORATION

A Member of Parliament who wants to leave Europe joined another parliament that wants to leave Earth.

The Conservative Party's Nigel Evans is a strong supporter of Brexit, and has been a serving member of the British Parliament for 26 years. This year he became

Donald Trump
announced his new
'space force', the sixth
branch of the American
military after the air
force, army, coast guard,
Marine Corps and navy.
Former NASA astronaut
Mark Kelly has called it
a dumb idea, pointing
out that the air force
already does everything
Trump wants the space
force to do. 'What's
next,' he tweeted; 'we
move submarines to
the 7th branch and
call it the "under-the-
sea force?"'

a member of another parliament: of the Space Kingdom of Asgardia.

Founded in 2016 by billionaire Russian rocket scientist Igor Ashurbeyli, Asgardia is the world's first space nation. Its plans include setting up colonies on the Moon and 'Space Arks' where humans can live permanently in outer space. Since its launch, over 200,000 people around the world have signed up as 'residents' (giving Asgardia a greater population than many actual nations including Samoa, the Isle of Man and Saint Lucia) and it has already launched its first shoe-box-sized satellite into space.

This year Ashurbeyli focused on establishing a democracy for Asgardia. He did this by creating a 147-seat parliament, tasked with representing the best interests of Asgardia's 200,000 citizens. The parliament attracted two other British politicians apart from Evans, including former Lib Dem Lembit Öpik, who was voted 'head of parliament'.

Elsewhere, Australia established its first ever space agency. Their budget isn't huge – they currently only have enough money to employ 20 members of staff. However, they hope to have as many as 20,000 by the year 2030. The director of the agency, Dr Megan Clark, isn't a space scientist. In fact Dr Clark has spent her career looking down rather than up – she is a mining geologist.

When the agency was first announced in 2017, many Australians were fooled by a satirical website with the convincing domain address www.spaceaustralia.com.au that it was going to be called Australian Research and Space Exploration (ARSE). ARSE claims to be 'an independent campaign designed to promote the space program and all related efforts in Australia' and states that it is 'dedicated to understanding the nether regions of our universe'.

SPAIN ▶

The Spanish prime minister was ousted after a scandal involving bribery, corruption and clowns.

Prime Minister Mariano Rajoy denied knowing about a secret, illegal financial structure within his own People's Party. Those involved had committed various acts of fraud and money laundering, and had awarded government contracts in exchange for bribes to party members, including luxury clothes, cars and even, on one occasion, a clown to perform at a children's birthday party. In the end, Rajoy was forced to resign as head of the party after losing a vote of no confidence in parliament, although he wasn't actually present for the debate. As MPs voted to remove him, he was down the road enjoying an eight-hour lunch.

Rajoy was replaced as prime minister by Pedro Sánchez, known in the press as 'Mr Handsome'. It was quite a comeback for Sánchez, who had previously led his party to two crushing electoral defeats in 2015 and 2016 and who had then resigned from his role as the Socialist Party's leader before ultimately regaining it. His nickname is due, unsurprisingly, to his good looks, which according to commentators have held him back in the past, because they make him appear vacuous and inexperienced. His new cabinet included Spain's first ever astronaut, Pedro Duque, as minister for science, innovation and universities, but was otherwise dominated by women by almost two to one.

—————— ▼ ——————

A Spanish festival, known as 'boloencierro' ('running of the balls') took place near Madrid in August. Designed to be a safer alternative to the traditional 'running of the bulls', it involved revellers running away from giant, rolling, 250-kilogram resin balls. However, a man had to be airlifted to hospital with head injuries after getting hit by one of the balls.

SPIES

Some of Australia's most secret documents were accidentally sold to a used furniture shop.

Not even the animal kingdom was safe from charges of spying this year. In India, officials captured and X-rayed a pigeon, suspecting it of being a Pakistani spy, and in Iran a general accused the West of using lizards to spy on the country's nuclear reactors.

The shop in Canberra sold some old filing cabinets at a discount – they were locked and nobody could find the keys. When the eventual purchaser drilled them open, they discovered thousands of top-secret documents stretching back more than a decade, including papers detailing the government's defence strategy in the Middle East and updates on the war in Afghanistan. The papers also revealed that the Australian police had lost 400 national security files between 2008 and 2013. The deputy prime minister, Barnaby Joyce, explained that 'Obviously someone's had a shocker', and Australia's spies rushed to seize the documents from the Australian Broadcasting Corporation, which had been sent them. Ex-PM Tony Abbott said it was 'not so much a Cabinet leak as a leaked cabinet'.

Next door, New Zealand's prime minister, Jacinda Ardern, announced that in the wake of the Salisbury Novichok poisoning, her country would expel Russian spies. But, she added, they hadn't located any, and that 'If there were [any], we would already have taken action'. A former KGB agent reassured New Zealanders that 'of course' there were Russian spies in New Zealand – they just hadn't been found yet.

STONED

For an app that tells you if you're high, *see* **Apps**; for a quick-thinking Brownie, *see* **Drugs**; for mice munching marijuana, *see* **Excuses**; for a Dogg with the munchies, *see* **Fast Food**; and for a royal weeding, *see* **Markles, The**.

Statues of the Year

And the statuettes go to . . .

A statue of Yuri Gagarin in Belgrade: It was taken down within a week after complaints that the head was too small. The bust was deemed an insult to the memory of the first man in space, especially as it was erected right next to a McDonald's.

The last remaining naked Donald Trump statue: Sold at auction for $28,000, it was one of five created in 2016 in a series entitled *The Emperor Has No Balls* (and, indeed, they lacked testicles, although they did all feature a micropenis).

The world's largest statue: A 182-metre monument twice the height of the Statue of Liberty, which was unveiled in India in October. It's of Vallabhbhai Patel, the patron saint of Indian civil servants, who was central to the country's independence movement.

A statue of David Bowie in Aylesbury: Loudspeakers mounted above it played a David Bowie song on the hour, every hour. The statue was vandalised within 48 hours of being unveiled.

A 10-foot-tall statue of a bear: This was taken down from the entrance of a park in Wales after a driver swerved off the road thinking it was real. There are no bears in Wales. Locals protested against the removal by holding a teddy bears' picnic.

SURGERY ▶

A surgeon was found guilty of branding his initials into patients' livers.

Simon Bramhall used an argon beam to burn the letters 'SB' into two patients' livers while performing transplants. He was caught when another doctor spotted them while performing follow-up surgery on one of the patients. In fact, a nurse had noticed them previously and asked Bramhall about it. On that occasion he'd simply replied: 'I do this.' Bramhall continues to practise, but was given a 12-month community order and fined £10,000 because although the process does no physical harm to patients, it was, unsurprisingly, deemed inappropriate.

Some rather more constructive work came from the surgeons who in April performed the world's first ever penis-and-scrotum transplant. Eleven doctors operated for 14 hours on a soldier who'd had his genitals blown off by a bomb in Afghanistan. He didn't receive new testicles, though, because, for ethical reasons, that isn't permitted.*

Since testicles transplanted on to a new body would continue to produce their old body's sperm, their transplantation would constitute a sperm donation without consent, especially if, as would be more than likely, the testicle donor was dead.

While penile and scrotal transplants may be new, another surgical process has been found to date back thousands of years. Archaeologists analysing ancient cow skulls this year found that Neolithic people 10,000 years ago performed brain surgery on their cattle. It could have been an attempt to relieve brain disease in them, but the lead researcher thought it most likely they practised on cows before doing the actual procedures on humans.

In which we learn . . .
How NASA screwed up its new telescope, which
author got too cocky for their own good, what to do
with 10 million pounds of poo, why Donald Trump
took Angela Merkel up to his bedroom, and why the
Turkish election was a piece of cake.

TANKS

The British army made plans to blow up its own tanks.

A Chinese high school in Hebei Province unveiled two decommissioned army tanks on its grounds in the hope of instilling 'fighting spirit' in students before their upcoming university entrance exams.

When a study on urban warfare concluded that troops and equipment need beefing up, the British military suggested building a fleet of inflatable tanks that could be used as decoys to confuse the enemy. They were proposed as part of Defence Secretary Gavin Williamson's push to increase defence spending. Similar models are already used in Russia and America.

For their *real* tanks, the Americans have developed a 'metal foam' armour that consists of steel plating with lots of little holes in it. It's three times lighter than normal armour, and its Swiss-cheese-like structure enables it to soak up bullets' energy as they strike it. At the same time, the hard outer layer shatters bullets that would go straight through traditional armour. In effect, the armour attacks the bullet. And a tank that's see-through (at least, from the inside) was invented by a company in the Ukraine. The tank is fitted with external cameras, so its driver can effectively look through its sides via a VR headset.

TAT

For congealed-fat-themed fudge, *see* **Fatberg**; for communist cookie cutters, *see* **Marx, Karl**; for Pope-pourri, *see* **Pope, The**; for Meghan Mark-ale, *see* **Royal Wedding**; for Kim-ñatas, *see* **Singapore Summit**; and for the Condom Who Must Not Be Named, *see* **Trademarks**.

TATTOOS

For e-tattoos, *see* **Bitcoin**; for rogue letters in a tattoo, *see* **Families**; for eye tattoos, *see* **Laws**; for ewe tattoos, *see* **Oldest**; and for inkriminating inkings, *see* **Yakuza**.

TELESCOPES

The hunt for two missing screws cost NASA a million dollars a day.

The launch of the brand-new, cutting-edge James Webb Space Telescope has already been postponed at least 10 times (it was originally scheduled for 2019 but now won't deploy until at least 2021). The latest delay came during the telescope's 'acoustic environmental testing' when around 70 screws and washers came loose. Within two months, all but two screws and two washers had been found, but because it's such a delicate instrument that could easily be damaged by loose bits and pieces floating around inside, it was essential that those two missing screws were tracked down as well. Every day the scientists couldn't find them cost NASA $1 million; the delays in total are expected to cost an extra $1 billion.

The James Webb Telescope will be so powerful that if it were deployed on Earth it would be able to spot a bumblebee on the moon.

Another telescope, which promises to be the world's second-largest, has also hit problems. The plan is that the Thirty Meter Telescope will rise 18 storeys above the summit of Mauna Kea in Hawaii. Objectors have pointed out that not only is the mountain sacred in traditional Hawaiian culture, but that it already houses 13 other telescopes, and they have taken their protest to the Hawaiian Supreme Court. Advocates of the project argue that Mauna Kea is the best possible site: there is almost no light pollution there, and the air above is dry, so there are more clear nights for stargazing than almost anywhere else on the planet. If built, the Thirty Meter Telescope will be 10 times more powerful than the largest Earth-based telescopes currently in use.

There was better news for stargazers at the Royal Observatory at Greenwich, which installed its first working telescope in more than 60 years. London's smog had previously forced astronomers to shut up shop, but now that the air is cleaner (and the technology more advanced), they have had a change of heart. The new telescope will be mainly used to encourage public interest in astronomy, although the chances of most people seeing it will be limited: the building which houses it has a capacity of only 12.

TIANGONG-1 ▶

An out-of-control Chinese space station crashed in the best possible place.

Tiangong-1 was China's first attempt at a space station. It was small (about the size of a bus) and it had no cooking or toilet facilities, meaning that visiting Chinese astronauts had to return to their shuttle whenever they had a call of nature. In 2016, China lost control of the space station and it began to fall towards Earth. By late 2017 it was clear that it would crash-land within a few months, but it wasn't clear exactly when or where. Although scientists calculated the chances of anyone being hit by the space station at 300 trillion to 1, they nevertheless acknowledged that a long strip of mainland America was potentially at risk, along with parts of Japan, China, Italy and Spain. In the final couple of days, millions of people looked up at the skies on the off chance of seeing the last moments of Tiangong-1.

In the end, something extremely unlikely *did* happen, but in an extremely fortuitous way. The station landed, on April Fool's Day, very close to 'Point Nemo' – a region of ocean further away from land than any other, and the area where space agencies deliberately aim for when crashing their crafts in a controlled way.

TO ME

See **To You.**

TO YOU

See **To Me.**

TOSSERS

For ball tossers, *see* **Cricket, Just Not**; for salad tossers, *see* **Excuses**; and for bottle tossers, *see* **Messaging, Very Much Not Instant**.

TOYS R US

Toys R Us auctioned off the domain names toysrussucks.com, turkeysrus.com and sextoysrus.com.

The company, which went bust in March, owned all the above, as well as cigars-r-us.com and adult-toys-r-us.com, along with the more conventional toys.com and toystoystoys.com. In fact, it owned a whole string of odd-sounding domain names, its goal being to prevent rival or inappropriate companies getting hold of them and thereby damaging the Toys R Us brand. All were put up for sale at auction as a way of making some money back to repay the firm's debts.

When Toys R Us closed, former employees set up a Facebook group called Dead Giraffe Society to serve as a forum for all alumni who wished to share happy memories of working for the company. The name was a reference to their famous mascot Geoffrey the Giraffe, as was the address of the company's head office: One Geoffrey Way. When the last branch shut in June, Geoffrey was pictured dragging a tiny suitcase out of an empty store, alongside a sign saying 'I guess everyone has grown up'.* Social media was, predictably, devastated. The company founder, Charles Lazarus, only just outlived his creation, dying a week after the closure was announced. But Toys R Us may yet live up to the Lazarus name: former CEO Jerry Storch announced a few months after the shutdown that he'd be back to try and resuscitate the store.

*It wasn't all bad news. San Antonio Zoo offered Geoffrey the Giraffe a new job as an ambassador for giraffe conservation, although they did say they wanted the rights to use the character for free.

TRADE WARS

The US made it more expensive to import spaceships and nuclear reactors from China.

These were just two of the 1,102 Chinese products on which the Trump administration raised import taxes by 25 per cent in the hope of boosting US industry. Others included lawnmowers, cruise ships, pacemakers and traffic lights. They would later cut the list down following public and political pressure, removing flame-throwers, hot air balloons and golf carts. It wasn't just China that felt the impact; Trump also made it much more expensive for Canada, Mexico and the EU to export various products to the US.

———— ◆ ————

US sanctions against China meant that Donald Trump's own flags and hats, manufactured in China, got stuck at the border.

To justify the move, the president cited 'national security'. When Canadian Prime Minister Justin Trudeau asked what Canada could possibly have to do with security issues, Trump replied, 'Didn't you guys burn down the White House?' referring to the War of 1812, which occurred 55 years before Canada became a country. He wasn't the only one to resort to playground rhetoric. When the duties on European goods were announced, Jean-Claude Juncker, president of the EU Commission, responded by saying, 'We can also do stupid.'

The affected countries responded in kind. Canada imposed new tariffs on US-made products including quiche (which, incidentally, is making a comeback – *see* **Quiche**), shaving foam and sleeping bags; Mexico put extra levies on American cold cuts and lamps; and the EU did the same with peanut butter, cranberries and orange juice.

While the taxed items may appear random, they are actually very specifically chosen to minimise harm at home while inflicting the greatest damage on the opponent. For instance, the EU raised tariffs on Harley-Davidsons and bourbon because they're made in Wisconsin and Kentucky. These are states represented by Paul Ryan and Mitch McConnell, two of the most influential Republicans. The EU hoped Ryan and McConnell would petition Trump to soften his tariffs to avoid a trade war that could destroy industry in their states.

Harley-Davidson immediately announced they'd have to shift production abroad because it would be too expensive to sell to Europe from the US. Trump sent out a series of tweets criticising this decision, which must have stung all the more because straight after his inauguration he'd thanked the company for being supportive, helping him to victory, and making their bikes in America.

TRADEMARKS ▶

An erotica author tried and failed to trademark the word 'cocky'.

Rapper Lil Wayne reportedly attempted to trademark the name 'New Dirty Bastard', in tribute to the rapper Ol' Dirty Bastard, who died in 2004 – only to receive a cease and desist letter from Ol' Dirty Bastard's estate. The name has stayed in the family: Ol' Dirty Bastard's son performs under the name 'Young Dirty Bastard'.

Faleena Hopkins is the self-published author of books including *Cocky Senator*, *Cocky Biker*, *Cocky Roomie* and *Cocky Cowboy*. This year she was granted a trademark for the word's use in book titles, and immediately started writing to other romance authors demanding they stop putting 'cocky' in their own book titles. The authors of novels such as *Mr Cocky* and *Cocky Fiancé* received legal letters; the latter was persuaded to change her novel's title to *Arrogant Fiancé*. But Hopkins became unpopular – *Chocolat* author Joanne Harris said it was a 'dick move' – and both the Authors Guild and the Romance Writers of America, whose membership includes the authors of *Her Cocky Doctors* and *Cocktales*, took Hopkins to court. She was eventually found to have been too cocky herself when a judge set aside the previous decision and ruled that other novels could include 'cocky' in their titles.

There were also trademark problems for Swiss novelty condom company Magic X, whose 'Harry Popper' branding is a wizard-shaped condom brandishing a wand and with distinctive round glasses. Warner Brothers, who with J. K. Rowling own the trademark to Harry Potter, launched legal proceedings against the company in 2008, and finally won their case this year. One of their lawyers stated: 'Everyone who sees the condoms automatically thinks of Harry Potter.'

One firm that *has* successfully trademarked something this year is Play-Doh, who have now registered 'the smell of Play-Doh'. The scent is described as a 'sweet, slightly musky, vanilla fragrance, with slight overtones of cherry, combined with the smell of a salted, wheat-based dough'.

In April, Formula 1 was granted a trademark for the word 'shoey', which describes the act of drinking alcohol directly from a shoe – a celebration made popular by racing driver Daniel Ricciardo. This was despite shoeys having been (relatively) common in Australia for at least 15 years.

TRAINS

When 10 million pounds of poo got stuck in Parrish, Alabama, everyone in town got a free can of Febreze.

The waste, which was on a train bound from New York, was due to be dumped in a landfill in nearby West Jefferson. The locals there objected and filed an injunction against the enormous load entering their town limits. But since the poo train had already left New York, and couldn't really be sent back, it got stuck in administrative limbo outside Parrish. The town's 982 residents said that luckily it didn't smell too much like poo; it apparently had more of a 'rotting carcass smell'. After two long months, the biowaste was taken to a private landfill about 30 kilometres away.

While this was happening in America, Britain had train problems of its own, as rail companies across

A railway line in Russia added a stop specifically for one girl so she can be picked up to go to school every day.

the country struggled with new timetables and a lack of drivers. Northern Rail was perhaps the worst offender: on 1 April, 94.5 per cent of its trains in the north ran to time, but by 1 June that figure had fallen to just 57.5 per cent. As angry passengers made their views known, the Department for Transport published a document suggesting that some busy trains could be 'hidden' from them, the idea being some services would not appear on digital noticeboards, and would stop only to let passengers off, not to let them on.*

In the midst of the crisis, one train actually did disappear: a service from Newcastle to Reading somehow got lost and ended up just outside Pontefract.

Another country with train trouble is Ethiopia, whose brand-new, Chinese-built railway line was responsible for the death of 50 camels during its first month in operation. Trains were forced to run at half speed to avoid further accidents, and the train company felt compelled to offer nomads who lost livestock double the market price for each camel killed. It has been suggested that this generous compensation might explain why there have been so many collisions: as an *Economist* correspondent wrote, 'a profit-maximising camel-owner would chivvy the whole herd onto the tracks'.

Japan, meanwhile, has been struggling to cope with deer on the tracks: the animals like to lick the rails to get more iron in their diets. Various unsuccessful attempts have been made to deter them, but the latest one, which involves a train that barks like a dog, does seem to be having an effect. A previous trial – spraying lion excrement on the tracks – very definitely didn't work and so stands no chance of being generally adopted – which is no doubt a relief for the people of Parrish, Alabama.

TRANSGENDER ▶

For the first time ever, a transgender woman breastfed.

The process involved the woman taking hormones produced by biological mothers, a drug that can stimulate milk production, and a male hormone blocker. She used a breast pump to stimulate her breasts. While there is anecdotal evidence on the Internet that other transgender women may have done it before, it was certainly the first to be officially recorded in medical literature. As Joshua Safer of Boston Medical Center said in an interview, 'There's a lot on the Internet that's true or untrue to varying degrees. It's a very big deal to have this recorded in a reliable document.'

In other transgender news: Yance Ford became the first transgender director to be nominated for an Oscar; Angela Ponce became the first to win Miss Universe Spain; Victoria Smith became the first to race as a professional jockey; Danica Roem became the first to take office in Virginia's House of Delegates; and Marvia Malik became Pakistan's first transgender news anchor.

More importantly, perhaps, the World Health Organization declared that being transgender should no longer be considered a mental illness, though it's still classified as a 'sexual health condition'. Some people object to this, but others argue that the classification makes it easier for transgender people to seek hormonal or surgical treatment.

Brazil chalked up one other first: allowing transgender contestants to enter the Miss Bumbum beauty contest to find the country's most attractive bottom. Some of the other competitors were not happy. But one transgender contestant, Oliveira, shrugged off the criticism, saying, 'I'm not offended by what they said, because it's clear they want me out because I've got a much sexier ass.'

Trump, Donald

This year, Donald Trump's work to Make America Great Again continued, as he . . .

Signed great deals: The President claimed the US would soon be selling F52 planes to Norway. There is no plane called the F52, except in the game *Call of Duty*.

Broke new records: In June, Trump broke the record for the number of false statements he had made in a week, racking up 103 lies, confusions or incorrect remarks. This smashed the previous one-week record of 60, set in March.

Supported the arts: Trump asked to borrow a fragile Van Gogh painting from the Guggenheim during his presidency. They refused, but said they would happily loan him a solid gold toilet called *America* instead.

Inspired entomologists: A new species of moth was named *Neopalpa donaldtrumpi* because of its blonde hair and small genitalia.

Stayed diplomatic: Trump showed Angela Merkel his bedroom while she toured the White House. A spokesman said that proved their relationship was close: 'That was very personal. No president has shown that to her before.'

Boosted American jobs: Trump routinely rips up sheets of paper after reading them, even ones that need to be kept for legal reasons. So a man named Solomon Lartey was hired to sellotape the pieces back together. He eventually left the role this year.

Communed with God: Trump led America's National Day of Prayer, shortly after acknowledging he'd repaid his lawyer for paying off porn star Stormy Daniels with $130,000 of hush money.

Was threatened by a swamp: A sinkhole opened up on the North Lawn of the White House, caused by a 'legitimate swamp' around the building. It's almost exactly a year since a sinkhole opened outside Trump's Florida home, Mar-A-Lago.

Fought disease: Bill Gates revealed that on two separate occasions, he had to explain to Trump that HIV and HPV are not the same thing.

Coined memorable phrases: One of Trump's new trade bills was the US Fair and Reciprocal Tariff Act – immediately dubbed the FART Act.

Considered new overseas ventures: It was revealed that last year Trump consulted several foreign policy experts about invading Venezuela. He was advised against it. One advisor explained, 'He just thinks out loud.'

Boosted big pharma: Police in Indiana reported that drug traffickers are making ecstasy pills shaped like Donald Trump. They are orange and have his face stamped on them and the words 'Great Again' on the back.

Considered the future: Trump's team tried to trademark the phrase 'Keep America Great' for his 2020 re-election campaign. The phrase first appeared in the 2016 horror movie *The Purge: Election Year*.

Despite all these disasters, Trump has enjoyed some of his most favourable ratings since his inauguration.

TURKEY

Recep Tayyip Erdoğan won the Turkish presidential election after promising the whole country free tea and cake.

———— ▼ ————

One of the candidates standing for Recep Tayyip Erdoğan's party in the election was a Syrian migrant who admired the president so much that he changed his name from Muhammad Sheikhouni to Muhammad Erdoğan.

It remains to be seen whether President Erdoğan will follow through on his promise of giving every neighbourhood in Turkey its own state-run cafe where tea and cake will be free. But one thing Erdoğan definitely is delivering on is giving himself sweeping new powers to detain dissenters, issue new laws and remove civil servants at whim.

The 2018 election marked an important victory for Erdoğan, but was by no means a walkover. Even though he was given 181 hours of coverage on state television during the campaign, he ended up with only 52.6 per cent of the vote. His main opponent, Muharrem İnce, by contrast, was allowed only 15 hours, while the candidate who came third was granted just 32 minutes (though he was in prison the whole time).

Muharrem İnce is a former physics teacher whose election promises included one to turn Erdoğan's 1,150-room presidential palace into an educational centre. He ran a dynamic campaign, staging more than a hundred rallies, but he couldn't overturn the massive built-in advantages that Erdoğan had. Some of his supporters claimed the election was not fair, but İnce accepted the result, saying that although he hadn't been able to fight on a level playing field, his final numbers were in line with earlier polls, and so were probably correct. His surname translates into English as 'gracious'.

TWITTER ▶

On World Password Day, Twitter revealed a glitch that compromised 330 million passwords.

Twitter said they didn't have any proof the passwords had been stolen, but nonetheless advised all 330 million users to change their passwords just in case. (They had been stored in an unencrypted form for some time, meaning hackers *could* easily have stolen them.) The company wasn't the only one to recommend changing passwords on World Password Day. The Nutella Twitter account suggested that people should change their password to 'A word that's already in your heart. Like Nutella', despite the fact that 'Nutella' would be an incredibly easy password to break.

In America, a New York judge ruled that Donald Trump can't block people on Twitter, because it violates their right to free speech under the First Amendment. The judge didn't directly order Trump to unblock users he'd blocked (including authors Stephen King and Anne Rice, among others) but did say that in future he should just use the 'mute' function instead if he doesn't want to see what they've written. Lawyers on both sides said they'd consider the ruling, but to date there is no evidence that the president has changed his ways.

Meanwhile, a study of American tweeters has established that if you make people look at opposing political opinions, it only strengthens their original views. When Republicans and Democrats had to follow an anti-polarising Twitter bot that tweeted opposite views, Republican voters became much more conservative and Democrats slightly more liberal.

In which we learn . . .
Where you can get a self-driving umbrella, why a
pervert hot-footed it to the police, where to get a pint
for 75p, why you shouldn't borrow a friend's urine,
and where Cubans can stick their Internet.

UGANDA ▶

Uganda's president taxed gossip and warned against oral sex.

This year Uganda issued a 'social media tax' to stop gossip, levying 5 cents a day on those who use sites such as Facebook and Twitter. Critics have pointed out that the tax is almost wholly unenforceable – and, indeed, many people have simply moved over to private networks to avoid detection. Some observers warned that in a world that relies so heavily on social media, the tax could be a blow to jobs.

Speaking of blows to jobs, Uganda's president, Yoweri Museveni, announced his strong opposition to oral sex and warned his people off it. 'The mouth is for eating, not for sex,' he declared in a speech. 'We know the address of sex; we know where sex is.' It was interpreted as a coded attack on homosexuality, which is already illegal in Uganda.

If Museveni's critics have been hoping he might step down, their hopes received a setback this year when MPs voted to scrap the rule that presidents should retire at 75. By sheer coincidence, Museveni is approaching his 75th birthday. He's now free to stand again in 2021, having been in power since 1986. Opposition MPs are not happy with this, and in April challenged the ruling, pointing out that last year the decision-making process was interrupted by politicians pushing, punching, and hitting each other over the head with chairs.

For the moment, then, Museveni stays in office and so can continue to make his views known. This year he praised Donald Trump for his comments about various African countries being 'shitholes', saying, 'I love Trump because he tells Africans frankly.' He also announced

—————— ▾ ——————

After the Ugandan president's car was stoned in August, Museveni's political opponent, Bobi Wine, was arrested and allegedly tortured, leading to huge protests. As well as being one of Uganda's most popular politicians, Wine is a pop star, a movie star, a YouTuber and a licensed boxer. Despite his name, Wine is teetotal.

that African nations aren't earning as much as they should because their citizens sleep too much. Ugandans responded by posting pictures of the 73-year-old Museveni sleeping through meetings.

UMBRELLAS

An art installation of 120 umbrellas had to be removed due to rain.

In late spring, the promise of heavy rainstorms in a yellow weather warning from the Met Office resulted in the colourful brollies suspended over Exeter High Street being taken down, so they didn't fall and hit unwary shoppers. A small proportion of the umbrellas that were in an indoor section of the arcade were allowed to stay up.

Slightly more sophisticated brollies have been developed in Japan, where the Asahi Power Service Company unveiled an umbrella attached to a drone. Designed for golfers, it will follow them along the course and keep them dry (or shaded). The drone umbrellas

could actually make a big difference to the game, since while the rules state that no other person can hold a brolly over you while you play, even if the rain is making your hands slippery, they don't have anything to say about drones keeping you dry.

Coral on the Great Barrier Reef also benefited from umbrella technology this year. To protect them from sun damage, the sea creatures have been given what's called a 'liquid umbrella', a white spray that forms a layer 50,000 times thinner than human hair. It will reflect the sun's UV rays and light away and prevent bleaching – but it won't, of course, keep the coral dry.

UPSKIRTING

A man handed himself in to police after the secret camera on his shoes exploded.

He was using the camera to try to take photos up women's skirts in Wisconsin, but ended up with severe burns to his feet after the battery caught fire. He confessed to a clergyman, who suggested he hand himself in to the police, but the authorities didn't press charges, as the explosion happened before any photos had actually been taken. In the very same week, another man in Leicester who had attached cameras to his shoes was arrested after his face appeared in some of his images – a co-worker came across a USB stick, opened the files, and recognised him.

Upskirting has become such a concern in the UK that Theresa May announced she wanted to see it made an explicit offence. Initial attempts to pass a law against it were, however, scuppered by Conservative MP Christopher Chope. Chope claimed he had blocked the law because he disagreed with the way it was pushed through Parliament: it was being proposed as a Private

Members' Bill, by which non-government ministers can suggest changes to law without a full debate. Indeed on the same day, he also derailed a proposed law to make it illegal to stab a police dog. In a bizarre display of hypocrisy, though, the very next time MPs were allowed to suggest their own Private Members' Bills, more than half of those proposed were by Chope himself. They included laws on fruit and vegetable classifications, mobile homes and the habitats in which bats are kept.

Despite Chope's best efforts, MPs persisted and pushed the new law through more conventional parliamentary channels. Politicians from all parties worked on the legislation, and they added a clause that confirmed the law would also protect men in kilts.

URINE TROUBLE

A drug user who swapped her urine sample with a friend's was jailed after it still tested positive.

Ohio resident Kiana Wallace was sentenced to a year and a half in prison after pleading guilty to attempting to tamper with the evidence. Judge Frank Fregiato, who sentenced Wallace, was incredulous: 'Let me get this straight,' he said. 'To avoid the positive test with your own urine, you used someone else's urine which turned out to be positive also. That's bizarre.'

Urine testing in sport faced its own problems this year, when Swiss company Berlinger announced that it would be discontinuing the manufacture of bottles used to store urine for doping tests. Berlinger explained that Russian officials had worked out how to tamper with the seals without being detected, and that an alternative type of bottle didn't work properly when frozen. This led to a shortage of the containers, but there were at least enough available to catch Nadezhda Sergeeva, a Russian bobsledder, who was spotted at the Winter Olympics wearing an 'I don't do doping' T- shirt at her training sessions, before later being disqualified after failing a urine test.

It wasn't all bad news for urinators. In Britain, the High Court ruled that dogs have the right to urinate on lamp posts. Richmond Council in London had tried to impose an order allowing it to prosecute anyone whose dog caused damage to 'any council structure, equipment, tree, turf or other council property', but an annoyed dog owner took the council to the High Court and won.

USBs ▶

A study revealed that most Cubans get their Internet on USB sticks.

Hardly anyone has access to the World Wide Web in Cuba, so people there have developed a replacement called El Paquete Semanal, a weekly Internet package that's uploaded on to USBs, CDs and hard drives and distributed to subscribers. It includes TV shows, music, video games, digital magazines, books and entire copies of websites like Wikipedia and a Craigslist equivalent, and the content changes every time. The system has existed for years, but it wasn't until recently that the three groups that keep it functioning were specifically identified: Los Maestros, who compile the material each week; Los Paqueteros, who deliver, edit and produce additional content; and La Gente: the people.

All this seems set to change, though, now that Havana is hoping to roll out mobile Internet throughout the country in 2019. Commentators believe this will weaken the grip of government by allowing people to access a wider range of news, although when trials first began, the online access was limited to employees of the state-run news agencies and embassies. Free Internet was later extended to the whole country so that everyone could try it out – but only for eight hours.

UZBEKISTAN ▶

The president of Uzbekistan overthrew the man who was actually in charge of Uzbekistan.

————— ▼ —————
The Uzbek capital, Tash-kent, was found to be the cheapest city in the world in which to live. A 'good bottle of red table wine' costs the equiva-lent of £2.27, and the average cost of a pint in the local pubs is 75p.

Shavkat Mirziyoyev has been president of Uzbeki-stan since 2016, but for decades the real power has been wielded by the much-feared Rustam Inoyatov, head of the country's security services, the SNB. So when Mirziyoyev fired his security chief in January, Uzbekistan became a little more free, bucking the world trend of regimes becoming more and more autocratic.

There are still human rights abuses in the country, of course, and Mirziyoyev remains the unchallenged leader, but the firing of Inoyatov is not the only sign that things are changing. In March, for example,

Yusuf Ruzimuradov, a reporter for opposition newspaper *Erk* (Freedom) and the world's longest-imprisoned journalist, was finally freed, 19 years after being incarcerated on trumped-up charges. And the *Yashirin Kamera* (Hidden Camera) TV show in Uzbekistan was criticised by the country's justice ministry for shaming couples who were showing affection in public. The official warning stated that *Yashirin Kamera* went 'against basic human rights and privacy laws'.

It wasn't all good news for civil liberties in Uzbekistan, though. Uzbeks have been told that if they don't use their gardens 'efficiently', agreeing to grow vegetables and keep chickens, they face a huge tax hike. And strict restrictions on weddings have been proposed that would limit the number of guests to a maximum of 150, and the maximum of cars and singers to one of each.

In which we learn . . .
Which emoji went vegan, the most dangerous
place you can roast a marshmallow, which part
of his garden Jeremy Corbyn likes to piss on,
and why Austrians are allowed to tell
their politicians to piss off.

VALENTINE'S DAY ▶

*Dozens of couples were arrested in Indonesia for
celebrating Valentine's Day.*

Valentine's Day was outlawed
in at least 10 Indonesian cities
this year, including Mataram
City, Lombok, where police
entered schools to check that
no students were getting too
amorous. Those lovers who
were arrested were eventually
released without charge. In Pakistan the holiday was
banned nationwide for the second year in a row – as
was any media coverage of the day. In India's Lucknow
University, all classes and exams were cancelled to stop
students from celebrating it on campus. One country
that did embrace Valentine's Day was Thailand, where
the government handed out vitamin pills in the hope of
boosting its falling birth rate.

In Britain, bakery chain
Greggs opened five
branches for Valentine's
Day dinners, so offering
couples the prospect
of celebrating their
love with a sausage
roll. And it worked: in
one London branch,
graphic designer Joe
Callingham proposed to
his girlfriend, Pineapple
Featonby. She said yes.

VAR ▶

*A Cardiff school warned parents to stop using VAR
at school sports days.*

Video assistant referees (VAR) were the talk of the
World Cup this year, but this wasn't the only major
sporting event in which they were involved. At Mynydd
Bychan primary school in Cardiff, some parents who
had videoed their children's sporting events on phones
and iPads then used the footage to challenge the official results, even resorting to social media to express
their dissent.

Head teacher Siân Evans wrote to parents asking them
to stop, and making it clear that: 'The members of staff at

the finish line, and nobody else, have the absolute final say as to the first, second and third place positions.' She also suggested it might prove necessary to 'consider changing the competitive nature of our sports morning'.

While video assistant referees may have been a disaster for school sporting events, in the world of professional football they have been largely successful. According to FIFA, referees at the World Cup this year achieved a 95 per cent accuracy rate in the decisions they made; but when these decisions involved VAR the figure rose to 99.3 per cent. Not everyone was happy, though. When a referee didn't give Serbia a penalty against Switzerland, Serbia's coach suggested the referee should be put before a war-crimes tribunal.

VEGANS

Google made its salad emoji vegan friendly.

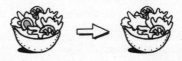

A company called Ecotricity launched the world's first vegan electricity. Unlike most other energy companies, it avoids any of the by-products of animal farming – like slaughter-house waste and animal slurry – that produce gas that can then be used to generate electricity.

When the egg was removed from the icon in June, an executive explained it was part of Google's drive to be more inclusive. She also announced they were adding redheads to their people emojis and making the goat less angry and the turtle less sad.

Veganism continued to grow in popularity. One survey suggested there has been an almost sevenfold increase in the number of Britons following a fully plant-based diet since 2016, from 540,000 to 3.5 million. Topshop jumped on the bandwagon, launching a shirt branded with the word 'Vegan' under a picture of a herbivorous dinosaur, and with a cake recipe on the label. The label gimmick was rather undermined by the fact that the recipe called for 6 oz of butter and three large eggs.

Veganism nevertheless continues to divide opinion. Its supporters include two brothers from Lymington who became the first people to row across the Atlantic, fuelled by a fully vegan diet, in order to prove that a plant-based lifestyle doesn't preclude success in extreme physical challenges. (They successfully raised £82,000 for skin cancer research in the process.) The less enthusiastic included the head chef at a Shropshire restaurant who spiked a vegan's meal with non-vegan ingredients, and subsequently posted on Facebook: 'Pious, judgmental vegan (who I spent all day cooking for) has gone to bed, still believing she's a vegan.' Outrage and even death threats followed, and the chef resigned.

French butchers aren't too happy about vegans, either. This year they successfully lobbied MPs to ban food firms from giving vegetarian meat substitutes names like 'bacon', 'steak', 'sausage' or 'cheese', on the grounds that it's misleading. And Baroness Deech, a peer in the House of Lords, managed to offend two different groups at once when she called vegetarians who eat fake meat 'transgender vegetarians'.

VEGETABLES

Jeremy Corbyn's beetroot sold for over £5,000.

The vegetable, fresh from the Labour leader's allotment, first attracted attention when he brought it to a Jewish Passover dinner. His attendance was controversial, as the dinner was hosted by Jewdas, a group that some argue downplays anti-Semitism in the Labour Party. The *Daily Mail* reported that during the feast, the beetroot was held aloft while guests shouted 'Fuck capitalism'. The anti-capitalist vegetable was later put

Barnet councillor Richard Cornelius suggested that in light of the row over alleged anti-Semitism in the Labour Party, Jeremy Corbyn should have his allotment taken from him.

on eBay, and initial (presumably fake) bids topped £50,000. eBay then removed and relisted the item, at which point it sold for £5,101.

Corbyn also brought a sample of home-grown horse-radish to the event and, according to the *Sunday Times*, had a 'nice chat' with a guest about the best way to grow it, as well as talking knowledgeably about the International Horseradish Festival held every year in Illinois.

The Labour leader is equally knowledgeable about the best way to keep compost, revealing in an interview that adding urine is important, and that everyone with allotments wees on their heaps. It's not clear whether he adopted this approach when a fire broke out near his patch this year. Luckily, Corbyn's vegetables are thought to have escaped the blaze unscathed.

VENEZUELA

Virtually everyone in Venezuela became a millionaire, but many struggled to afford even basic items.

'We are millionaires, but we are poor,' said 43-year-old Maigualida Oronoz, whose nurse's salary, which in July stood at 5 million bolívars a month, made her a multimillionaire but was worth only US$31. To make matters worse, most Venezuelans are unable to change money at the official rates and have to rely on the black market, where 5 million bolívars could get you as little as $1.

Later in the year, as the currency crashed and inflation rates rose sharply, things got even worse. By August, a burger and chips could cost as much as 20 million bolívars, a sum so high that credit card machines couldn't cope, and sales had to be broken up into smaller transactions. In fact, the only commodity that could be bought in the usual way was petrol, which the government keeps artificially cheap for locals (*see* **Haiti**). At one stage, the price of a cup of coffee would be enough to fill your SUV 9,000 times.

President Nicolás Maduro, a former bus driver who found himself in power after the death of Hugo Chávez in 2013, won his first election this year. The vote was called a 'sham' by the US government, an analysis that appeared to be borne out when a video appeared of Maduro waving to his supporters: when the camera panned out, it became clear that he was waving to an empty plaza.

Later, an attempt was made on Maduro's life as he spoke to a (real) crowd in Caracas. It was thwarted only because the two explosives-laden drones involved were stopped by radio jammers that caused one to crash into a building and the other to explode a safe distance from the president. The attack represents the first time drones have ever been used to target a head of state, but it appears that Maduro's team had long known of the threat – it was already illegal in Venezuela to fly drones within 3.7 kilometres of the president.

Venezuela cancelled its version of quiz show *Who Wants to Be a Millionaire?* once runaway inflation meant that a million Venezuelan Bolivars was no longer a prize worth playing for.

VENICE

The city of canals ran short of water.

In February, Venice ran dry. Thanks to cold winter weather, an unusual lack of rain and abnormally low tides caused by a 'super blue blood moon', the city's canals turned into muddy lanes, while almost all the gondolas were beached on muddy, unromantic channels. It's the third year in a row the problem has struck, although annoyingly flooding remains a problem there at other times of the year.

And *human* flooding is a perennial problem. Every day 60,000 tourists arrive in a city that is home to only 55,000 people. The locals are not happy. In June, 4,000 of them took part in a 'March for the Dignity of Venice' to protest against the cruise ships that discharge thousands of daytrippers. In an attempt to stop tourists snacking while standing at historic landmarks and ruining the view for everyone else, new kebab shops were banned. And turnstiles were installed at the ends of two major bridges in an attempt to control overall numbers of visitors.

Some Venetians, however, can't resist cashing in on the city's popularity. In January, a restaurant charged a group of Japanese tourists €1,143 (£994) for four steaks, a plate of grilled fish, two glasses of wine and some mineral water. Fortunately, three other members of the same tour group suspected the restaurant might be dodgy and went to another one – where they were charged €350 for three plates of pasta.

VOLCANOES

The US Geological Survey warned people not to roast marshmallows over volcanic vents.

The Hawaiian volcano Kilauea has been erupting, on and off, since 1983, but in May it entered a much more violent phase. Boulders the size of washing machines were thrown hundreds of metres, ash clouds rose 10 kilometres high, and the air filled with toxic gases. Lava destroyed 657 houses (including the mayor's), as well as a GPS station, a car park and lots of roads – so naturally, some people asked if it was all right to use the volcanic vents to roast marshmallows.

The USGS advised not to, pointing out that the vent would cover them in dangerous gases like sulphur dioxide, hydrogen sulphide and perhaps even sulphuric acid. In addition, it warned tourists against swimming near the lava as it hit the ocean, and especially against hanging out near lava flows to take selfies – 40 people were arrested for the offence, which now carries a $5,000 fine or up to a year in prison.

Residents were also warned to look out for and to avoid 'laze', or 'lava haze' – clouds of hydrochloric acid generated when lava hits the sea. And they were advised to steer clear of 'vog' (volcanic smog) if possible. Thankfully, there weren't too many casualties, although Hawaii resident Darryl Clinton was badly injured in the leg by a 'lava bomb' – a globule of molten lava that had blasted into the air and solidified into a red-hot cannonball.

In Guatemala, where the Fuego volcano erupted in June, at least 150 people were killed. But tourists soon returned to the volcano when things had calmed down – and, ignoring all official advice, toasted marshmallows there.

VOTES

For vomiting while voting, *see* **Brexit**; for an opposition candidate who didn't oppose anything, *see* **Egypt**; for flying home to vote, *see* **Eighth Amendment**; for a country run by 'Mr Nobody', *see* **Italy**; for a sore loser who inaugurated himself anyway, *see* **Kenya**; for coming face to face with your own campaign material, *see* **Leaflets**; for the world's first sports star leader, *see* **Liberia**; for a 92-year-old courting the youth vote, *see* **Malaysia**; for the world's second sports star leader, *see* **Pakistan**; for promises of discount peas, *see* **Russian Election**; for promises of tea and cake *see* **Turkey**; for the first transgender member of the Virginia House of Delegates, *see* **Transgender**; and for promises of the fastest trains the world has ever known, *see* **Zimbabwe**.

VULGAR

An Austrian court ruled that the public has the right to swear at politicians.

The ruling was made after the leader of the far-right Freedom Party, Heinz-Christian Strache, attempted to sue a group of left-wing activists over a video in which they attacked his policies. In the video the activists are seen yelling 'Fuck Strache' while giving the middle finger to the camera. The court ruled that Austrians are entitled to express 'provocative and shocking' political opinions and that these are a 'fundamental part of freedom of expression'.

In other vulgar news, tennis player Nick Kyrgios was caught simulating a sexual act with a water bottle while on court at the Queen's Club Championships. He was fined £13,190. And a shop in Canada refused to put cum on a student's graduation cake. The student's mother had asked for the words 'Summa Cum Laude' (Latin for 'with the highest distinction') to be written in icing. However, the cake she got back read: 'Summa — Laude'. In a Facebook post the mother said that not only was her son humiliated, but she also had to explain to a lot of family members what 'cum' meant.

In which we learn . . .
Where whales go to retire, where iguanas fall out
of trees, where clever pigs cross borders, where
firefighters can get free fish, and where Al Qaeda and
ISIS differ when it comes to women's rights.

WAITER, WAITER ▶

A waiter who was fired for being too rude claimed he's not rude, he's just French.

Guillaume Rey, who worked at Milestones restaurant in Vancouver, Canada, believes he has been the victim of cultural discrimination, and is suing his former employers for violating his human rights. Rey had received many warnings for his behaviour towards fellow staff members, and was finally fired when he left a member of staff almost in tears when he criticised her for not finishing a task. His manager said he was 'aggressive, rude and disrespectful'. Rey said he was just employing his 'direct, honest and professional personality'. Winning the case won't be easy. According to a tribunal member, 'Mr Rey will have to explain what it is about his French heritage that would result in behaviour that people misinterpret as a violation of workplace standards of acceptable conduct.'

WATER, WATER ▶

Dirty hair became fashionable in Cape Town.

At the start of the year, it was being predicted that Cape Town would run out of water in April. Residents were banned from watering their gardens and washing their cars, most swimming pools were shut, the water pressure was cut, and Capetonians were rationed to just one toilet flush a day.

At the same time, showers were restricted to just 90 seconds per person (some musicians came up with songs precisely that long, so you could hit the play button and know you had to be out by the time the track finished). And some hairdressers took to charging extra for the water used to wash customers' hair, unless they brought

———— ▼ ————

A boater in a rush accidentally drained a section of the Kennet and Avon Canal by forgetting to shut the lock gates. Boats were left in the mud, and fish flailed around in the shallow puddles that remained.

their own. *Time* magazine reported that 'unwashed hair is now a symbol of upright citizenship' in the city.

The crisis was eventually averted thanks to farmers outside the city agreeing to risk their livelihoods by donating their precious water supplies. It was a gesture that gave Cape Town some breathing space before the much-needed rains arrived. Had dam levels fallen below 13.5 per cent of their capacity – an event that would have been known as 'Day Zero' – all taps would have been turned off, and residents would have had to queue for water rations.

Cities around the world sat up and paid attention: Los Angeles, Beijing and São Paulo are also suffering water shortages, and so have kept a close eye on how Cape Town coped. And it's not just big cities that are affected: the town of Vittel in north-east France, famous for its water, complained that thanks in part to a lack of rain, and in part to Nestlé extracting and selling too much local spring water, it too was running out.

WEAPONRY

A Mexican police force had their guns replaced with slingshots and rocks.

Researchers studying weapons prized by the people of New Guinea used computer simulations and stabbing tests with bird and human bones to show that human thigh bones make the best bone weapons.

The entire police department of Alvarado in Veracruz was stripped of its guns this year, after 100 of its 130 personnel failed a weapons competency test. In protest, the mayor of Alvarado, Bogar Ruiz Rosas, decided to equip all police officers with slingshots and bags of rocks.

The mayor believes the decision to disarm the officers was a political one, as it happened just ahead of state and national elections. As he handed out the slingshots, Rosas told Alvarado police that their vote

in the elections was their most powerful weapon.
In response, Veracruz state governor and rival
party member Miguel Ángel Yunes Linares advised
all police officers that if they actually patrolled the
streets with the slingshots, they would be subject to
prosecution.

Over the border in America, 5-gallon buckets full of
rocks were placed in 200 classrooms across Blue Mountain School District in Pennsylvania for use in the event
of a school shooting. Superintendent Dr David Helsel
said, 'If an armed intruder attempts to gain entrance
into any of our classrooms, they will face a classroom
full of students armed with rocks and they will be
stoned.' He had initially considered arming the students
with golf balls, but decided against it as they bounce
around too much.

In other weapons news: Russia unveiled an impressive
new missile system that boasts a 'practically unlimited' range, and an ability to travel so fast that no
anti-missile system can stop it. In its first test, it flew for
around two minutes and travelled 35 kilometres before
it lost control and crashed. And in China, researchers
claimed they had invented a laser assault rifle the size

Weather, Severe

Extreme weather took many forms this year . . .

The icy cold: In Florida in January, frozen iguanas fell out of the trees; in Massachusetts, frozen sharks washed up on beaches; and in North Carolina, alligators had to make holes in the ice and stick their snouts up out of them like snorkels in order to breathe.

The very windy: A historic building was blown from the US to Canada. One of the last traditional smoked-herring facilities in America was blown out of the ground in Maine and deposited on the other side of the border. The building was eventually returned, and the local preservation society are working to turn it into a fishing industry museum.

The expensively hot: Los Angeles sprayed some of its streets white in a bid to reduce ambient temperatures, at a cost of $40,000 a mile. It used squeegees to spread the tarmac with a product called CoolSeal, which reflects more of the sun's rays and so can reduce the temperature by over 10 degrees.

The inconveniently snowy: Russians complaining about local government's slowness in clearing away snowdrifts spray-painted them with the name of government opposition leader Alexei Navalny to ensure their swift removal by the authorities. It wasn't a foolproof method, however. One woman reported that officials simply covered the name with more snow.

And finally, the undeniably miserable: In January, it was revealed that during the whole of December 2017, Moscow had just six minutes of sunshine.

of an AK-47 that can shoot a distance of 800 metres. According to Chinese media reports, the ZKZM-500 rifle can 'instantly carbonise' human skin and tissues, set a person on fire and make them feel 'pain beyond endurance'. It is currently classified as 'non-lethal'.

WHALES ▶

The world's first retirement home for celebrity whales is being constructed . . . right next to a restaurant that serves whale.

Next year, two performing belugas, Little Grey and Little White, will be airlifted almost 9,000 kilometres from Shanghai to the sea off the coast of Iceland, where they will live out the rest of their days in a netted-off section. There's a lot of preparation required before they go – the temperature of their tank is slowly being cooled to prepare them for colder water, they're being fed lots of herring to build up their blubber, and they're being trained to hold their breath so they can dive for long periods. Finally, they're being 'introduced' to the stretchers that they're going to be lifted on when they make the journey, so they don't get upset when the time comes.

It was announced that killer whales can 'talk' – sort of. Professor Josep Call and his team wrote that they've been trained to mimic words like 'hello', 'bye bye' and 'one two three', and to imitate the sound of a creaking door and a trumpeting elephant. They can also blow a raspberry.

Awkwardly, the sanctuary itself is very near a shoreline restaurant that serves minke whale steak in Béarnaise sauce. Not only that, but a week after the announcement, the Icelandic government spoiled its green credentials by announcing the country would take up hunting endangered fin whales again, and granted itself the authority to catch 238 of them every year. The new prime minister has promised to review the local whaling industry – it's a lot less popular than it used to be and in Iceland only 3 per cent of the population eat it.

WILD BOAR

Poland announced the world's longest boar-der.

Pigs weren't the only beneficiaries of steel barriers this year. During the World Cup, a 4-metre-high steel fence was put round the England training ground in Russia to stop any foreign swine spying on the England team's tactics.

The sole aim of the 2-metre-high, 1,200-kilometre-long galvanised steel fence along Poland's borders with Ukraine, Russia and Belarus will be to stop foreign pigs wandering into the country. Foreign boar often carry African swine fever, a deadly disease that can kill a farm pig in 10 days and could decimate Poland's pork industry. The fence will even run underground, to stop the animals tunnelling beneath it.

Poland wasn't the only nation to plan an anti-boar barrier this year. The Danish government announced its own 70-kilometre fence along the German border, to protect the country's £4 billion-a-year pig industry from ASF-infected *German* wild boar. It's unlikely to be foolproof: one expert on boar immigration warned, firstly, that the animals don't live in the area where the fence is going to be erected; and, secondly, that even if the fence stops them arriving by land, they will easily be able to swim into Denmark via a fjord. The Polish wall faces the same challenges since there will be gaps at rivers and lakes which clever boar might well exploit.

So it may turn out that massive fences aren't the answer to the boar problem. But there is an alternative. One local politician in Belgium suggested that the exploding wild boar population could be curbed by putting females on the Pill. According to the mayor of Beringen, it should be possible to establish special feeding zones where the food left out for the boar contains contraceptives. The authorities have yet to respond to this idea. One sceptical expert pointed out that other animals might take the contraceptive by mistake, and that even if the boar did eat it, there was no way to ensure they would actually consume the requisite dose.

WILDFIRES ▶

The Manchester moor fires were blamed on a lack of fires.

The blaze on Saddleworth Moor in Greater Manchester burned over 1,800 hectares and forced 50 households to evacuate. But experts suggested it could have been minimised had fires been deliberately set. In other parts of the UK, controlled burning of heather, the main fuel for moor fires, is carried out throughout the year. But it's banned in places such as Saddleworth because it's feared it will damage the peat and local wildlife. Had the ban been lifted, some academics have argued, the fires here and in other parts of Lancashire would have been easier to deal with.

In fact, when the Saddleworth blaze did start, firefighters considered torching the heather to create fire breaks. But it was too late. Instead, they dug trenches around buildings and even individual family homes to keep the flames at bay. They also dropped vast quantities of water from helicopters. The effectiveness of this approach, however, was limited: much of the water

▼

The Europe-wide heatwave in July led to at least 11 wildfires burning in the Arctic.

sprayed on the blaze evaporated before it reached the ground, and according to the editor-in-chief of the journal *Fire Technology*, any water that makes it to the ground won't penetrate deeply enough. Professor Guillermo Rein argued that in such circumstances it's much better to pump water through tubes deep into the peat to stop it burning.

One possible long-term effect of the moorland fires may be the release of pollutants trapped in the peat since the time of the Industrial Revolution. But in the short term, it wasn't all bad news: those fighting the fire were offered free fish and chips by a chippie in Stalybridge.

WINE ▶

A study found that women make better wine tasters but that men get more emotional about it.

A team from Cambridge analysed 411 wine glasses from different periods and found that they have undergone a sevenfold increase in size between Georgian times and today.

This was the conclusion after blind taste tests involving 208 people. Women, it emerged, were better at distinguishing between wines, and reported greater differences between them. But they gave them lower 'emotional ratings' than the men, who seemed to be more passionate about them, even if they couldn't taste them as well. The study also found that older people, who have fewer taste buds, were 'more likely to enjoy any glass of wine whatever its attributes'.

In France, where wine is virtually a religion, there was outrage when it emerged that up to 66 million bottles of cheap plonk had been passed off as Châteauneuf-du-Pape or other Côtes du Rhône. It can only be hoped that most of the bottles were drunk by men who couldn't tell the difference.

One Frenchman who might have the expertise to tell the difference is President Macron, who got in trouble with French doctors for encouraging his countryfolk to drink wine. After he said he had wine every day with both lunch and dinner, and that it was much better than drinking beer or spirits, nine eminent killjoy doctors wrote to the newspaper *Le Figaro* telling him off, and saying alcohol policy should be tightened.

Britain, meanwhile, got its first 'wine A-level' in the form of an Advanced Technical Certificate in Viticulture. Plumpton College in East Sussex, which launched it, is hoping to turn out graduates who can help build the British wine industry. Because the course is aimed at 16- to 18-year-olds, most who take it won't be of legal age to buy wine.

The coffin of one of England's greatest poets, Samuel Taylor Coleridge, was found in a wine cellar in a church. It had lain there since his death but had been completely forgotten until it was rediscovered during a renovation.

WINNIES

For the Pooh, *see* **Auctions**; for the anti-apartheid campaigner, *see* **Mandela, Winnie**.

WOMEN'S RIGHTS

Al-Qaeda launched a women's magazine.

The new publication is called *Beituki*, which translates as 'Your Home', and it tells women how to support and please their jihadi husbands. One piece of advice encourages wives to always greet their husbands with a smile, and never dabble in their work, because: 'Can you imagine all the bloodshed and bones he sees every day? Your fussing only increases the pressure.' The magazine strikes a slightly lighter note when suggesting: 'Stealing is legal when you're stealing your man's heart.' The magazine is thought to be a response to ISIS's policy of encouraging women to engage in fighting. Al-Qaeda thinks they should remain in the home.

Formula 1 racing
recently phased out 'grid
girls' – female models
wearing clothes embla-
zoned with sponsors'
names whose role was
to form a glamorous-
looking accompaniment
to F1 events – in favour
of 'grid kids' – child
mascots.

Elsewhere in the Middle East there were genuine victories for women's rights, notably in Saudi Arabia (*see* **Saudi Arabia**) and also in Iran, where women were allowed in a football stadium for the first time since 1979: they watched the Iran vs Spain World Cup match on a huge screen in the country's largest stadium in Tehran. After the game, Sergio Ramos, the Spanish captain, shared photographs of Iranian female fans on Twitter, declaring: 'They are the ones who won tonight. Hopefully the first of many.' Although, in a strictly sporting sense, Spain won.

In Japan, sumo was the focus for the battle against sporting sexism. Two female spectators caused contro-versy when they ran over to give CPR to a sumo wrestler who was having a heart attack. Since the rules of sumo clearly state that women are not allowed in the ring, the referee ordered them to leave – and a furore ensued. The Japan Sumo Association have since agreed to review the rule. Perhaps they could take their lead from Japan's bullfighters, who recently dropped their own long-standing rule that prohibited women from entering the bullfighting ring.

Back in Britain, on International Women's Day, Oxford University was criticised for asking a female cleaner to scrub some 'Happy International Women's Day' graffiti off a staircase.

WONGA

Wonga got some emergency cash before ending up bankrupt.

The payday loan company, which went into admin-istration in late August, was famous for lending people money on very short-term contracts but with extremely high levels of interest. This year, Wonga itself struggled financially thanks to a surge in compensation claims by customers who, it is claimed, borrowed money that Wonga should have known they had no hope of paying back. Wonga also had to write off a large number of debts that it no longer had any hope of recouping.

In an attempt to prevent their collapse, the company asked for an emergency injection of money, raising £10 million of capital from a group of early investors. The exact terms of the deal were not released, but it was presumably slightly better than Wonga's own advertised interest rate of 1,460 per cent per year.

WORDS ▶

A group of schoolchildren bullied dictionaries into changing their definition of the word 'bully'.

This year, as children around the world took part in the #IAmNotWeak campaign, many voiced their objections to existing definitions of the word 'bully' that included the word 'weak' when describing the victim. The *Oxford English Dictionary* (*OED*), for instance, defined 'bully' as 'a person who uses strength or influence to harm or intimidate those who are weaker'. Following the campaign, the *OED* altered its definition to 'a person who habitually seeks to harm or intimidate those who they perceive as vulnerable'.

This year the *OED* also asked the public to put forward local words from around the world that weren't already included in the dictionary. As a result, it now boasts Hawaii's 'hammajang', meaning 'in a disorderly or shambolic state'; New Zealand's 'munted', meaning 'broken or wrecked'; and 'frog-drowner', which Americans might use to describe a torrential downpour of rain. Closer to home, the north-east of England turned out to be a

Merriam-Webster added more than 800 words to its dictionary this year, including millennial terms such as 'adorbs', which is short for adorable, and 'embiggen', which was invented by *The Simpsons* as a fake word that is only used in Springfield. The dictionary says that it now means 'make bigger or more expansive'.

particularly fruitful source, offering 'spuggy', a house sparrow; 'cuddy-wifter', a left-handed person; and 'mard-arse', 'a sulky, petulant, or grumpy person'.

WORLD CUP, FIFA ▶

For advice on making passes, *see* **Advice, Worse**; for fake fake injuries, *see* **Crazes**; for avoiding a drugs ban, *see* **Incas**; for avoiding a chicken ban, *see* **Football Fans**; for gaming-inspired celebrations, *see* **Fortnite**; for passing balls between world leaders, *see* **Gifts, Diplomatic**; for football-inspired revolutions, *see* **Haiti**; for predicting winners, *see* **Quokkas**; for eating weiners, *see* **Sausages**; for what's not allowed at school sports days, *see* **VAR**; for what *is* allowed in Iran, *see* **Women's Rights**; and for something that's absolutely not related to the FIFA World Cup in any way whatsoever, *see* **World Cup, Non-FIFA**.

WORLD CUP, NON-FIFA ▶

An international tournament called itself the World Football Cup to avoid being sued by the Football World Cup.

———— ♥ ————

The tournament was run by CONIFA, the Confederation of Independent Football Associations. Its head, who began his career as a referee, is called Per-Anders Blind.

The competition, held in London, was for countries and regions not recognised by FIFA. Teams participating included ones from Abkhazia, Northern Cyprus, the Isle of Man, and Cascadia, a region of north-west America where some people wish to start their own environmentally conscious country. The county of Yorkshire also wanted to take part, but didn't send in its application in time.

The tournament was won by Karpatalya, an area of Ukraine that has a predominantly Hungarian population, but the Ukrainian government wasn't happy. Its sports minister was quoted as saying, 'I call on the Security Service of Ukraine to respond appropriately to such a frank act of sporting separatism. It is necessary to interrogate the players of the team.'

Several other national governments objected to the tournament, too. The Cypriot High Commission, angry that Northern Cyprus was fielding a team, tried to get the whole tournament cancelled; and under pressure from China over Tibet's inclusion, four major sponsors withdrew. The Kabylia team, representing an ethnically Berber area that wants to split from Algeria, refused to release the names of their squad before the tournament, in an attempt to thwart an Algerian government that in the past has detained players to stop them from playing. Even so, six of the team were denied visas.

One tournament innovation this year was the introduction of green cards alongside the usual red cards and yellow cards. Designed as an 'intermediate disciplinary measure', green cards signify that a player who has argued with the referee is being sent off but that a substitution can be made in order to avoid the team being reduced to 10 men.

In which we learn . . .
Why Martians shouldn't panic,
how China went loopy for luxury loos,
and what links Fort Dick and Big Beaver.

SpaceX launched a rocket that could theoretically kill all Martians, emblazoned with the slogan 'DON'T PANIC'.

According to a report by scientists at Purdue University, Elon Musk's Falcon Heavy, the most powerful rocket to launch into space since the 1970s, may have carried a number of unwanted passengers in the form of a colony of bacteria. That colony could, in theory, be enough to wipe out any aliens they come in contact with – or, more positively, they could be seen as a backup copy of the type of life found on Earth.

Later in the year, SpaceX used its rockets to send ice cream, mice and the world's strongest coffee to the International Space Station.

It wasn't the rocket that was at fault: it was made in sterile conditions, just as NASA's spacecraft are. But Musk also sent a Tesla roadster car that was built in a clean rather than a completely sterile environment. (The Tesla also had the phrase 'DON'T PANIC' stamped on the dashboard – referencing *The Hitchhiker's Guide to the Galaxy* – and had David Bowie's 'Space Oddity' playing on an endless repeat from its speaker.) Musk's plan was to crash the car – and the similarly unsterile mannequin inside – into the surface of Mars. There is, of course, currently no evidence that there is any life on Mars, but if there is, then Earth bacteria could easily outcompete it, and cause its extinction.

XL

Increasing waistlines featured prominently across the world's news this year.

Pony-trekking: A company in Dartmoor announced it was closing because people are becoming too overweight to ride its horses. Over the past seven years it's had to turn away 30 per cent more customers on the grounds that their weight would damage the horses.

Mortuaries: More plus-size fridges are now needed to accommodate the rising number of chubby cadavers. And a company called LEEC, which makes mortuary equipment, has had to produce a new 'bariatric body trolley' that can bear a corpse weighing up to 65 stone.

Rollercoasters: A Chinese theme park granted free entry to any women fatter than a celebrated concubine. Women were invited to sit on giant weighing scales before entering and those heavier than 61.8kg, the weight of Yang Guifei, an 8th

YOU MUST BE THIS WIDE TO RIDE

century consort and one of China's 'four great beauties', were then allowed in for free.

Palaeontology: A study concluded that birds that lived around the time of the dinosaurs would have been too heavy to sit on their eggs without breaking them. They would have had to sit beside them instead.

XS

While people were getting larger, everything else seemed to be getting smaller.

Fish: A chef at a restaurant in Tokyo that sells the world's smallest sushi, made from a single grain of rice garnished with a tiny flake of seafood, said that overseas diners tend to be 'extra enthusiastic' about the dish. Indeed one European woman was so moved by it that she proceeded to cry for an hour and a half.

Chips: The University of Michigan made the world's smallest computer, which, at 0.3 mm cubed, is smaller than a grain of salt. It's hoped it could be used to diagnose glaucoma from inside the eye, monitor biochemical processes and study tiny snails.

Spaceships: Japan launched the world's smallest rocket into space. It's 9.54 metres long and about the width of a scaffolding pole, and it carries a 34.6-centimetre-long satellite that will take photos of Earth and relay them back.

Homes: Robots managed to build the world's smallest house. It has a tiled roof, seven windows, a door and a chimney, but since it's only about one fifth the width of a human hair, it's too small for even an amoeba or a sperm to live in. Scientists working on the project said that they did it in order to prove that it can be done. They also said that the reason they'd installed a chimney was: 'It snows in winter [in Besançon – the French town where it was made] and it is cold.'

XI JINPING ▶

Chinese councils built luxury loos to impress Xi Jinping.

China is in the middle of a 'toilet revolution'. Since 2015, President Xi Jinping has been urging local governments across the country to modernise public conveniences to a decent standard. (When Xi visits rural areas he often checks people's loos to see how good they are.) But this year, the revolution finally went too far. In January, the Chinese National Tourism Administration was forced to ask local officials to stop spending so much money on toilets, because in their zeal to improve the nation's loos, they have had an arms race: competing with one another to build the most lavish lavatories. Some hired only university graduates as toilet managers, while others spent up to £100,000 on a single bog.

Xi will be revolutionising toilets for a while. This year 99.79 per cent of China's People's Congress voted to abolish the 10-year limit on how long he can stay in power. The government immediately proceeded to block people from searching the Internet for the phrase 'serve another term'. Other blocks included 'personality cult', 'lifelong', 'shameless', '1984' and 'ascend the throne' (although that one might have had something to do with the toilets).

For whatever reason, Xi's personality cult is definitely getting stronger. This year China dedicated a whole train to his political thoughts, with carriages covered in Xi quotes. Xi slogans are all over billboards across China, and school pupils are instructed to 'plant Xi's thought in their minds'.

XXX ▶

When Hawaiians thought they were going to be hit by a North Korean missile, the number of people using Pornhub fell by 77 per cent.

When they got the all-clear, there was a spike of 48 per cent. And it wasn't only imminent death that pulled people off porn sites: Pornhub traffic went down by 21 per cent in the UK when the royal wedding took place. There was a small increase after the coverage finished, with a 2,812 per cent increase in Pornhub searches for 'Meghan Markle', though around 75 per cent of people spelled her name incorrectly – either as Megan Markle or Megan Markel. In America, there was a big drop in malware infections in late February, which was ascribed to Christians giving up pornography for Lent.

Though maybe these increases in viewer numbers were not just down to porn. It emerged this year that there was more on Pornhub than just pornography. The site announced that users were misusing the site by posting family-friendly material, including the Disney film *Zootropolis* and clips of the musical *Hamilton*. As a result, the website was having to remove content for breaching copyright. To make the videos less conspicuous, uploaders had given them porn-like names: *Zootropolis* had been renamed 'Hot Animal Action' and *Hamilton* had been renamed 'Revolutionary Twinks Have Historical Fun'.

———— ▼ ————

As part of a publicity campaign, Pornhub gave free premium access to anyone living in a rude-sounding place. So residents of the following places all get free content: Fort Dick, California; Hooker, Oklahoma; Horneytown, North Carolina; Big Beaver, Pennsylvania; Threeway, Virginia; and Blowhard, Australia.

In which we learn . . .
Why the Y chromosome might be Yuseful after
all, who Yelped about diarrhoea, why Donald
Trump is banned from Sheffield, and why
Koreans love robots who have no fun.

Y CHROMOSOME

The Y chromosome might not be completely useless after all.

The Y chromosome has long been the butt of scientific jokes due to its relative puniness in comparison with the X chromosome. Biological females carry a pair of X chromosomes (clusters of genes) in their cells, which are robust, healthy and contain about 1,600 genes with a multitude of purposes. Males have one X and one Y, the Y being shrivelled, constantly degrading and carrying only about 27 genes that aren't found elsewhere.

But new research suggests men's Y chromosome might have more functions than previously thought. It may, for example, unblock arteries, keep cancer at bay and prevent plaque from building up in the brain. Certainly there's a direct correlation between the rate at which individuals shed Y chromosomes as they age and their susceptibility to certain diseases. One reason why men don't live as long as women may well be that they keep tossing out their Y chromosomes.

Because Y is mostly made up of purposeless piles of 'junk DNA' and has degenerated significantly over the past 166 million years, many scientists give it just another 4.6 million years to live. One of the few attributes that might save it from extinction is its ability to host 'palindromes'. These are strings of DNA that read the same backwards as forwards and somehow keep the chromosome from shrinking further.

As it stands, the scientific community is divided as to whether Y will disappear, with geneticists split into groups nicknamed 'leavers' and 'remainers'.

YAKUZA ▶

Mafia gangs in Japan are making as much money smuggling sea cucumbers as they are drugs.

The Yakuza are a Japanese organised crime syndicate. They have office buildings, a website and a theme tune. They produce their own magazine with articles on topics such as fishing; gossip about them frequently features in Japanese tabloids; and they are the subject of a popular long-running PlayStation game series. They are notorious for their drug smuggling, money laundering, prostitution rings, illegal gambling, and now, sea cucumber trafficking.

Sea cucumbers are a culinary delicacy in Asia and a valuable export for Japan – in 2017 the country sold £143.8 million-worth of them. It's no surprise, therefore, that for the past few years Yakuza gangs have been getting in on the act by illegally fishing for the animals themselves and then selling them abroad.

To clamp down on the Yakuza's cucumber racket, the Japanese government announced this year that it would be initiating a 'catch certificate' system for all domestically caught sea cucumbers. When it launches in 2020, customs offices will be able to monitor and prevent illegal exports by requesting 'certificates of origin' issued by fishermen's associations. Needless to say, the Yakuza are not official fishermen.

One way and another, it wasn't a great year for the Yakuza. Membership was reported to be at an all-time low, with fewer than 20,000 core members remaining;* and Japanese banks announced that because they now had access to police databases, they could ensure that loans did not go to people associated with the Yakuza. According to one member, some gangs have now become so poor they have had to resort to stealing watermelons from farms.

Even the Yakuza's overseas members couldn't catch a break this year. Shigeharu Shirai, a 74-year-old gang member who had managed to evade the police for 14 years, was arrested after being recognised when photos of his full-body tattoos were put online by a Thai man who happened to like the look of them. Unfortunately for the Yakuza member, the photo was shared 10,000 times and, owing to his very recognisable tattoos, he was arrested.

In 1963 there were over 180,000 members.

YELP

Investigators tracked food poisoning outbreaks by searching Yelp reviews for 'diarrhoea'.

The New York City Department of Health and Mental Hygiene noticed that when people have bad restaurant experiences, they are very likely to share them on sites such as Yelp and TripAdvisor. So they partnered with Columbia University to set up a program that searched for words such as 'sick', 'vomiting' and 'diarrhoea'. The algorithm was able to identify 8,523 complaints of food-borne illness stretching back over the last five years.

Yelp and cleanliness also featured in a row that turned into a battleground between the American Left and Right. First, the Red Hen restaurant in Lexington refused to serve White House Press Secretary Sarah Huckabee Sanders because she was associated with Donald Trump. Then the president himself got involved. In a furious tweet, he wrote: 'The Red Hen Restaurant should focus more on cleaning its filthy canopies, doors and windows (badly needs a paint job) rather than refusing to serve a fine person like Sarah Huckabee Sanders. I always had a rule, if a restaurant is dirty on the outside, it is dirty on the inside!'*

The tweet had the desired effect and the Red Hen was 'Yelpbombed' with negativity. The restaurant had received 5,000 reviews in their first five years, with a median score of 5 stars. Within a single weekend, the number of reviews had tripled, and the average had gone down to 1.5 stars. Other completely unrelated restaurants that were unfortunate enough to have the same name found themselves Yelpbombed into near collapse.

But even Trump himself hasn't been immune to Yelp-bombing. After he allegedly called a number of different

For the record: the Red Hen has been found guilty of three health violations since 2013, whereas Trump's Doral Golf Club has managed 524; these include incidences of cockroach infestations, 'slimy/mold-like build-up' in freezers, and holes in kitchen walls.

countries 'shitholes' in January, people logged into Yelp and began describing his hotels as shitholes – and much worse. One user gave the following one-star review to one of Trump's gold-coloured hotels in Las Vegas: 'If you like your hotels how Trump likes his prostitutes, then you'll love this golden hotel.'

YORKSHIRE

Sheffield's mayor was inaugurated to the sound of 'The Imperial March' from Star Wars.

The Steel City's new mayor, Magid Magid, is the first from the Green Party, the first to have come to the country as a child refugee from Somalia, and the first to have appeared on the TV reality show *Hunted*. When he was sworn in this year and realised he could choose his own music, he went for Darth Vader's famous, ominous tune. Once that song finished, and he had the chains of office around his neck, the music morphed into the *Superman* theme.

Magid hit international headlines when he appeared in a video wearing a sombrero and announcing that he would not allow Donald Trump to enter Sheffield. He later wrote: 'I Magid Magid, lord mayor & first citizen of this city hereby declare that not only is Donald J Trump a WASTEMAN, but he is also henceforth banned from the great city of Sheffield!' He also declared 13 July – the date of Trump's UK visit – to be Mexico Solidarity Day.

Magid has taken to inviting members of Sheffield's creative community to perform at council meetings, in a kind of half-time show. In the first one, a scientist called Hassun El Zafar performed tricks that included one in which a water rocket was launched across the chamber. Magid's welcome attitude in a world of career politicians was summed up in an interview with the *Guardian* when he said, 'Do you know what, I wake up in the morning and I think: "I couldn't give a fuck today, I couldn't give a shit," I'm just going to do what I want to do. Of course, I've had a lot of stick. But I don't care.' When asked about his political ambitions he pragmatically said, 'Nobody joins the Greens to have a career in politics.'

YOUTUBE

One of YouTube's biggest new stars became famous for doing nothing.

The YouTube channel in question is called Bot-No-Jaem – which translates as 'a robot which is no fun' – and it's become hugely popular in South Korea. It features a young man sitting and reading a book for hours on end. His face stays blank, he's always alone, and he never says anything. One of his videos is seven hours long. He has gained a third of a million subscribers.

At least Bot-No-Jaem's videos feature a person. Arguably even more dull are the videos of Australian YouTuber Sebastian Tomczak, who a few years ago uploaded 10 hours of white noise (scratchy electronic hissing with no clear sounds in it). This January he learned that five copyright infringement claims had been brought against him including some by people who make 'white noise' sleep therapy products and who claimed his indistinct electronic sounds were too much like *their* indistinct electronic sounds.

In other YouTube news:

▶ When YouTube removed alt-right campaigner Alex Jones's channel InfoWars, it added insult to injury by keeping a column of 'Related Channels' running down the side that advertised nothing but such left-wing shows as *The Late Show with Stephen Colbert* and *Saturday Night Live*.

▶ Two YouTubers fought in one of the year's biggest boxing matches. Despite the fact that Logan Paul and KSI make their living filming themselves, the 20,000 fans in attendance were banned from recording the event.

▶ In protest against a video posted online that criticised the prophet Muhammad, Egypt banned the entirety of YouTube in the country for a month.

▶ YouTube's head of music announced plans to 'smoke out' anyone who could afford a paid subscription, and 'frustrate and seduce' them into signing up by showing them more adverts. A spokesperson quickly clarified that what she'd meant was that YouTube's 'top priority is to give users a great experience'.

In which we learn . . .
How Zuma faced Zexit, who promised zippy trains in
Zimbabwe, and what the Zuists did with their ziggurat.

ZEXIT ▶

While Britain faced Brexit, South Africa encountered Zexit.

In other 'Zuma' news, the US lost a highly secret spy satellite with that name after it took off from Florida in January. The failed mission was thought to have cost the American government billions of dollars, despite the fact that it didn't officially exist.

That was the term used throughout the country to refer to the departure of President Jacob Zuma, who finally failed to live up to his middle name, Gedleyihlekisa, a Zulu word meaning 'I laugh at you as I destroy you'. He was forced out of office by his party after clinging on to power for eight years, during which time, according to one prominent economist, Zuma's poor governance cost South Africa more than a trillion rand (£50 billion) in GDP.

One of the reasons he was so keen to stay in power may well have been that he knew as soon as he could no longer claim presidential immunity from prosecution, he'd face criminal charges. One of the crimes he is accused of is accepting 24 cows and a bull as a gift, when he knew they had been bought with government money set aside to help struggling farmers. Other charges include corruption, fraud, money laundering and racketeering. He's defending himself against these with the help of his long-time lawyer, Kemp Kemp.

At one point it looked as though Zuma might be replaced by Zuma: Nkosazana Dlamini-Zuma, his former wife, came a close second to Cyril Ramaphosa in the vote that elected the latter as new leader of the party. By coincidence, Ramaphosa has also been in cow trouble in the past. In 2012 he had to apologise for getting carried away at an auction and bidding more than £1 million for a cow in a country where poverty is rife. He didn't even win the cow.

ZIMBABWE ▶

The runner-up in the Zimbabwean presidential election promised trains that travel 200 km/h faster than the world's fastest train.

Nelson Chamisa's 600 km/h trains were widely ridiculed, as was his promise to bring the Olympics to Zimbabwe. But he still came top out of the 22 people running against the incumbent president, Emmerson Mnangagwa of ZANU-PF, in the first election in Zimbabwean history without Robert Mugabe on the ticket.* As the preferred candidate of the MDC opposition party, Chamisa looked good going into the election, especially as, according to MDC spokesman Welshman Ncube, he had been blessed by spirit mediums. When torrential rain fell at his first campaign rally, Ncube said it was evidence of Chamisa's 'annointing'.

Other candidates, all of whom struggled for votes, adopted very different campaigning strategies. The New Patriotic Front (NPF) candidate, Peter Munyanduri, promised every Zimbabwean egg, bacon and milk for every breakfast, while the only independent candidate, Bryn Taurai Mteki, when asked how he was going to campaign in the election, said that he wouldn't tell: 'There is no way Barcelona will disclose its strategy to Real Madrid,' he said, 'but I can tell you, you are looking at the next President of Zimbabwe.' When pushed, he admitted: 'I will just chill at home. I will not have any public campaign.' He did not become president.

In the end, it was Mnangagwa who was victorious, helped in no small degree by the way the voting cards were printed. As there were 23 candidates in total, the names had to be placed in two columns, in alphabetical order. In theory, that should have placed Mnangagwa near to the middle of the second row. In the event, though, fourteen names were placed in the first column

Mnangagwa came to power in 2017 following a bitter dispute with former president Robert Mugabe's wife Grace over who would succeed Robert. When Mnangagwa fell ill after eating ice cream from the first family's dairy, his supporters even went so far as to suggest he had been poisoned. He briefly fled the country, before returning to seize the presidency with the help of the military.

and nine in the second column. This meant that Mnangagwa's name appeared, rather conveniently, at the top of the second column where it was very easy for people to find.

ZOOS ▶

A man named Valentine quit Edinburgh Zoo after failing to matchmake the pandas.

Iain Valentine was a member of the team that negotiated to bring a pair of giant pandas, Tian Tian and Yang Guang, to Edinburgh Zoo and get them to breed with each other. He then set up a 'love tunnel' between the pair's enclosures, the idea being that they would open it whenever their calls became especially amorous, or when Tian Tian's urine contained enough oestrogen and Yang Guang was eating enough bamboo – both signs that they might be ready to mate. (They only opened it once.) Pandas are only fertile for about 36 hours a year, and so whenever things looked promising the viewing gallery was closed to the public and the online 'panda cam' was turned off to give the couple some privacy. Valentine would also let them loose in each other's enclosures on their own so that they could spray their scents around, his hope being that they'd attract each other that way. Sadly, the spark never fully ignited, and subsequent attempts to artificially inseminate Tian Tian were also unsuccessful. Valentine quit in February after 10 years in the job, and the panda procreation programme is now on hold.

It isn't just pandas' sex lives that humans interfere with. On Valentine's Day, a Devon zoo removed single males from its penguin colony to give breeding couples time and space to mate with each other. The curator said that bachelor penguins tended to disturb the loved-up ones.

Detroit Zoo ran a promotion this year that involved giving each of the first thousand people to visit its new anaerobic digestor unit a free bucket of 'Detroit Zoo poo'.

And in Canada, wildlife officials took a bear on a date. Keepers from the zoo in Alberta, Canada, later admitted they'd made a mistake in putting an adult Kodiak bear in their car passenger seat, taking it to a Dairy Queen drive-through and having the seller hand-feed it ice cream through the car window.

ZUCKERBERG, MARK ▶

Mark Zuckerberg's private data was compromised while he was talking to Congress about compromised data.

Mark Zuckerberg was called to give evidence to the US Congress at the height of the Facebook scandal – a scandal that involved the accessing of the data of nearly 90 million Facebook users and sharing it with third parties (including Donald Trump's presidential campaign). Even Zuckerberg's own Facebook data was accessed by the political consultation firm at the centre of the storm, Cambridge Analytica. And in between sessions, Zuckerberg had his own data compromised yet again: he left his extensive briefing notes behind on the table during a break, meaning a photographer was able to swoop in and snap them. Zuckerberg's decision to give his evidence while sitting on a four-inch booster cushion prompted a lot of derision, although a Facebook spokesperson insisted the cushion had been provided by Congress and had definitely not been brought in by Facebook or Zuckerberg.

Ahead of Zuckerburg's appearance in front of Congress, 100 Mark Zuckerberg carboard cut-outs appeared on the lawn of the US Capitol, wearing a T-shirt reading 'fix fakebook'.

Zuckerberg's firm experienced other problems this year, too, not least when it was revealed that Facebook had connected thousands of ISIS extremists to each other through the 'suggested friend' feature, due to their shared interest in destroying the West. A spokesman for Facebook clarified that 'there is no place for terrorists on Facebook'.

All this bad publicity, the corporate crisis and angry shareholders led to . . . a big rise in Facebook's share price, meaning that in July, Zuckerberg briefly overtook Warren Buffett to become the third-richest person on the planet.

ZUISM

Iceland's Zuists announced plans to build a ziggurat.

Zuism, an ancient religion involving the worship of gods such as An, Ki, Anki and Nanna, has found itself extremely popular in Iceland over the last few years, thanks to the fact that it offers local people a tax loophole (an explanation that, it should be said, Zuists (predictably) deny). The country has a 'church tax' that it places on all of its citizens, giving the money to their chosen denomination. Zuism takes that tax and simply hands it back to its worshippers.

According to spokesman Águst Arnar Ágústsson, Reykjavik's newest building would be a place where adherents to the ancient Sumerian religion could host name-giving celebrations, weddings and 'beer and prayer' meetings. Whether it will eventually be built or not, the announcement of a Zuist ziggurat was excellent news for people who were writing an A–Z of the year's news and struggling to find things beginning with 'Z'.

LATE NEWS

Huge thanks go to:

Our QI family: John Lloyd, Anne Miller, Alice Campbell Davis, Ed Brooke-Hitching, Coco Lloyd, James Rawson, Liz Townsend, Gaby Jerrard, Natascha McQueen, Simon Urwin, Emily Jupitus, Esther Fearn, Isaac Deayton, Joe Mayo, Frances Arnold and Hannah Dunsmore, who constantly fed us news stories, advice and biscuits throughout the long writing process. Special thanks to Sarah Lloyd, who has tirelessly guided and championed us over the years, and given us a 2018 we'll never forget. And to Alex Bell who is undoubtedly the Best member of the podcast team – specifically, the 'Pete Best' member.

Our Random House family: Fergus Edmondson and Laura Brooke for all they've done to let the world know about our book; Henry Petrides for our brilliant cover; Lindsay Nash, our can-do-anything text designer; Alison Rae, our assiduous copy-editor; and Lindsay Davies, our eagle-eyed proofreader. Thanks again to Adam Doughty, who delivered another collection of inspired illustrations. And to Rowan Borchers, the tireless multi-tasking wunderkind who, among countless other things, took on the daunting task of fact-checking our entire book.

Our Fish family: All those who helped with our live shows: Ash Gardner, Mick Perrin, Viki Sever, Bec Cliff, Marnie Foulis, Ifan Thomas, Matthew Grundy and David Geli; our merchandise gurus: Kevin Douch, Jack Clothier and Mark Chatterley; and our team at Audioboom: Ruth Fitzsimons, Shaun Wilson and Oli Walters.

Our actual families: Bean, Fenella, Molly, Polina, Wilf and all the Harkin, Murray, Ptaszynski and Schreiber clans, whose 2018 was very much dominated by being told again and again about things happening in 2018.

Finally, we have to thank Nigel . . . the gannet, whose devotion to true love has helped us through the darkest of times when writing this book. We must also thank Nigel . . . Lawson, whose decision to get a French residency card despite being a Brexiteer made us realise we must always look at both sides of each story. But, of course, none of these is nearly as important as the most important Nigel . . . Owens, the referee whose appearance in a sub-titling mishap reminded us of the importance of accuracy when writing the book.

. . . Oh, and thanks to Nigel Wilcockson, our editor, as well. The real 'Nigel of the Year'. We couldn't (and wouldn't) have written this book without you.

Okay, that's it, that's all of our thanks, we'll see you again next year, goodbye!

PHOTO ACKNOWLEDGEMENTS

Photos are reproduced by kind permission of the following: Art: 'Unhappy Meal' © Carol May. Astronauts: Fake astronauts © Bhavatosh Singh. Babies: Happiness executive © UAE General Civil Aviation Authority. Beano: Walter the Softy © Beano Studios. Bell End: street sign © Matthew Cooper/PA Wire/PA Images. Bombs: bag via Twitter. Cricket, Just Not: book © Benjamin Schultz, Dymocks Brisbane. Desserts: shoe via Instagram. Fatberg: T-shirt © Museum of London. Fingernails: Shridhar Chillal © 2018 Ripley Entertaiment Inc. *Fire and Fury*: Ayatollah Khamenei © Khamenei.ir. Football Fans: Ikea sign © Capital North East. G7: summit © Jesco Denzel/Handout/Getty Images. Hawking: time traveller party © Lwp Kommunikáció/Flickr. Heatwaves: ghost garden © Lancashire County Council. Invasive: tumbleweeds © James Quigg/VVDailyPress.com. ISIS: actor © Meysam Mah'Abadi/FARS News Agency. Judo: football tackle © Genya Savilov/AFP/Getty Images. Koko the Gorilla: Koko with cat © The Gorilla Foundation. Mars: helicopter © NASA/JPL-Caltech. Marx, Karl: ducks © DPA Picture Alliance/Alamy Stock Photo. New Species: Arnold Schwarzenegger via Wikimedia Commons; fly drawing © Tyler Hayden. Oldest, Second: IV drip tree © ANI. Plastic: Swiss Guard helmet © WENN UK/Alamy Stock Photo. Queues: Amazon Go © VDB Photos. Quokkas: prophetic quokka © Melanie Dinjaski. Smuggling: oranges in car © Emergencias Sevilla. Statues of the Year: Yuri Gagarin head © @cenzura via Twitter. Tanks: inflatable tank © Vitaly Kuzmin. Urine Trouble: athlete via Youtube. Vegetables: Jeremy Corbyn © Jonathan Brady/PA Archive/PA Images. Yorkshire: Magid Magid © Chris Saunders.

Every effort has been made to trace copyright holders and to obtain their permission for the use of copyright material. The publisher apologises for any omissions and will be pleased to make the appropriate acknowledgements in any future reprints or editions.

ALSO AVAILABLE
ON AUDIOBOOK

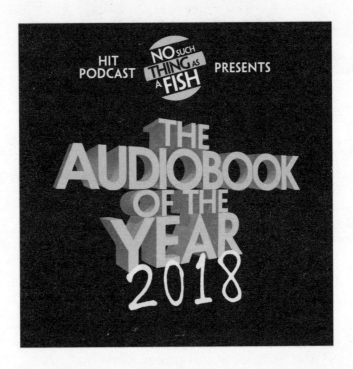

HIT
PODCAST

NO SUCH
THING AS
A FISH

PRESENTS

THE
AUDIOBOOK
OF THE
YEAR
2018

NARRATED BY THE AUTHORS

This page intentionally left blank

So is this one

This one was an accident

This is not a blank page (for blank pages, see pp.339–41)